The Productive Efficiency of Container Terminals

An application to Korea and the UK

DONG-WOOK SONG and KEVIN CULLINANE
Department of Shipping and Transport Logistics
Hong Kong Polytechnic University

MICHAEL ROE
Institute of Marine Studies, University of Plymouth

Ashgate

Aldershot • Burlington USA • Singapore • Sydney

© Dong-Wook Song, Kevin Cullinane and Michael Roe 2001

Published by
Ashgate Publishing Limited
Gower House
Croft Road
Aldershot
Hampshire GU11 3HR
England

Ashgate Publishing Company
131 Main Street
Burlington, VT 05401-5600 USA

Ashgate website: http://www.ashgate.com

British Library Cataloguing in Publication Data
Song, Dong-Wook
  The productive efficiency of container terminals : an
  application to Korea and the UK. - (Plymouth studies in
  contemporary shipping and logistics)
  1.Harbors - Korea 2.Harbors - Great Britain 3.Harbors -
  Economic aspects - Korea 4. Harbors - Economic aspects -
  Great Britain
  I.Title II.Cullinane, K. P. B. (Kevin P. B.) III.Roe,
  Michael, 1954- IV.Plymouth Polytechnic. Deparment of
  Shipping & Transport
  387.1'0941

Library of Congress Cataloging-in-Publication Data
Song, Dong-Wook.
  The productive efficiency of container terminals : an application to Korea and the UK /
  Dong-Wook Song and Kevin Cullinane, Michael Roe.
    p. cm.
  Includes bibliographical references.
  ISBN 0-7546-1639-8
    1.Harbors--Government policy--Korea (South) 2. Harbors--Government policy--Great
  Britain. 3. Privatization--Korea (South) 4. Privatization--Great Britain. I. Cullinane,
  Kevin. II. Roe, Michael, 1954- III. Title.

  HE559.K8 S66 2001
  387.1'64'094--dc21   2001022167

ISBN 0 7546 1639 8

Printed and bound in Great Britain by Antony Rowe Ltd.,
Chippenham, Wiltshire

90 0498704 X

SEVEN DAY LOAN

This book is to be returned on
or before the date stamped below

- 1 APR 2003	3 0 OCT 2003
2 9 APR 2003	1 8 NOV 2003
	2 7 NOV 2003
1 2 MAY 2003	1 5 DEC 2003
	2 0 JAN 2004
1 6 JUN 2003	1 3 APR 2004
3 0 SEP 2003	1 7 MAY 2004
1 5 OCT 2003	2 5 MAY 2004

THE PRODUCTIVE EFFICIENCY OF CONTAINER TERMINALS

Contents

v

List of Figures

List of Tables

Preface

This book is the outcome of research conducted by the authors while they all worked at the Centre for International Shipping and Transport, University of Plymouth, UK. The current book aims to review critically the characteristics of international port privatisation together with the economic theory of privatisation, to apply an econometric technique for efficiency measurement (i.e. the frontier model) to container ports in Korea and the UK, and to assess the policy implications of the results obtained. The book pays particular reference to the range of privatisation strategies and their implementation within a nation's seaports and terminals.

When the research idea was initiated in 1995, there were few studies available in related fields. Since then studies on the chosen topic have significantly expanded. This volume makes an original contribution to knowledge in three respects: firstly, port privatisation, in particular the Korean case, for the first time, has been scientifically investigated on the basis of the economic theory of privatisation; secondly, the port industry was analysed through the application of a recently developed econometric efficiency measurement method based on the estimation of two frontier models (i.e. cross-sectional and panel models); and finally, the results of the research undoubtedly provide governments, port authorities and other interested parties with information and guidelines for implementing the policy of port privatisation.

We owe debts of gratitude to many individuals for their comments, suggestions, and encouragement. In particular, Dong-Wook Song wants to dedicate this book to his beloved wife, Sung-Hee, for her never ending devotion and the God for the good; Kevin Cullinane's contribution to this work is dedicated to his wife, Sharon, for her continued and much valued patience, help and advice; and Michael Roe has cause to thank Liz, Joe and Sian for their continued good humour.

October 2000

D.W.S., K.P.B.C., M.S.R.

1

1 Introduction

RESEARCH BACKGROUND

The Republic of Korea (South Korea, hereafter referred to as just Korea) has achieved remarkable economic growth over the last four decades: from a poor developing country with a small manufacturing sector and heavily dependent on foreign aid in the 1960s to a fully industrialised country currently ranked as the world's 11th largest trading nation[1]. This impressive development within a short period of time is largely thanks to the adoption of outward-oriented and export-led economic policies.

This inspiring economic growth has resulted in a rapid increase in export and import cargoes and this trend has recently been accelerated by the better trade relations with the Chinese economy: the fastest growing economy in the world. Since the foreign trade of Korea is carried predominantly by sea transport (approximately 99.8 % in terms of volume), its ports play a crucial role in the process of economic development; any Korean port can, therefore, be regarded as a 'trade facilitator'.

The recent development and operation of Korean ports has kept pace with the ever-growing seaborne cargoes. However, they still have a number of problems including, amongst other things, insufficient port and terminal capacity, inefficient managerial and operational behaviour, and bureaucratic administration. As a consequence, Korean ports suffer from serious port congestion. This problem is particularly acute in the port of Pusan, the country's main seaport and the fifth largest container port in the world. By adding to the logistics costs of manufactured products, the delays caused by this congestion seriously undermine their competitiveness in world markets and detract from Korea's further development capability.

---

(1) At the time when this text was being finalised, the Asian financial crisis had seriously affected the Korean economy. The country's inherent economic structure (e.g. the government's heavy-handed intervention into business activities and inflexible bureaucratic system) was one of the main reasons behind the nation's deep economic woes. This economic crisis is discussed in a section of Chapter 2 from the perspective of the opportunity it provided for rationalisation.

Until recently the development and operation of ports and terminals was entirely dependent upon government funds. This system caused problems due to the inflexibility of the budget and the bureaucratic procedures for obtaining the necessary funds. Fortunately, under the new ongoing economic policy allowing more freedom to businesses, the government and the public port authority regard private sector participation in an industry whose activities used to be dominated by the public sector, as an important means of reducing their administrative and financial burden. This new tendency has resulted in massive private sector participation in several projects, including new container terminal developments.

In the past, all ports and terminals were controlled and administered by the Korea Maritime and Port Administration (KMPA), which was a public port authority. In 1996, by merging three maritime-related organisations, the Korean government established a new government organisation, the Ministry of Maritime Affairs and Fisheries (MMAF), with a mission to administer and manage its seaports and other maritime-related activities and to improve management efficiency in the maritime area.

Just as the 1970s and the 1980s were known for enormous capital investments into the port industry, it can be asserted that the late 1980s through the 1990s will become known for port sector reorganisation. In an attempt to improve efficiency and performance and to reduce the government's financial burden in supporting a very capital intensive industry, a number of countries have considered or have already undertaken some form of institutional reform of their port industry (e.g. commercialisation and privatisation).

Parallel with the general privatisation and liberalisation policies of the government and following the dominant current trend in the world's port industry, Korea's new port authority, MMAF has launched several new port and terminal development schemes as a means of solving problems related to port congestion and other sources of inefficiency. As the MMAF implements its plan to attract private capital into both existing and new port facilities by seeking some degree of privatisation where the costs and returns to port businesses can be shared between public and private sectors, competition has also been introduced into the Korean port industry. This is an environment which the country's port industry is totally unused to.

The motives for privatisation are complex and varied, but one key claim made is that the transfer from public to private ownership improves economic efficiency and, hence, ultimately financial and operational performance. Economic theories and existing empirical studies, however, fail to establish any clear-cut evidence of private enterprises performing better than their public counterparts. This phenomenon may reflect, to some extent, a paucity of performance indicators which can be systematically applied across enterprises and industries to allow a comparative analysis of performance to be undertaken. It is essential, therefore, to have a system for evaluating the impact of privatisation which can be widely applied and to provide a systematic and pragmatic analytical framework to assess the process of privatisation and its results.

RESEARCH OBJECTIVES

In light of the above context, this text aims to critically review the characteristics of international port privatisation along with the economic theory of privatisation; to introduce a novel method for efficiency measurement which is applicable to the port industry; and to assess policy implications for the Korean government and port authority, paying particular attention to the privatisation strategy and its implementation within the nation's seaports and terminals.

RESEARCH METHODOLOGY

To achieve the objectives, the current research employs a recently developed econometric method for efficiency measurement known as the 'frontier production function model' as an analytical tool to determine whether or not port privatisation has improved the efficiency of Korea's port industry.

Under the hypothesis that the productive efficiency of terminal operators improves as their ownership transforms from public to private sectors, the frontier model is divided into two types: the cross-sectional and panel models. The former is concerned with calculating an average efficiency level of terminal operators during each sample period, while the latter deals with the time-invariant terminal operator-specific efficiency over the period of analysis.

The data necessary for empirical investigation are taken from the annual reports and financial accounts published by each container terminal. The time span is from 1978 to 1996 inclusive. For an international comparison with a country where port privatisation policies have had more time to work, the main container terminals in the UK are also included in the analysis. The UK terminals sampled for inclusion account for a significant proportion of the UK container traffic and have different ownership attributes not only among themselves but, most importantly, as compared to their Korean counterparts.

STRUCTURE

The text consists of eight chapters. Following the introductory Chapter 1, Chapter 2 reviews the Korean national economy with an emphasis on trade promotion strategy and its effects on foreign trade, the role of the public sector in the process of economic development, and the newly adopted economic policies of privatisation and deregulation. Chapter 2 ends with by a brief examination of the current economic crisis which is severely influencing the nation's economy in terms of restructuring opportunities. Chapter 3 details the importance of Korean ports to the national economy and discusses increasing container traffic due to the trade-oriented development policy, port and terminal congestion as a result of the aforementioned policy, and new port and terminal development plans. The administrative system which controls the port industry and the increasing participation of the private sector in port activities are also examined in Chapter 3. In Chapter 4, economic theories and empirical evidence relating to privatisation are critically assessed. The principles applicable to, and the practice of port privatisation are evaluated in Chapter 5. After a review of the basic concepts related to production functions and economic efficiency, Chapter 6 justifies the application of two types of frontier model (i.e. the cross-sectional and panel models) for the empirical analysis. Chapter 7 applies the analytical tool developed in the previous chapter to the selected container terminals in Korea as well as the UK and provides the results of the application. Finally, Chapter 8 presents the interpretation of the findings and their implications for port privatisation in Korea, together with an objective assessment of the contribution to knowledge of this research, its limitations and ideas for further research areas. A flow chart illustrating the structure of the research is shown in Figure 1.1.

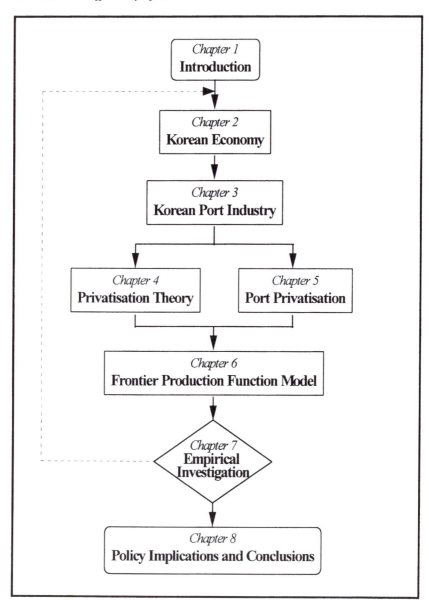

Figure 1.1 Research Flow Chart

2 An Overview of the Korean National Economy

INTRODUCTION

Strategically located in the north-eastern part of the Asian continent, the Korean Peninsula thrusts to a southerly direction for about 1,000 kilometres. To the north lie regions of China and Russia, while the Chinese mainland lies directly to the west. To the east, the peninsula faces the islands of Japan. The shortest distance from the west coast of Korea to China's Shantung Peninsula is about 190 kilometres. The shortest distance from the southern port of Pusan to the Japanese island of Honshu is about 180 kilometres. The total area of Korea is 221,607 square kilometres (about 85,563 square miles). At present, the land is divided into two parts: the Republic of Korea (South Korea) and the People's Republic of Korea (North Korea). Due to this political situation, Korea is engaged in foreign trade as an island nation like Britain and Japan, thus forcing the country to actively participate in the maritime industry for effectively carrying its own trade. The administrative area of the country is 99,237 square kilometres or about 45% of the Korean Peninsula, which is slightly larger than Hungary or Portugal, and a little smaller than Iceland.

With 44.6 million inhabitants at the end of 1994, Korea is one of the most densely-populated countries in Asia and also has one of the smallest land areas per capita in the world. Moreover, its terrain is very hilly, with only one-fifth of the land being arable. It is not, however, well endowed with natural resources. Morita (1987) remarks on Japan's natural resource poverty, that the land provides almost no raw materials except water, and that less than a quarter of the land is usable. This statement describes Korea's situation almost exactly as well. Therefore, like Japan, Korea has to rely on foreign countries for most mineral resources such as oil, iron ore, copper, gold, silver, etc., which are crucial for industrialisation. This poverty in natural resources has forced the country to pursue an outward-oriented economic policy.

NATIONAL ECONOMY

In 1960, Korea was a poor developing country with a small manufacturing sector and heavily dependent upon foreign aid. It had seemingly few prospects for increasing and sustaining economic growth. Over the last three decades, however, Korea has achieved what is widely acclaimed as 'the economic miracle of the Han River' (World Bank, 1993). Since Korea embarked on an economic development plan in 1962, its economy has grown at one of the fastest rates in the world. This remarkable success can be largely attributed to the outward-oriented and export-centred economic policies implemented by the Korean government and to the determination of the Korean people. As a result, Korea has successfully transformed itself from a largely agrarian based economy in the 1960s to a fully industrialised one today, and is currently ranked as one of the largest trading nations in the world.

The importance of ports for national economic development is widely recognised, for example, by Nagorski (1972), Faust (1978), Hoyle (1983), and UNCTAD (1985). There is a close relationship between ports and the prospects for economic development. The port is not only a determinant of economic development, but also a decisive factor in it. Moreover, ports not only have an influence on economic development but, at the same time, are also directly affected by economic development. The influence of a port on the economy extends beyond its boundaries into the industrial, commercial and business sectors of the nation at regional and national levels (Frankel, 1987).

The impact of the port industry on economic development can be discussed in the context of the process of Korean economic development over the last three decades. A useful starting point before proceeding into an analysis of Korea's ports industry is to look at the overall growth of the economy, its reliance upon foreign trade, the roles of the public sector in the process of development and finally, at the new economic policies oriented towards privatisation and deregulation. This overview provides the context within which this process of economic growth has emerged.

Economic Growth

A large infusion of economic aid during the period 1953-1958, following the Korean War, enabled the country to reconstruct its war-damaged production facilities and to achieve a moderate level of economic growth, although with a very high rate of inflation. During the period 1959-1962, the rate of inflation eased, but so did the pace of economic expansion with the annual growth of national output per capita declining to nearly zero in the early 1960s. Following this period of moderate growth and then near stagnation, a rapid economic expansion began in 1963. Supported by a rapid and sustained expansion in its exports, the country's gross national product (GNP) grew rapidly during the course of six successive Five-Year Economic Development Plans (hereafter referred to as 'FYP'). Rapid increases in output, income and exports were accompanied by rising investment, savings, exports and imports. These became more important for the national economy and were achieved by a fundamental change of economic structure, away from agriculture and towards manufacturing.

The rate of GNP growth, however, has slowed considerably in recent years. After recovering from the recession of 1989 and reaching a rate of GNP growth of 9.1% in 1991, it slowed to 5.0% and 5.6%, respectively, in 1992 and 1993. However, helped by such favourable international factors as stable petroleum prices, the strong Japanese yen, and a relatively robust world economy (in particular, the performance of the US economy), the growth rate recovered in 1994, rising to 8.3%. In that year, Korea's real GNP was 303,773 billion won (US$ 378,086 million[1]), compared with 265,518 billion won (US$ 330,793 million) in 1993. These figures made Korea one of the largest economies in the world. Table 2.1 shows some major indicators of Korean economic development over the last three decades. The growth of Korea's GNP since 1962 shows a truly remarkable performance: from 356 billion won (US$ 2,738 million) in 1962 to 348,284 billion won (US$ 451,572 million) in 1995, resulting in an economy which has grown by one-hundred-and-sixty-five times over a period of only 33 years.

Rapid economic development since 1963 can partly be explained by the country's strategy of maximising growth by pursuing outward-orientated, export-centred economic policies (Chung, 1996). This strategy was adopted in 1962, when the First Five-Year Economic Development Plan was introduced, replacing the policy of import-substitution which was in effect up until that time. Effective formal economic planning in Korea started with the First FYP (1962-1966). The country has now completed six five-year planning cycles.

---

(1) Throughout the chapter, US$ equivalents are calculated by corresponding exchange rates based on each period average.

Table 2.1 Major Indicators of Korean Economic Growth (1962-1995)

Year	Popula -tion[1]	GNP[2]	GNP per Capita[3]	Exports[4]	Imports[5]	Govern- ment Consum- ption[6]	Private Consumption[6]
1962	26.15	356	87	18	55	50	294
1965	28.33	806	105	69	123	75	672
1970	32.24	2,736	243	382	616	265	2,041
1975	35.28	10,065	591	2,855	3,521	1,121	5,323
1980	38.12	36,672	1,589	12,765	13,541	4,268	24,786
1985	40.80	72,850	2,150	27,327	27,089	7,893	44,126
1990	42.87	178,262	5,659	65,016	69,844	18,187	96,388
1995	45.09	348,284	10,037	125,058	135,119	36,387	185,899

Notes: (1) Millions (mid-year estimates); (2) Actual Prices (Billions of Won); (3) US$ (in Actual Prices); (4) F.O.B (Billions of Won); (5) C.I.F. (Billions of Won); and (6) Billions of Won.

Sources: International Monetary Fund (1989, 1996), and Song (1994).

The objectives of the successive FYPs, shown in Table 2.2, have changed over time with rising income, shifts in economic structure, and changes in economic issues and priorities. The changes in the objectives of the government's economic policy can be examined in relation to four major government economic functions (Song, 1990, p. 129):

- Creating the economic and legal framework: i.e., the constitution, the rules of the economic game, and economic laws;
- Ensuring stability - macroeconomic functions;
- Promoting efficiency - microeconomic functions (industrial policy, trade policy, agricultural policy, and social infrastructure policy); and
- Promoting equity (personal, regional, and industrial equity).

As shown in Figure 2.1, prior to the Fourth FYP, the forecast rate of economic growth increased gradually with successive plans, and, without exception, was always exceeded. The planned average annual rates of growth for GNP (and actual performance) for the first three FYP were: 7.1% (7.9%), 7.0% (9.7%) and 8.6% (10.2%), respectively. In contrast, the planned average GNP growth rate of 9.2% per year during the Fourth FYP was not achieved, owing to the world economic recession of 1979-1980. The actual rate achieved during the Fourth FYP period was only 5.7%. The average annual rates of economic growth, however, envisaged during the Fifth and Sixth Plans (7.5% and 7.3%, respectively) were in fact exceeded, with actual growth rates achieved of 8.7% and 10.0%, respectively.

Table 2.2 An Overview of Korea's Five-Year Economic Development Plans

Plan	Period	Growth Rate	Objectives	Major Policy Directions
1st FYP	1962-66	7.1[*] (7.9)[**]	Breaking the vicious circle of poverty Establishing the foundations for self-sustaining economic development	• Securing energy supply sources • Correcting structural imbalances • Expanding basic industries and infrastructure • Effective mobilisation of idle resources • Improving the balance of payments • Promoting technology
2nd FYP	1967-71	7.0 (9.7)	Modernising of industrial structure Promotion of self-sustaining economic development	• Self-sufficiency in food, development of fisheries and forestry industries • Laying the foundation for industrialisation • Improving balance of payments • Employment creation, family planning and population control • Raising farm household income • Improving technology and productivity
3rd FYP	1972-76	8.6 (10.2)	Harmonising growth, stability, and equity Realising a self-reliant economy	• Self-sufficiency in food staples • Improving the living environment in rural areas • Promotion of heavy and chemical industries • Improving sciences, technology, and human resources

			Compreh-ensive national land development and balanced regional development	• Development of national land resources and efficient spatial distribution of industries • Improving the living environment and national welfare
4th FYP	1977-81	9.2 (5.7)	Achievement of self-sustaining economy Promoting equity through social development Promoting technology and improving efficiency	• Self-sufficiency in investment capital • Achieving balance payments equilibrium • Industrial restructuring and promoting international competitiveness • Industrial restructuring and enhancing intentional competitiveness • Employment expansion and manpower development • Improving living environment • Expanding investment for science and technology • Improving economic management and institutions
5th FYP	1982-86	7.5 (8.7)	Establishing foundations for price stability and self-sustaining economy Technology improvement and quality of life	• Eradicating inflation-oriented economic behaviour • Increasing competitiveness in heavy industries • Improving agricultural policy • Overcoming energy constraints • Improving financial institutions

			Restructuring government's economic functions	• Readjusting government functions and rationalising fiscal management • Solidifying competitive system and promoting open-door policy • Manpower development and promotion of science and technology • Establishing new labour relations • Expanding social development
6th FYP	1987-91	7.3 (10.0)	Establishing socio-economic system. Promoting creative potential and initiative Industrial restructuring Improvement of technology Improving national welfare through balanced regional development and income distribution	• Expanding employment opportunities. • Solidifying foundation for price stability • Realising balance of payments surplus and reducing foreign debt • Industrial restructuring and technology improvement • Balanced regional and rural development • Improving national welfare through improved social equity • Promoting market economic system and readjusting government functions
New FYP	1993-97	6.9	Revitalisation of economy Promotion of technology Promotion of the role of private sectors	• Stimulation of small and medium-sized firms • Reform of tax system, government expenditure, financial sector, and administration regulations • Boosting investment

			Enhancing quality of life	•	Deregulation and liberalisation of the economy
			Expanding social overhead capital	•	Employment and price stabilisation
				•	Increasing productivity

Notes: (*) Planned Growth Rate; and (**) Achieved Growth Rate.
Sources: Song (1990) and Korean Overseas Information Service (1993).

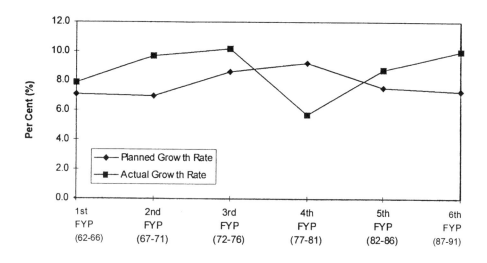

Figure 2.1 Planned and Actual GNP Growth Rates
(First FYP to Sixth FYP)
Source: Derived from Table 2.2.

The Five-Year Economic Development Plans

The main objectives of the *First FYP* (1962-1966) were to break the vicious circle of poverty and to build a foundation for self-sustaining growth. In addition to export expansion, which consistently received priority in all the subsequent plans, the First FYP emphasised the expansion of infrastructural capital in electric power, railways, ports and communications, with the aim of overcoming the impediments to development.

During the *Second FYP* (1967-1971), special attention was paid to the microeconomic functions of the government: namely, promoting efficient allocation of resources through agricultural, industrial, trade and social infrastructure policies. The objectives of the Second FYP aimed at the development of electronic and petrochemical industries, and to increasing income in the agricultural sector by maintaining high prices for rice, the staple crop.

The rapid growth of the economy caused increasing disparity between income classes, export and domestic industries, firms of different sizes, and regions. As a result, the *Third FYP* (1972-1976) implemented policies for the promotion of equity. Priority was given to the development of heavy and chemical industries and this materialised during the period, with the construction of integrated steelworks, the expansion and construction of petrochemical plants, and the expansion of shipyard capacity.

The *Fourth FYP* (1977-1981) placed its emphasis on the industries making intensive use of technology and skilled labour and focused on machinery, electronics and shipbuilding. The Fourth FYP gave an even higher priority to social development as a means to promoting a more equitable distribution of income. For this purpose, government spending on education, housing, public health and medical care was increased substantially over what had been present in previous plans. From the Fourth FYP the government's key goals shifted from the quantitative aspects of economic growth to the qualitative aspects of life. As a consequence, the Fourth FYP was even officially named the Five-Year 'Socio-economic' Development Plan.

As its rural-agricultural economy began to change into an industry-oriented one, the Korean economy became increasingly complex and subject to business fluctuations and inflation. In these circumstances, economic stability emerged as a new policy issue. The *Fifth FYP* (1982-1986) specified achieving economic stability as its major policy objective.

Because the principal source of instability in a mainly agricultural economy was the weather, rather than business conditions, maintaining economic stability had not been considered as a very important government function until the first oil crisis in 1973. The strategy of export-led growth was to be maintained, and the policy of liberalising the domestic market was to be actively implemented. The Fifth FYP envisaged a moderate reduction of both the trade deficit and the deficit on the current account of the balance of payments. The manufacturing sector, with its high potential for competing in the world market, was to receive priority. The Fifth FYP also envisaged a more balanced development of the regions and industrial sectors, an enhancement of the private sector and a further increase in economic efficiency.

The relative importance of the government and private sectors has changed substantially since the First FYP. During the early planning periods, the public sector played a dominant role as the market system was not well developed. It was only as the urban-industrial sector expanded that market activities and the function of the market system began to modernise. In consequence, the private sector expanded greatly relative to that of the public sector. Since the Fifth FYP, particular emphasis has been given to enhancing free competition. In addition, as of 1986, the Korean economy experienced high economic growth, stable prices and a trade surplus, and thus faced a new phase of growth. The broad policy direction of the *Sixth FYP* (1987-1991) was to enhance the efficiency, and strengthen the international competitiveness, of its economy in general through reforming the free enterprise market system. The principal contents of policy reforms included the simultaneous drastic reduction of various government regulations constraining growth of enterprises, together with extensive liberalisation of financing, imports and foreign exchange. Song (1990) highlights the major changes in economic policy including the gradual reduction of various fiscal subsidies, the privatisation of public enterprises, the shift from direct to indirect monetary controls, the reduction of foreign borrowing and the improvement of exchange rate management.

The *Seventh FYP* (1992-1996) was replaced in 1993 by the *Five-Year Plan for the New Economy* (1993-1997) in an unprecedented move by the newly-elected government. The main aim of the New FYP with an envisaged average annual growth rate in GNP of 6.9% was to raise the Korean economy to the ranks of the advanced nations and to lay the economic foundations for an eventual Korean unification. The elimination of official corruption was emphasised, as was the introduction of reforms in the economic structure, including government regulations, public financing and the deregulation of financial markets. One of the ways of measuring national economic progress is that, on 11 October 1996, Korea became a member state of the Organisation for Economic Co-operation and Development (OECD).

In the light of the fact that the new administration considered revitalisation of the economy as its most important task, the following short term measures were taken (Korean Overseas Information Service, 1993, p. 374):

- Boosting investment;
- Structural improvement of small and medium-sized firms;
- Promotion of technology development; and
- Deregulation of the economy.

In an effort to promote private initiatives in the business sector, the government eliminated a variety of regulations and removed obstacles to fair competition. In 1993 alone, of the 1,079 business restrictions reviewed, the government decided to ease or abolish 757 of them. Moreover, ad hoc committees continue to review other cases in order to further ease the restrictions on business activities.

The ultimate objective of the economic policy of the New FYP is to enhance the quality of life through employment stabilisation and higher real incomes. Real income can be increased through price stability and increases in productivity, which can be made possible by enhancing the quality of labour and increasing investments. The achievement of these goals, however, also requires the evolution of supporting institutions; the reform and advancement of such institutions will guarantee the free activity of companies and the equitable distribution of economic rewards.

With regards to port development under the New FYP, the government released an overall plan for expanding the social overhead capital in order to build up an efficient transport system throughout the country, and thus to properly distribute import and export goods in an effort to accelerate economic growth. Port development was one element of this plan. A problem raised in the process of developing a port is how to finance the project, as a huge amount of funds are normally required. The government has taken the participation of the private sector into consideration as an alternative method of reducing its financial burden, and has encouraged the private sector to take part in investment projects. The port industry is no exception.

In short, as noted by Collins (1990), the main reasons for the success of Korea's economic growth are that (i) stable and sensible economic policies have provided a solid platform for adjusting to internal and external economic shocks like the oil crisis in the 1970s; and (ii) investment in both physical and human capital has been recognised as a key to economic growth. This rapid development, however, has resulted in negative consequences. Since national security and economic development, among others, were the most important objectives of the past authoritarian regime, a centralised system of rule over the economy was strengthened while business autonomy and market-driven activities remained relatively inactive (Ro, 1996). This system has hampered the proper development of the nation's economic policy.

TRADE PROMOTION STRATEGY AND FOREIGN TRADE

As has already been mentioned, initially the Korean government attempted an economic policy of import substitution as a means of domestic economic growth. The national economy relied heavily on foreign aid to finance domestic sectors and imports of manufactured goods were virtually prohibited by the import substitution policy which revolved around high tariffs, quotas and a variety of non-tariff barriers. This policy, however, was ineffective in generating national wealth during the 1950s. Korea switched its national economic policy from import substitution to export-led growth around 1963, which is known as the 'switching point' (Ranis, 1989). At that time, the government embarked on an export-led and an outward-orientated policy (Hanink, 1994). With the adoption of an export-oriented industrialisation strategy and the subsequent reform of various trade and economic policy measures, exports from Korea have increased rapidly since 1963. Because trade-oriented industrialisation has been the basic growth strategy for Korea since the early 1960s, increases in the foreign trade of Korea are inseparable from its industrialisation.

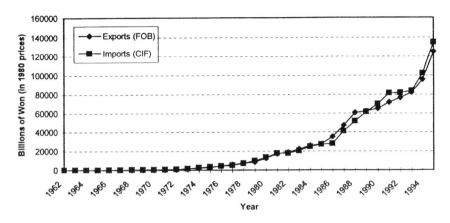

Figure 2.2 Growth of Exports and Imports (1962-1995)
Source: International Monetary Fund (1989, 1996).

Figure 2.2 illustrates the ever-increasing volume of Korea's exports and imports since the First FYP was launched in 1962, when the total value of Korean exports and imports amounted to only 18 billion won (US$ 138 million) and 55 billion won (US$ 423 million). By 1995, however, the real value of exports and imports (in 1980 prices) had increased to 125,058 billion won (US$ 162,146 million) and 135,119 billion won (US$ 175,190 million), respectively. This rapid expansion of exports and imports is closely related to Korea's growth strategy. In particular, the rate of increase in the 1980s is considerable although it is followed by even sharper growth in the 1990s. Figure 2.2 also shows the balance of trade where the value of exports was lower than that of imports from 1962 to 1975. Since then and until 1989, the value of exports has been higher than the import value. In the 1990s, the value of imports has again been higher than exports.

Growth strategies must be compatible with the country's resource endowment, population size, economic system and other characteristics (Song, 1990). The adoption of an appropriate growth strategy appears to be crucial to initiating as well as maintaining economic growth and is a necessary pre-condition to development. Korea's sustained growth since the early 1960s is largely credited to the identification of, and adherence to, a growth strategy that was right for the country, i.e., an outward-, industry- and growth-oriented (OIG-oriented) strategy. Again, Song (1990) argues that these OIG-oriented strategies are the only choice available to Korea for economic development, and that this has become even more true with the increasing globalisation of national economies.

The most important choice for nations wishing to develop their economies is between an internal policy emphasising the efficient mobilisation of, and reliance on, domestic resources, and an external policy stressing the promotion of foreign trade. In resource-rich countries, economic development tends to be based on their resources and starts from resource-based activities. In contrast, resource-poor countries like Korea do not have the opportunity to opt for a primary sector-oriented growth strategy. By necessity, their economies have to be developed by focusing on manufacturing industries.

On the basis of the choice between inward- and outward-oriented policies, resource endowment and population size, Chenery and Syrquin (1986, pp. 91-94) classified development strategies into four types:

- Outward- and primary-oriented economies;
- Inward-oriented economies;
- Neutral economies; and
- Outward- and industry-oriented economies.

Under the Chenery and Syrquin taxonomy, Korea falls into the outward- and industry-oriented categorisation of economies. This policy could be regarded as the key to Korea's rapid economic growth.

Korea's industrialisation depends mainly upon the import of raw materials and the export of processed and finished products. Since the beginning of its rapid economic growth, Korea has adopted this economic strategy based on export expansion plans. The national economy, as a consequence, has developed remarkably with substantial increases in exports. In particular, manufacturing industries have led this growth. The export expansion policy has brought about a rapid increase in the volume of exports and imports and, therefore, has a direct impact on the development of the port industry, because seaborne trade through ports accounts for almost 99% of Korean trade.

Krause (1981) classifies the export promotion strategies of the Asian newly-industrialised countries (NICs) according to the degree of government intervention, as shown in Table 2.3. Depending on the pattern of government trade promotion, the strategy is either interventionism or *laissez faire* according to the degree of government intervention. The second dimension Krause uses concerns the trade pattern: either free trade or a deviation from free trade. Deviations can be divided into right-wing and left-wing deviations. Right-wing deviations, resulting from excessive export subsidies or tariffs on imports, are trade-promoting. Left-wing deviations, however, entailing excessive restrictions on exports or imports are trade-reducing.

Table 2.3 Types of Trade Promotion Strategy relative to Government Intervention

Type	Free Trade	Deviation
Interventionism	Singapore,	Taiwan, Korea
Laissez Faire	Hong Kong	

Source: Krause (1981).

In the context of the Krause framework, Korea, like Taiwan, follows a right-wing deviationist and interventionist strategy. There is, therefore, great scope for Korea to lessen the degree of government intervention still further and move closer to a free trade position.

As a result of the adoption of an export-oriented trade policy, Korea's industrialisation has greatly depended upon imports of raw materials for the manufacturing industries, and the export of processed and finished products. Comparing their ratios of foreign trade (exports and imports) to national product whatever their stage of development, Amsden (1989) and Wade (1990) show that none of the countries in Europe, USA, Canada or Japan have ever had anywhere near as high a dependence upon foreign trade as Korea. Table 2.4 and Figure 2.3 show the very high dependence of Korea's economy on foreign trade (exports and imports); up to 74.7% in 1995 after a peak in 1988 of 85.6%.

Table 2.4 Dependence of Korean Economy on Foreign Trade (Billion Won, %)

Year	GNP	Total Foreign Trade	Exports	Imports	Dependence (%)		
	(A)	(B)	(C)	(D)	(B/A)	(C/A)	(D/A)
1962	356	73	18	55	20.5	5.1	15.4
1965	806	192	69	123	23.8	8.6	15.3
1970	2,736	998	382	616	36.5	14.0	22.5
1975	10,065	6,376	2,855	3,521	63.3	28.4	35.0
1980	36,672	26,306	12,765	13,541	71.7	34.8	36.9
1985	72,850	54,416	27,327	27,089	74.7	37.5	37.2
1990	178,262	134,860	65,016	69,844	75.7	36.5	39.2
1991	214,240	153,395	71,870	81,525	71.6	33.5	38.1
1992	238,705	158,407	76,632	81,775	66.4	32.1	34.3
1993	265,518	166,036	82,236	83,800	62.5	31.0	31.6
1994	303,773	198,361	96,013	102,348	65.3	31.6	33.7
1995	348,284	260,177	125,058	135,119	74.7	35.9	38.8

Sources: International Monetary Fund (1989, 1996).

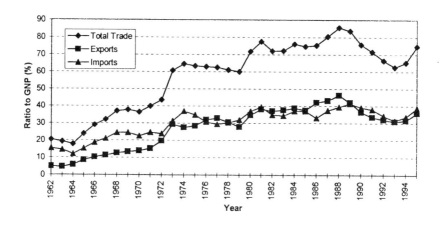

Figure 2.3 Ratio of Total Foreign Trade to GNP
Source: International Monetary Fund (1989, 1996).

THE ROLE OF THE PUBLIC SECTOR

In the rapid industrialisation of the Korean economy, the active role of the government has often been cited as a major source of strength. The government has been involved in the process by developing industrial policies and fostering close relationships with priority and related industries. Its interventions were justified on the grounds that the Korean government wanted to catch up with the advanced industrialised nations within the shortest possible time. Porter (1990, p. 474) describes the role of the Korean government in the process of industrialisation as follows:

> "The Korean government has played a relatively heavy and important role in the economy. Governments have enjoyed unusual power and continuity in Korea and have been blessed with a national consensus for decades about the importance of economic growth. This has provided a capacity to carry out sustained programmes in slow-to-change areas such as education. ...Some aspects of the role of the Korean government have been unqualified successes. Most significant were a series of actions that laid the foundation for upgrading. Substantial investments in education and infrastructure, efforts to promote exports, and the elevation of international competitive success to the level of a national priority have been important stimuli to Korean industry."

A primary role of government is to provide the legal framework within which all economic transactions occur (Stiglitz, 1986). Beyond that, the activities of government can be divided into three categories: (i) production of (public or/and private) goods and services, and regulation and subsidisation of private producers; (ii) purchase of goods and services; and (iii) redistribution of income by making payments to particular groups of individuals to enable them to spend more than they otherwise could, for example, through welfare payments and social insurance.

Begg *et al.* (1991) suggest reasons why governments may wish to intervene and/or nationalise their industries. These include the natural monopoly problem, externalities, and equity distribution. The *first* reason is concerned with large economies of scale; meaning that marginal cost lies below average cost. Social efficiency requires that prices be close to marginal cost, but this will imply smaller profits or even losses for the natural monopolist. Therefore, public subsidy may possibly be needed. The public commitment to pick up the bills, however, requires public monitoring to ensure that the monopolist continues to minimise production-related costs and to produce efficiently. Public ownership may be an obvious solution because private shareholders cannot be expected to subsidise the goals of society as a whole.

The *second* is regarding externalities, which exist when the production or consumption of a good directly affects businesses or consumers not involved in purchasing and selling it, and when those spillover effects are not fully reflected in market prices (Begg *et al.*, 1991). Whenever there are externalities, the resource allocation provided by the market may not be efficient. Since individuals do not bear the full cost of the negative externalities they generate, they will engage in an excessive amount of such activities. On the other hand, since individuals do not enjoy the full benefits of activities generating positive externalities, they will engage in too little of these. Thus, there needs to be some kind of government intervention.

The *third* reason is involved with important judgements of equity distribution. Where goods or services are crucial in contributing to the welfare of citizens but are not attracting production possibilities to the profit-seeking private sector, society faces two options; either it can order a private supplier to provide these goods or services with some kind of subsidy, or it can directly take over production to run the industry in the interests of the nation as a whole.

In addition to these three sources of market failure as a rationale for government intervention, Cullis and Jones (1989) add one more problem: uncertainty. Whatever the reasons, the fact that risk is not fully insurable in a market economy may give rise to a case for government involvement.

Several observers like Pack and Westphal (1986) and Kuznets (1988) have documented an active government role beyond correcting market failures. The role of government, however, differs country by country. Amsden (1989) and Wade (1990) point out that the governments of Taiwan and Korea had clear industrial priorities and did not hesitate to intervene, through subsidies, trade restrictions, administrative guidance, etc., to reshape comparative advantage in the desired direction. From a different perspective, Park (1990) argues that the government of Taiwan has been supportive rather than interventionist, whereas its Korean counterpart has been collaborative and even coercive in relations with the private sector. Furthermore, Chen (1995, p.151) suggests in relation to Japan and Korea:

"However, the existence of intimate government-industry relations in Japan and Korea does not testify to a 'Japan Inc.' or 'Korea Inc.' conspiracy. Japanese and Korean businessmen are not motivated much differently from their Western counterparts, despite their differing interests. Their willingness to collaborate with government is not because they are exceptionally patriotic, or culturally devoted. Rather, it is because they have known through their experience that such collaboration can bring material benefit. It is also true that industrial policy is not unique to these two countries. Close governmental relationships with priority industries and related big businesses are also quite commonly seen elsewhere in the world. For many developing countries, these phenomena are more sources of trouble than of strength. This is because they contributed to widespread favouritism, corruption and suffocation of competition. Nevertheless, in Japan and Korea, the result seems to have been quite remarkable and the channel seems to have been fairly effective."

In short, Japan and Korea have shared a similar historical legacy of heavy government involvement in economic activities which was justified on the grounds that, in order to catch up with the advanced countries, the government should assume responsibility for defining industrial policies and for using whatever means available to achieve its identified goals. With this economic philosophy, it is understandable why public enterprises in Korea have played an important role in its economic development.

A public enterprise can be broadly defined as a productive entity which is owned and/or controlled by public authorities and whose output is marketed (Jones, 1975). In Korea, public or nationalised enterprises are defined as independent organisations producing goods or services for the benefits of the public under direct or indirect control of the government (Economic Planning Board, 1988). The motivation for establishing public enterprises in Korea is to attain economic development objectives through providing basic materials for industrialisation in the early stage of a national economic development plan when private counterparts have no concept of how to manage and operate a business activity. This ideology is further confirmed by the notes of the former president:

"Private ownership of production should be unconditionally encouraged except in instances where it is necessary to control it to stimulate national development and protect the interests of the people." (Park, 1970, p. 218)

Thus, public ownership in Korea can be viewed as a necessary evil. Jones (1975) named this motivation as 'developmental motives'. This motivation can, therefore, be considered different from conventional reasons for establishing nationalised or public enterprises.

When the First FYP began, there were 52 public enterprises. The number had increased to 143 by 1993. If local public enterprises are included, the total number of public enterprises rises to 345 which, as can be seen in Table 2.5, comprises 4 government enterprises, 23 government invested enterprises (GIEs), 8 subsidiary companies of GIEs, 108 government-backed enterprises and 202 local public enterprises.

Table 2.5 Status of Public Enterprises in Korea (1993)

Type of Public Enterprise	Number	Employment[1]	Budget Size[2]
Government Enterprises	4	72.2	3.8
Government-Invested Enterprises	23	177.4	44.7
Subsidiary Companies of GIEs	8	42.4	10.9
Other Government-Backed Enterprises	108	69.5	9.0
Local Public Enterprises	202	-	-
Total	**345**	**361.5**	**68.4**

Notes: (1) In thousands; and (2) Trillion Won.
Source: Korea Chamber of Commerce and Industry (1995).

According to the Economic Planning Board (1988), these categories of public enterprise in Korea can be defined as follows. *Government enterprises* are those staffed and operated by government officials and take the form of government offices; a *government-invested enterprise (GIE)* is when the government owns more than 50% of the shares of an enterprise; *subsidiary companies of GIEs* are those only indirectly invested in by the government but where the activities of these companies are closely related to those of the GIEs; *local public enterprises* provide local services related to water, health and other local utilities and are financially supported by the local or municipal government. There were only 7 local public enterprises in 1969, but this had increased sharply to 202 by 1993 thanks to a rise in the standard of living in Korea and the government's decentralisation policy.

Public enterprises in Korea increased in number and expanded with the burgeoning of rapid economic growth in the early 1960s. In terms of the share in total investment, the public enterprises reached their peak in the mid-1970s (See Table 2.6). Investment in public enterprises began to accelerate with the initiation of the Development Plan for Heavy and Chemical Industries (1972-1981). Since the mid-1970s, the share of total investment in public enterprises appears to have declined. This declining trend accelerated somewhat in the 1980s with the development of a privatisation policy which was one of the key policy directions of the Fifth FYP (1982-1986).

Table 2.6 The Public Enterprise Sector in Korea

	1963	1970	1975	1980	1987
Number of enterprises	52	119	116	111	107
Sectoral value-added (Billion Won)	31.8	262.1	848.5	6,680	6,859
GDP (%)	7.0	9.2	8.3	8.3	9.1
Sectoral Employment (000)	-	-	-	280	341.9
Total Employment (%)	-	-	-	1.9	2.0
Sectoral Investment (Billion Won)	21.6	216.3	918.6	3,253.7	3,897.3
Total Investment (%)	31.7	18.9	33.2	27.6	15.6

Note: Local public enterprises excluded.
Source: Derived from Song (1986) and Kang (1988).

The public enterprises in Korea before 1960 were largely confined to the public utilities and to basic necessities such as salt as well at to monopolies selling high-value consumer products such as ginseng, cigarettes and banking. With the beginning of the Five-Year Economic Development Plans in the 1960s, these boundaries for public enterprises were dissolved and the government established public enterprises in any industries they considered appropriate. From the 1980s, many public enterprises took the form of development corporations, such as the Agriculture and Fisheries Development Corporation, the Korea Land Promotion Corporation, the Industrial Sites and Water Resource Development Corporation, the Petroleum Development Corporation, the Korea Trade Promotion Corporation, the Overseas Development Corporation and the Korea Development Bank.

In the 1960s and 1970s, government policy was aimed at establishing public enterprises in any area considered essential to expanding the country's export capacity and, at the same time, could not be properly handled by private enterprise. The government established public enterprises, therefore, even to handle such items as iron, steel, petroleum, chemicals and tourism that in some countries are generally regarded as traditional areas for private sector business. In the 1980s, government policy towards the public enterprises changed greatly and attempts were made to privatise the public enterprises as much as possible. The main reason for this action was simply that the private sector was perceived as being capable of operating such enterprises at least as efficiently as the public organisation.

TOWARDS A NEW ECONOMY: PRIVATISATION AND DEREGULATION POLICIES

In the 1960s, Korea had to cope with a formidable array of structural and institutional problems. The low savings rate and chronic current account deficits required a continuous inflow of foreign lending unavailable without government guarantees. It was believed that the financial system could not direct resources to export-led industries and that there was a shortage of entrepreneurs and managers to undertake the development of export-oriented industries. The industrialist class that had been nurtured during the import substitution period had little knowledge of foreign markets and international marketing, and, therefore, was unprepared to take the high risks associated with selling abroad. In many cases, greater efficiency required the adoption of increasing return technologies. This conflicted with the country's limited resources, and hence forced the government to support a few, selected large producers in targeted industries. During the 1960s, these large firms became successful exporters and, with the growth of the economy, also developed into industrial groups (referred to as *chaebol*) which dominated the manufacturing sector.

Park (1990) argues that, with the exception of the 1970s, Korea's export-oriented industries could have sustained rapid growth without government support. However, instead of deregulating state-controlled sectors, the Korean government tightened its grip over manufacturing industries and financial intermediaries. The confidence the government gained from its success in the 1960s encouraged a large, but unsuccessful, import substitution of capital and technology-intensive products in the 1970s.

Government involvement and support for industrial groups created its own problems and moral hazards. By the early 1970s, the industrial groups were highly leveraged (or geared) with loan guarantees through the banks owned by the government. Park (1990) describes the situation as one where the government had literally become a partner responsible for their failure as well as success.

Problems were at their most serious during the 1970s when the government attempted to develop a number of heavy and chemical industries simultaneously. The development was deemed necessary to take advantage both of complementarity on the demand side and forward and backward linkages among these industries. This approach, however, resulted in excessive investment and duplication. In order to export with the benefits of scale economies and minimum efficient size, the industrial groups were encouraged to build large plants from the earliest stage of their development. Park (1990) also notes that because of the lack of marketing, quality and technology, export earnings were low and losses heavy and that, furthermore, complementarity as well as the forward and backward linkages made the situation much worse. This setback motivated the economic liberalisation which took place at the end of the 1970s.

Currently, Korean industry is on the brink of a transformation as the trade barriers and financial protectionism that have supported its economy over a period of impressive growth are dismantled. The central issue is whether or not Korean companies can successfully move from the safety of state protection to an environment driven by market forces (Financial Times, 1995). In order to provide business with greater freedom and to cope with the ever changing world economic environment, the Korean government have several times attempted to launch privatisation and deregulation programmes. These programmes, however, have not yet proved successful. The country's ambitious privatisation programme is faltering and frustrated by the slow pace of privatisation, the country's President has urged that the reform of state-run industry be accelerated (Financial Times, 1996). Resistance to the programmes is strong in the country's bureaucracy and amongst public sector workers. This implies that privatisation will slow down not only because it represents a big political problem for the government, but also because Ministries are reluctant to relinquish control of the empires they command. At the same time, public sector workers are worried about losing their jobs due to privatisation.

Programmes for privatising government-run enterprises in Korea go back to 1968, with ensuing programmes taking place in 1981, 1987 and

1993. The main characteristics of each privatisation programme are described as follows (Korea Chamber of Commerce and Industry, 1995; Maekyung Business, 1997).

The First Privatisation Programme (1968-1973)

The first programme took place during the period 1968 to 1973, with the purpose being the rationalisation of the management of inefficiently-run or insolvent public enterprises. At the time, privatisation was mainly carried out through the public sale of government owned shares and cash transactions via commercial banks. The enterprises which were privatised through these methods were the Korea Machinery Corporation, the Korea Shipping Corporation and the Korea Shipbuilding Corporation in 1968; with Inchon Heavy Industry and Korean Airlines being privatised during the period 1968 to 1970.

The Second Privatisation Programme (1981-1983)

In early 1980 the second programme was instigated by the government. The main objective of the second privatisation programme was to deregulate and liberalise domestic financial markets, with the expectation of improving and developing the market. One distinguishing characteristic of this programme was the imposition of strict rules to limit share holdings to prevent majority stockholders from dominating companies. The chosen method of privatisation involved placing half of the state owned shares with corporations and selling the other half to individuals through public sales.

The Third Privatisation Programme (1987-1989)

The third programme was carried out more systematically than the previous programmes through the establishment of the 'Privatisation Committee of Public Enterprises' in 1987. The aim of the third privatisation programme was to help meet the challenge of a changing economic environment which was confronted by a national economy enjoying a high growth rate, the upgrading and advancement of economic market structures and the business know-how which the private sector had accumulated since the First FYP had been launched in 1962.

Furthermore, the central issue was how to transfer a domestic economic system driven by government or the public sector to one driven by the private sector, a situation that was in line with the open economic policy that had resulted in the growth of the domestic economy. Among the enterprises privatised during the third programme were the Pohang Iron and Steel Corporation (POSCO), the Korea Energy Power Corporation and the Korea Foreign Exchange Bank. Some of the government-owned shares of these public enterprises, valued at about 5 billion won (US$ 6.1 million), were distributed as public shares with the aim of public welfare improvement. Thirty-four per cent of the government-owned shares of POSCO were sold to the public in October 1988, and 21% of Korea Energy Power Corporation in 1989. The third privatisation, however, was not successfully carried out due to political and social problems and finally ended in 1990. The major reasons for the failure of the third programme were a dull stock market and labour disputes at the public enterprises to be privatised.

The Fourth Privatisation Programme (1993-1997)

In December 1993, the government announced a large scale privatisation programme which was the biggest in the history of the nation. The public enterprises to be privatised were 8 out of the 23 government-invested enterprises (GIEs), 2 out of the 8 subsidiary companies of the GIEs, and 61 out of the 108 other government-backed enterprises. Thus, more than 50% of state-run or owned enterprises are included in this huge privatisation scheme.

In the fourth programme, government policies toward privatisation were changed in the following two main areas (Korea Chamber of Commerce and Industry, 1995). First, the privatisation policy was carried out in a much clearer way than under previous programmes. This means the government played a more active part in transferring the public owned companies to the private sector and, in discarding completely its role, thus truly leaving management and control of the enterprises in the hands of the private sector. Secondly, the aim of privatisation was made more definite by the government: that is, to obtain an improvement in efficiency.

Although these two points have significant meaning in the light of policy makers' intentions for implementing the programme, there still remained a lack of detail as to how the privatisation policy was to be implemented in reality. The World Bank (1995, p. 10) suggests three necessary conditions for the successful reform of state owned enterprises as follows:

- Reform must be politically *desirable* to the leadership and its constituencies. Reform becomes desirable to the leadership and its supporters when the political benefits outweigh the political costs. This usually happens with a change in regime or coalition shift in which those favouring the status quo lose power. It may also happen when an economic crisis makes subsidies to state owned enterprises so costly that reform becomes preferable to the status quo;
- Reform must be politically *feasible*. Leaders must have the means to implement change and to withstand opposition to reform; and
- Promises central to the reform of state owned enterprises must be *credible*. Investors must believe that the government will not renationalise privatised firms; the employees of state owned enterprises, and others who fear that they may lose out in reform, must believe that the government will deliver on any promises of future compensation.

Reforms such as privatisation invariably undermines a government's support base. This is because they almost always involve eliminating jobs and cutting long established subsidies and other forms of protection. Politicians, naturally, prefer policies that benefit their constituents and help them remain in power over policies that undermine support and may cause them to be turned out of office. How countries that want to successfully reform public enterprises actually overcome these political obstacles is dependent on the existence of these three conditions (i.e. political desirability, political feasibility, and credibility).

The fact that the Korean economy now faces changes in both the international and domestic environment requires industry to make structural adjustments in order to maintain healthy economic growth and advance into the ranks of the industrialised economies. In addition, Korea's desire to be a part of the OECD fostered these changes in the direction of greater liberalisation. For these reasons, the government should plan to strengthen private sector initiatives by supporting an increasing role for market forces and competition as a means of improving efficiency. Moreover, the government must strive to continue the major policy measures it has already implemented to liberalise foreign trade and investment regimes (Koo, 1991). Ro (1996) stresses the point that Korea is no longer a country that aims merely for economic development under a centralised and authoritative regime, while acknowledging many positive changes experienced over the past three decades, such as the development of the national economy, were made possible through the contribution of the bureaucratic elite in charge of public administration. The Korean government should not ignore the recommendation of Porter (1990, p. 690):

"Direct intervention in individual industries, reliance on the *chaebol* [industrial conglomerate] as a prime development tool, widespread protection, and directing capital through government decisions were appropriate in earlier stages.... But such policies must give way to a new set of priorities if Korean industry is to progress further. Moving to the next stage requires that economic decision making be decentralised into a growing number of private sector hands. The prime role of government must shift from direct intervention to providing the resource foundations for upgrading and creating a more challenging environment in which firms compete. Rule setting and signalling need to replace a direct role in decisions. Efforts to stimulate investment in advanced and specialised factors, institute world-class product and environment standards........deconcentrate economic power are prime government roles in moving to the innovation-driven stage.... It is hard for any government accustomed to an activist role to make these changes. The capacity of the Korean government to do so is yet to be determined. It must be said, however, that Korean government policy has been evolving, which bodes well for the nation's future."

This piece of advice should be kept in mind so as to successfully carry out the transformation of economic policy, i.e. from a nation-state economy with centralised planning to a free and spontaneous economy by reducing regulations and implementing a market-driven policy. Aoki *et al.* (1996) also suggest that the market-enhancing view be taken into account when governments on the stage of transformation like Korea make a master plan for their national economies.

CURRENT ECONOMIC CRISIS: AN OPPORTUNITY FOR RESTRUCTURING

The fundamental economic structures which have built Korea into the world's 11th largest economy in less than four decades appear to be drastically in need of reform and recent financial turmoil highlights the urgent need for change. As part of the Asian economic crisis (Financial Times, 1998), Korea's national economy has recently suffered near financial catastrophe, i.e. the national currency has depreciated sharply against the US dollar, almost 40% over only a few months in late 1997 and early 1998. A symptom of this crisis was first revealed in the middle of 1997, when several companies including some industrial conglomerates (*chaebol*) became insolvent due to their adoption of high-risk debt-ridden financial structures.

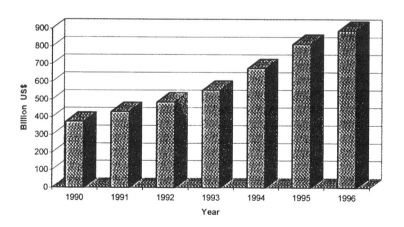

Figure 2.4 Total Corporate Debts in Korea
Source: Derived from Burton (1997, p. 8).

Figure 2.4 illustrates the accumulation of debts borrowed by Korean companies from domestic and overseas financing sources, indicating that these have been continuously increasing over the past few years. To make matters even worse, most of the debts shown in Figure 2.4 are short-term (with less than 12 months maturity). As of June 1997, Korea's short-term debt was more than three times as big as its foreign reserves, which is a higher ratio than any other country in Asia (Economist, 1998). Like other Asian countries in crisis (i.e. Indonesia, Malaysia and Thailand), Korea has suffered from too much borrowing, coupled with its financial system which fails to allocate resources efficiently. The Economist (1998) also points out that banks in the region did not properly assess credit risks, lending largely on the basis of previously established personal relationships, and taking on risks in the belief that the government would always bail them out. This kind of lending behaviour can be regarded as 'politically driven lending' (Montagnon, 1997), not a business oriented one.

Since the early stage of development, the Korean government has treated banks and financial industries, like other major sectors, as instruments of its industrial policy, directing them to lend to favourable sectors of the economy at cheap rates, hence resulting in the bank's reckless behaviour. Furthermore, cheap money from abroad encouraged the debt-laden conglomerates to diversify their business activities into too many areas. At the end of 1996, the top 30 conglomerates had an average debt-equity ratio of 400%, which is seriously high relative to the 70% for their US counterparts (Economist, 1998). Unfortunately, these top 30 huge business groups have a central role in the nation's economy; for instance, approximately 90% of the nation's GNP can be attributed to them in 1996 alone (Lee, 1998).

The cosy relationship between governments, banks and companies has isolated business from market forces, consequently fostering excessive borrowing and a wasteful use of resources. This financial instability combined with the economic structural reforms urged by the International Monetary Fund (IMF) has already produced a change in government and subsequently in economic policy and system. In this way, the country can deal with the problems of inadequate bank regulation, too much government intervention, corruption and a general lack of transparency in business affairs. In fact, the IMF's bail-out package was made in return for an agreement by the Korean government that it would provide the following conditions (Lloyd's Shipping Economist, 1998, p. 16):

- opening its financial markets;
- revising banking structures; and
- lowering trade barriers.

Under these circumstances, demanding more freedom for businesses and market-driven decision making, the government has realised that public administration can no longer lead the economy as it did in the past, and that the relaxation of regulation and greater privatisation are inevitable policies that may stand a chance of returning its national economy to the level previously enjoyed and to remain at a high level of growth into the future.

Recent research (Ryoo, 1997) mentions that the policy of privatisation is one of the most likely options available to the country's policy makers for solving the current economic and financial crisis. The claim is supported by another report (Baker, 1998) which maintains that the current crisis has its roots not in improvidence but in economic structures, indicating that:

> "The problems that must be fixed are much more microeconomic than macroeconomic, and involve the private sector more and the public sector less."

In short, Korea went through many different stages over the past four decades in building up the nation's economy. Since the first FYP commenced in the early 1960s, Korea has been able to rapidly develop its economy thanks to the enthusiasm of political leaders and commitment of its people. The developmental stage, however, seems to be over; now Korea is at a turning point of moving into a new stage. The old ways of central government planning, leading and guiding the people are to be altered with new policies such as deregulation, decentralisation and privatisation now being implemented. This role change is required under the condition that Korea is forced to open the market and be more global in terms of its business activities.

REFERENCES

Amsden, A. (1989), *Asia's Next Giant: South Korea and Late Industrialisation*, Oxford University Press, New York.

Aoki, M., Murdock, K. and Okuno-Fujiwara, M. (1996), Beyond the East Asian Market: Introducing the Market-Enhancing View, in Aoki, M., Kim, H.-K. and Okuno-Fujiwara, M. (eds.), *The Role of Government in East Asian Economic Development: Comparative Institutional Analysis*, Clarendon Press, Oxford, pp. 1-37.

Baker, G. (1998), US Looks to G7 Backing on Asian Crisis, *Financial Times*, 20 February.

Begg, D., Fisher, S. and Dornbusch, R. (1991), *Economics* (3rd ed.), McGraw-Hill International UK Ltd., London.

Burton, J. (1997), Asian Financial Markets: South Korea - A Puddle to Fight a Big Fire, *Financial Times*, 9 May, p. 8.

Chen, M. (1995), *Asian Management Systems: Chinese, Japanese and Korean Styles of Business*, Routlege, London.

Chenery, H. and Syrquin, M. (1986), The Semi-Industrial Countries, in Chenery, H., Robinson, S. and Syrquin, M. (eds.), *Industrialisation and Growth: A Comparative Study*, Oxford University Press, London, pp. 84-118.

Chung, J.S. (1996), Korean Economy, in *The Far East and Australasia 1996*, Europa Publications Ltd., London.

Collins, S. (1990), Lessons for Development from the Experience in Asia: Lessons from Korean Economic Growth, *American Economic Review*, Vol. 80, No. 2, pp. 104-107.

Cullis, J. and Jones, P. (1989), *Microeconomics and the Public Economy: A Defence of Leviathan*, Basil Blackwell, Oxford.

Economic Planning Board (1988), *White Paper on Public Enterprises*, EPB, Seoul.

Economist (1998), A Survey of East Asian Economies: Frozen Miracle, 7 March.

Faust, P. (1978), The Role of Ports in Economic Development, in Beth, H. L. (ed.), *Port Management Textbook*, Institute of Shipping Economics, Bremen, pp. 15-24.

Financial Times (1995), South Korea: Trade, Industry and Finance, 20 October.

Financial Times (1996), Kim calls for Accelerated State Sector Reform and Privatisation, 18 June.

Financial Times (1998), Special Report: Asia in Crisis, 13-16 January.

Frankel, E. (1987), *Port Planning and Development*, John Wiley and Sons, New York.

Hanink, D. (1994), *The International Economy: A Geographical Perspective*, John Wiley and Sons, New York.

Hoyle, B. (1983), *Seaport and Development: The Experience of Kenya and Tanzania*, Gordon and Breach, London.

International Monetary Fund (1989), *International Financial Statistics Yearbook*, IMF, Washington, D.C.

International Monetary Fund (1996), *International Financial Statistics Yearbook*, IMF, Washington, D.C.

Jones, L. (1975), *Public Enterprise and Economic Development: The Korean Case*, Korea Development Institute, Seoul.

Kang, S.I. (1988), *A Study on Privatisation of Public Enterprises*, Korea Development Institute, Seoul.

Koo, B.H. (1991), The Korean Economy: Structural Adjustment for Future Growth, in Lee, C.-S. (ed.), *Korea Briefing, 1990*, Westview Press, Oxford.

Korea Chamber of Commerce and Industry (1995), *Privatisation of Public Enterprises and Changing Role of Public and Private*, KCCI Working Paper No. 264, Seoul.

Korean Overseas Information Service (1993), *A Handbook of Korea* (9th ed.), Hollym Co., Seoul.

Krause, L. (1981), Summary of the Eleventh Pacific Trade and Development Conference on Trade and Growth of the Advanced Developing Countries, in Hong, W. and Krause, L. (eds.), *Trade and Growth of the Advanced Developing Countries in the Pacific Basin*, Korea Development Institute, Seoul.

Kuznets, P. (1988), An East Asian Model of Economic Development: Japan, Taiwan, and South Korea, *Economic Development and Cultural Change*, Supplement Vol. 36, pp. s11-s44.

Lee, T.W. (1998), Korea: Chaebol Dilemmas, *Lloyd's Shipping Economist*, April, pp. 10-12.

Lloyd's Shipping Economist (1998), Korean Crisis: Korean Pride Comes before a Fall, February, pp. 16-18.

Maekyung Business (1997), The History of Privatising Public Enterprises, 15 October, p. 18.

Montagnon, P. (1997), This is an Unusual Situation, *Financial Times*, 9 December, p. 19.

Morita, A. (1987), *Made in Japan*, Fontana and Collins, London.

Nagorski, B. (1972), *Port Problems in Developing Countries: Principles of Port Planning and Organisation*, International Association of Ports and Harbours, Tokyo.

Pack, H. and Westphal, W. (1986), Industrial Strategy and Technological Change: Theory versus Reality, *Journal of Economic Development*, Vol. 11, pp. 87-128.

Park, C.H. (1970), *Our Nation's Path*, Hollym Corporation, Seoul.

Park, Y.C. (1990), Development Lessons from Asia: The Role of Government in South Korea and Taiwan, *American Economic Review*, Vol. 80, No. 2, pp. 118-121.

Porter, M. (1990), *The Competitive Advantage of Nations*, Macmillan Press, London.

Ranis, G. (1989), *The Political Economy of Development Policy Change: A Comparative Study of Taiwan and Korea*, KDI Working Paper No. 8916, Korea Development Institute, Seoul.

Ro, C.H. (1996), Introduction: Korea in the Era of Post-Development and Globalisation - The Tasks of Public Administration, in Ro, C.-H. (ed.), *Korea in the Era of Post-Development and Globalisation: The Tasks of Public Administration*, Korea Institute of Public Administration, KIPA Publication Series II, Seoul, pp. 25-35.

Ryoo, S.Y. (ed.) (1997), *Privatisation and Korean Economy*, Samsung Economic Research Institute, SERI Economic Research No. 3, Seoul.

Song, B.N. (1990), *The Rise of the Korean Economy*, Oxford University Press, Hong Kong.

Song, B.N. (1994), *The Rise of the Korean Economy* (Updated ed.), Oxford University Press, Hong Kong.

Song, D.H. (1986), The Role of the Public Enterprises in the Korean Economy, in Lee, K-U. (ed.), *Industrial Development Policies and Issues*, Korea Development Institute, Seoul.

Stiglitz, J. (1986), *Economics of the Public Sector* (2nd ed.), W.W. Norton & Company, Inc., New York.

The Times Atlas of the World (1995), Times Books and Bartholomew, Edinburgh.

UNCTAD (1985), *Port Development: A Handbook for Planners in Developing Countries*, TD/B/C.4/175/Rev.1, New York.

Wade, R. (1990), *Governing the Market: Economic Theory and the Role of Government in East Asian Industrialisation*, Princeton University Press, Princeton.

World Bank (1993), *The East Asian Miracle: Economic Growth and Public Policy*, Oxford University Press, Washington, D.C.

World Bank (1995), *Bureaucrats in Business: The Economics and Politics of Government Ownership*, Oxford University Press, Washington, D.C.

3 The Korean Port Industry

INTRODUCTION

The previous chapter was devoted to describing the remarkable progress Korea has made in economic growth and in expanding the size of its economy over the last four decades. As was shown, this economic development has resulted in a rapid increase of exports and imports. Since the foreign trade of Korea is predominantly carried by sea transport, Korean ports have played a crucial role in the process of economic growth and, therefore, in dealing with the additional seaborne cargoes that have resulted from the development of the national economy. In particular, the ever-growing dependence of Korea's national economy on foreign trade has underlined the importance of its ports to consumers and producers. A widespread maritime connection with overseas countries is, as a consequence, one of the essential prerequisites for national economic growth and development. Korea is fortunate that the recent development and operation of its ports has kept pace with the ever-growing seaborne cargoes that have stemmed mainly from the adoption of an economic policy based on outward-oriented industrialisation. The ports, however, still have several problems that will be discussed in the following sections.

In this chapter, the importance of ports and terminals to the Korean national economy will be described, highlighting the sharply growing container traffic and insufficient port and terminal capacity. After an explanation of the port administration structures containing a discussion of some characteristics of port management and operation, this chapter will move on to the new port and terminal development plans for coping with the future expected increased demand for port facilities, especially for container terminals, and the prospects for greater private sector participation in ports.

41

THE IMPORTANCE OF KOREAN PORTS TO THE NATIONAL ECONOMY

Historically, ports have acted as the interface between national or regional economies and the rest of the world (Haynes *et al.*, 1997). A port provides direct access to world markets and an excellent opportunity for access to the developing trade with a wide range of countries; in other words, a port can be regarded as a gateway for international trade. There is a close relationship between ports and the prospects for economic development. The port is not only a determinant of economic development, but a decisive factor in it. The influence of a port on the economy extends beyond its boundaries into the industrial, commercial and business sectors of the nation at regional and national levels (Frankel, 1987). At the same time, ports are also directly affected by economic development.

Nagorski (1972) suggests that an important role of ports is to provide gates for global trade. Without an efficient port, the cost of living becomes higher, industrial development more difficult, and the export of domestic products unprofitable. Thus, the rate of economic progress is drastically curtailed. Western Europe could never have achieved such spectacular and rapid progress without Hamburg, Bremen, Rotterdam and Antwerp. Except for a small proportion as air cargoes, in island countries such as the UK and Japan, a formidable volume of imports and exports must, by necessity, be channelled by sea. Under this circumstance, the major British ports have been veritable bastions of British prosperity for centuries.

UNCTAD (1992) categorises ports according to three criteria: (i) port development policy, strategy and attitude; (ii) the scope and extension of port activities, especially in the area of information; and (iii) the integration of port activities and organisation. In addition, as service industries have replaced manufacturing as a dominant economic sector in the 1980s, the role of ports and their economic impact on their adjacent cities has shifted (Haynes *et al.*, 1997). The function of ports to their adjacent cities is substantial, offering a wide range of logistical and telecommunication activities, which are the main features of the third generation ports (UNCTAD, 1992). Whatever these activities may be, however, maritime-related industries carry on their businesses in competitive markets. Under these circumstances, a port is considered as merely one link in a chain of transport, trading facilities and services involved in any given transaction. In this context, as Suykens (1989) argues, any improvement in the economic efficiency of a port will enhance economic welfare by increasing the producers' surplus for the originators of goods being exported and consumers' surplus at the final destination of the goods being imported. Ports can no longer expect to attract shipping lines simply because they are natural gateways to rich hinterlands.

Turning to the Korean case, Hong (1995) listed three major factors affecting the country's maritime policy, one of which is the geopolitical situation. Bounded on the north by North Korea, on the south by the Korea Strait, on the west by the Yellow Sea and on the east by the East Sea, Korea is in fact a geopolitical island and a landbridge connecting the Pacific Ocean and mainland Asia. Sea transportation and ports, therefore, have played a strategic and crucial role in the country's industrialisation and naval defence. As for the importance of Korean ports to the national economy, Raven (1982, p. 82) describes the economic role of ports in developing countries as follows:

"Because ports play such a catalytic role in economic expansion, we find that many developing countries, where ports are able to function freely and efficiently, have made particularly rapid progress. Typical examples are Hong Kong, Singapore, Korea and Taiwan."

Table 3.1 Exports and Imports carried by Sea and Air
(Units: Billions, %)

Year	by Sea		by Air		by Sea		by Air	
	Tonnes	%	Tonnes	%	Tonne-kms	%	Tonne-kms	%
1985	1,330	99.8	3.3	0.2	11,498	99.8	24	0.2
1986	1,538	99.7	3.9	0.3	12,888	99.8	28	0.2
1987	1,780	99.7	4.7	0.3	14,514	99.8	31	0.2
1988	1,985	99.7	5.1	0.3	16,354	99.8	35	0.2
1989	2,039	99.7	7.1	0.3	16,652	99.7	43	0.3
1990	2,198	99.6	7.8	0.3	18,337	99.8	46	0.2
1991	2,630	99.7	7.9	0.3	21,686	99.8	45	0.2
1992	2,856	99.7	8.4	0.3	24,571	99.8	50	0.2
1993	3,169	99.7	9.5	0.3	27,684	99.8	62	0.2
1994	3,534	99.7	11.1	0.3	28,817	99.8	70	0.2

Source: Korean National Statistical Office (1996).

To export-led economies, like Korea, the most important role of ports is linkage in the transport chain for imports and exports. As shown in Table 2.4 in Chapter 2 and Table 3.1, the Korean economy has been heavily and continuously dependent upon international trade with almost 99.8% (in volume terms) of imports and exports carried by sea transport. The dependence of GNP on foreign trade amounted to 74.7% in 1995. This phenomenon explains the important role of Korean ports in national economic growth and development. In other words, the port sector has been treated as a 'trade facilitator' (Haralambides and Veenstra, 1996).

Ports contribute much to the economy of a nation, and port economic impact analysis is the major tool for assessing such contributions (De Salvo, 1994). Moon (1992) analyses the impact of the port industry on the Korean economy and identifies the spreading effects of port investment from a macroeconomic viewpoint. Using a standard input-output model, his analysis reveals that the Korean port industry was responsible, directly and indirectly, for gross sales within the economy of 375,241 million won (US$ 618 million – 1980 exchange rate) and the creation of a 202,261 million won (US$ 333 million) contribution to GNP as well as for 28,760 jobs. His study also shows that the chain reactions initiated by the demand for port operations gives the Korean port industry a multiplier effect of 1.68 and an employment multiplier of 1.29. The former means that each unit of sales by the port produces 1.68 units in sales throughout the economy, and the latter that ten million won worth of sales by the port creates 1.29 jobs in all industries.

CONTAINER TRAFFIC IN KOREA

When analysing the characteristics of a port wishing to serve the transportation needs of the future, Vogel (1994) has suggested that this really amounts to the container terminal of the future. His argument suggests that the container terminal will play a considerably more crucial role in international trade in the future. Several studies, for example, Gilman (1983), UNCTAD (1985), Pearson (1988) and Containerisation International (1997), classified the development of container ships into 'generations' as having characteristics typical of certain stages in container development and container shipbuilding. Table 3.2 shows us that increases in size and cargo handling capacity are the main characteristics of each generation of container ship. Baird (1996) and Cullinane and Khanna

(1997) discuss the on-going trend towards larger container ships and its impact on ports. Ports and terminals will not work properly and productively unless infrastructure is provided, as the container revolution increases momentum toward the year 2000 (Lloyd's List Maritime Asia, 1995). With regard to this situation, it might be worth noting the following quote:

> "In the highly competitive environment, ports have to make significant investments without any degree of assurance that traffic will increase. Their only guarantee is that unless there is a container handling facility, there will be little or no container traffic." (Haynes *et al.*, 1997, p. 99)

Table 3.2 Physical Characteristics of Container Ships

Generations	Year	Maximum Capacity (TEU)
First Generation	1964	1,000
Second Generation	1972	1,500
Third Generation	1980	3,000
Fourth Generation	1984	4,500
Fifth Generation	1995 ~	over 6,000

Sources: Gilman (1983), UNCTAD (1985), Pearson (1988) and Containerisation International (1997).

It is said that unitisation, particularly containerisation, has significantly altered trade patterns as well as the port industry. Containerisation was, in fact, introduced to international shipping in the late 1960s as an attempt to cut the costs of maritime transport by reducing cargo handling costs and the vessel's time in port. It has also allowed economies of scale to be reaped, has increased efficiency and service speeds, and has offered goods greater protection from loss and damage they would otherwise have received. In international liner shipping, containerisation represented a radical transformation of existing technologies which not only dramatically altered the processes in the ports and shipping industry, but also pervaded the entire socio-economic system (Baird, 1996). The number of advantages of this transportation system over conventional, labour-intensive cargo-handling techniques were of great significance and led to the transformation and modernisation of cargo-handling systems.

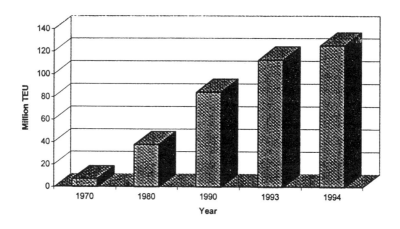

Figure 3.1 Development of World Container Traffic
Source: Containerisation International Yearbook (various years).

In consequence, it has increasingly gained favour in the carriage of international trade and has become one of the most important means of transport. Figure 3.1 illustrates the increasing volume of container traffic handled in world ports. In 1994, the recorded global total was 125 million TEU; an increase of 11 million TEU (10.4%) over the 1993 figure. This rate of growth is in line with the average annual increase of 10% experienced over the last decade and slightly above the 9% figure for the last five years (Containerisation International Yearbook, 1996). Container volume has increased 18 fold from approximately 7 million TEU in 1970 to 125 million TEU in 1994. In the context of container ship and port generations, the container terminal looks set, therefore, to still be playing a significant role in international trade in the future.

Parallel with the growth in world container traffic, the volume of containers handled in Korea has also risen sharply since the 1970s as a result of the country's rapid economic growth and development. This is illustrated in Figure 3.2. The latest rise has been fuelled by the rapidly developing trade between Korea and China and gives a clear signal that the Korean import and export economy, after a dip in the early 1990s, is back on course.

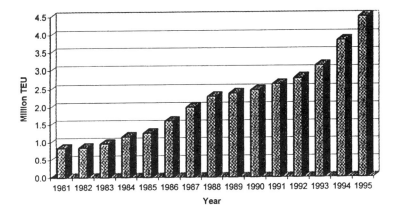

Figure 3.2 Growth of Container Traffic in Korea
Sources: Containerisation International Yearbook (various years); KMPA (1996).

Furthermore, the volume of container traffic is expected to increase in the future. A recent report by the Korea Maritime and Port Administration (1992a) shows that container volume in Korea is predicted to rise to 6.5 million TEU by 2001 and then 11.5 million TEU by 2011. Additionally, the forecast of regional container traffic by Drewry Shipping Consultants (1996) partly supports this expectation, arguing that Far East Asia (including Korea) will continue to outpace average global development, remaining the most dynamic container zone in the world and capable of registering double digit growth rates for several years to come (see Figure 3.3).

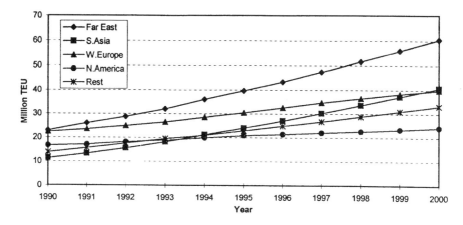

Figure 3.3 Forecast of Regional Container Activity to 2000
Source: Drewry Shipping Consultants (1996, p. 54).

Table 3.3 The World's Top 10 Container Terminals

Rank	Container Terminal	1995 (Million TEU)	1994 (Million TEU)	Changing Rate (%)
1	Hong Kong	12.6	11.1	13.7
2	Singapore	11.9	10.4	13.9
3	Kaohsiung	5.1	4.9	3.1
4	Rotterdam	4.8	4.5	5.5
5	**Pusan**	**4.5**	**3.8**	**17.6**
6	Hamburg	2.9	2.7	6.3
7	Long Beach	2.8	2.6	7.7
8	Yokohama	2.7	2.3	16.6
9	Los Angeles	2.6	2.5	1.58
10	Antwerp	2.3	2.2	5.4

Source: Cargo Systems (1996).

As can be seen in Table 3.3, Pusan, the principal port of Korea, is ranked the fifth largest container port after Hong Kong, Singapore, Kaohsiung and Rotterdam. One thing to be noted in Table 3.3 is the fact that the fastest rate of growth in container throughput from 1994 to 1995 occurs in Pusan with a changing rate of 17.6%. In addition, Robinson (1998) speculates that the port of Pusan will continue to play a crucial role in international trade, as the axis of trading patterns moves to eastern ports.

Table 3.4 Container Traffic through the Port of Pusan

Year	Pusan		Inchon		Others*		Total	
	TEU (000)	(%)	TEU (000)	(%)	TEU (000)	(%)	TEU (000)	(%)
1983	884	91.8	79	8.2	-	0.0	963	100
1984	1,054	91.3	100	8.7	1	0.1	1,155	100
1985	1,155	91.7	104	8.3	-	0.0	1,259	100
1986	1,491	93.1	101	6.3	10	0.6	1,602	100
1987	1,887	94.5	108	5.4	1	0.1	1,996	100
1988	2,135	93.4	150	6.6	2	0.1	2,287	100
1989	2,257	94.9	116	4.9	6	0.3	2,379	100
1990	2,348	95.1	112	4.5	9	0.4	2,469	100
1991	2,518	95.5	119	4.5	-	0.0	2,637	100
1992	2,673	95.5	118	4.2	8	0.3	2,799	100
1993	2,998	95.7	113	3.6	21	0.7	3,132	100
1994	3,575	93.2	227	5.9	34	0.9	3,836	100
1995	4,130	92.0	296	6.6	62	1.4	4,488	100

Note: * Others includes the ports of Ulsan and Masan.
Source: KMPA (1993, 1996).

One of the main problems the Korean port industry faces, however, is that almost all container traffic, shown in Figure 3.2, is handled through the port of Pusan, which is located on the south-eastern coast of the Korean peninsula. As can be seen in Table 3.4, between 90% and 95% of total container volume is handled through Pusan almost every year. Of this, transhipment cargo represents about 15% of total container traffic, mainly from China and Japan bound for Europe and south-east Asia. The portion of total container volume that Pusan port handled reached its peak in 1993 with 95.7% of the total. In 1995, it handled 4.1 million TEU accounting for 92% of the total container traffic of 4.5 million TEU. In contrast, the port of Inchon handled 0.3 million TEU accounting for only 6.6%, and the ports of Ulsan and Masan together handled only 1.4% of Korea's total container volume.

Park (1995, p. 11) gives the following explanation why a high volume of container traffic has concentrated on the port of Pusan:

"Despite the fact that the port of Inchon has 1,160 metres of container berths and about 40% of the containerised cargoes originates in and is destined for the *Kyungin* area (the province of *Kyunggi* and the capital city), which is the major area of industrial and population concentration in Korea, the port has not acted as a load centre. The reason for this is that it is one shipday away from the main container trunk line and has restricted passage through a lock to enter the port owing to its big tidal difference. As a result, the containers have been concentrated on the port of Pusan."

Moreover, a recent report (Port Development International, 1995) gives several reasons for congestion at Pusan. First, the country's industrial production grew at an average of 13.7% per annum over the last few years and trade with China increased remarkably (in 1994, imports from China were up by 39% in 1993 to US$ 5.4 billion, exports were up by US$2 billion, a 20.4% increase on 1993). Second, apart from the sheer volume of traffic using the port, the consolidation of the operations of the Hanjin Shipping Company at Pusan's Jasungdae container terminal has led to delays to the services of other lines.

The port of Pusan, as Fleming (1997) points out, serves the miracle-growth economy. Pusan is favoured as a load centre by two major Korean container lines, Hanjin and Hyundai, and additionally the transhipment segment of Pusan's container traffic has been growing sharply recently. Pusan is cost-competitive in container handling, especially in comparison to Japanese load centres (Drewry Shipping Consultants, 1996). It has consequently been selected to handle transhipments of Chinese cargo and, more remarkably, Japanese cargo that would normally use load centres in Japan were the container transfer and domestic transport costs not so high (Canna, 1995). Table 3.5 presents a comparison of costs incurred at the major terminals in the world and shows that port costs in Japan are 2.5 times those of Singapore, 2.2 times those of Rotterdam and 2.1 times those of Pusan.

Table 3.5 International Terminal Cost Comparison

Terminals	Costs (US$ per TEU)
Japan	350
Hong Kong	290
Los Angeles	250
Hamburg	230
New York	220
Seattle	200
Kaohsiung	190
Pusan	**170**
Rotterdam	160
Singapore	140

Source: Drewry Shipping Consultants (1996, p. 127).

INSUFFICIENT TERMINAL CAPACITY AND CONGESTION

There are at the moment four operating container terminals in Korea; (i) the *Jasungdae Container Terminal* which is run by the Busan Container Terminal Operation Corporation (BCTOC), (ii) the *Shinsundae Container Terminal* which opened in 1991 and is operated by the Pusan East Container Terminal Company (PECT), (iii) *Inchon Pier 4*, jointly operated by the Hanjin Transportation Company and the Korea Express Company, and (iv) the *Uam Container Terminal* (Phase One) which started operating in September 1996, and is operated by the Uam Terminal Company (UTC). Table 3.6 shows the container terminal facilities in Korea as of 1996.

Due to the concentration of container traffic in the port of Pusan, the lack of cargo handling capacity makes matters even more serious. According to two recent studies (KMPA, 1989 and 1992b), the problem of insufficient terminal capacity will become worse in the future. Table 3.7 shows the seriousness of the problem. The result has been that Pusan has been asked to handle more than it can cope with at times. In fact, congestion at Pusan in early 1995 was so considerable that it prompted the Far East Freight Conference to impose a port congestion surcharge (Fairplay, 1995).

Table 3.6 Container Terminals Facilities in Korea (as of 1996)

	Jasungdae Terminal	Shinsundae Terminal	Inchon Pier 4	Uam Terminal
Cargo Handling Capacity*	900,000 TEU	960,000 TEU	250,000 TEU	300,000 TEU
Berth Capacity	4 ships x 50,000 dwt	3 ships x 50,000 dwt	1 ship x 50,000 dwt	1 ship x 20,000 dwt 2 ships x 5,000 dwt
Operator(s)	BCTOC	PECT	Hanjin Co. Korea Express Co.	UTC
Operation Starting Year	September 1978	June 1991	December 1973	September 1996**

Notes: * annual capacity; and ** partly operated.
Source: Korea Container Terminal Authority (1996).

Table 3.7 Container Terminal Capacity and Shortages in the Port of Pusan (Unit: Million TEU)

Year	1989	1990	1991	1992	1993	1994
Demand	2.16	2.27	2.45	2.60	2.81	3.23
Terminal Capacities	1.26	1.26	2.22	2.22	2.22	2.22
Jasungdae	0.90	0.90	0.90	0.90	0.90	0.90
Shinsundae	-	-	0.96	0.96	0.96	0.96
Conventional Berths	0.36	0.36	0.36	0.36	0.36	0.36
(Shortage)	(0.90)	(1.01)	(0.23)	(0.38)	(0.59)	(1.01)

Note: Transhipment cargoes excluded.
Source: KMPA (1989, 1992b).

UNCTAD (1985, p. 1) points out the importance of port development to an export-oriented economy, like Korea, as follows:

"The paramount importance of a far-sighted port development policy does not appear to have been fully appreciated in the past by many governments. As a result, ports have often been unable to keep up with the rate of expansion of a country's overseas and coastal trade."

This argument could be applied to the Korean port industry. In spite of the considerable amount invested in port development by the Korean government, sufficient capacity has neither been planned nor constructed in time. This logic becomes even more convincing when one considers that the total cargo handling capacity, in particular at the country's main port of Pusan, has lagged chronically behind demand. Moon (1992) points out four consequences of inadequate port development that are, to some considerable extent, interlinked: port congestion, poor port performance, a negative impact on the nation's economy, and a negative influence on port users. Of these, port congestion most seriously affects the country's overall economy, because almost all commodities for export and import are carried through its seaports, in particular, container terminals.

Beth (1985) defines the concept of port congestion from the viewpoints of shippers and shipowners, but focusing on the standpoint of shipowners, port congestion means that ships are delayed spending more time in port than scheduled. The delay may occur either at berth or before berthing with the kind of delay depending on the cause. There is no doubt that the problem of congestion produces serious repercussions of all sorts, not only within the countries concerned but also for the users of the ports. Imakita (1978, p. 19) explains some consequences of port congestion by noting:

> "During such periods [time of congestion], time losses and damage or thefts and pilferage of cargo tend to occur more frequently than would otherwise be the case. And the entry of too many ships for anchorage within the mooring area of the port makes each one increasingly subject to collision. . . . . On the other hand, heavy congestion may result in a substantial diversion of traffic in the long run, or even stimulate the development of an alternative transport route."

The country suffering from congestion may, as a result, receive no share of the growing transport industry. Port congestion must thus be regarded as one of the foremost constraints to the economic development of any country and region. In particular, to trade-oriented nations.

Port congestion in Korea is widely recognised as being largely caused by the insufficiency of terminal cargo handling capacity (Moon, 1995). The problem is most prevalent at the container terminals in Pusan. Port costs constitute a significant proportion of total distribution costs and thus, ultimately, have an important impact on the value of commodities entering international trade. In order to obtain, therefore, increased benefits from international trade, ports and terminals should be operated as efficiently as possible. By adding to the logistics costs of Korea's manufactured products, however, the delay caused by this congestion seriously undermines their competitiveness in the world market and detracts from Korea's potential for further economic development. Chung (1995) estimates that congestion costs at the port of Pusan totalled 29.3 billion won (US$ 36.5 million) in 1994. In 1995, the situation became even worse, resulting in costs of more than 70 billion won (US$ 90.8 million). Furthermore, during the first quarter of 1995, some 15.7% of all vessels calling at Pusan had to wait more than 12 hours for a berth. Delays varied according to the terminals used, with ships having to wait an average of 29 hours for access to the Shinsundae container terminal and 54 hours for the Jasungdae container terminal (Containerisation International, 1996).

PORT ADMINISTRATIVE STRUCTURES IN KOREA

In general, types of port administration differ very widely in terms of patterns of ownership and administrative systems. Thomas (1976) points out that the management of most ports in the world is vested in a port authority. The constitution and objectives of these bodies differ quite considerably from country to country and indeed even within national boundaries. Perhaps the most remarkable feature of port administration in the major ports of the world are the diverse forms of ownership adopted and the numerous ways in which responsibility for providing facilities and services have been delegated.

Goss (1990) classifies the activities of a port authority into two different roles: one is a *comprehensive* role and the other a *landlord* role. The former involves providing all facilities and services with independent operators either prohibited from undertaking work within the port or permitted to perform only minor tasks (e.g. refuse collection). The landlord role, however, limits the activities of the port authority simply to providing and maintaining the basic infrastructure (e.g. breakwaters, quays, roadways) and essential services (e.g. fire service, security, etc.) with independent private or public companies allowed to provide all other facilities and services (e.g. cargo handling, towage, etc.). In this context, the administrative characteristics of Korean ports are discussed in the following sections.

Port Management and Administration

The Korean government has traditionally been responsible for the central control of the country's ports in such areas as port administration, management and development. In Korea, prior to 1996, the KMPA played an important role in the planning and development of the country's maritime industry including its ports. Moon (1992) gives details of Korea's port administration prior to the establishment of the KMPA. The turning point for the Korean port industry came in 1976 when the government established the Korea Port Authority (KPA) with the purpose of providing a central authority for port management and development. The KPA was renamed the Korea Maritime and Port Administration (KMPA) in 1977.

Prior to the creation of the KMPA in 1976, the fragmentation of authority and the lack of co-ordination between the bodies concerned with port planning and operations caused the development of the ports to proceed in a piecemeal and uncoordinated fashion. It also led to the duplication of effort and facilities due to the competition between ports and between the interested government agencies (Bang, 1984). The government, as a result, realised it was necessary to integrate port operations and development in an effort to maximise efficiency and to meet the rapidly increasing demand for port facilities. This is the reason why the KPA, later named KMPA, was launched. Until early 1996, the KMPA was subject to the supervision of the Ministry of Construction and Transportation. At this time, however, it became administered by and operated under the auspices of the Ministry of Transportation. Until very recently, the KMPA acted in a 'comprehensive role' having responsibility for and central control of the country's ports and terminals in such areas as administration, management and operation. The organisation structure of each division of the KMPA are illustrated in Figure 3.4. The KMPA was headed by an administrator who was appointed directly by the Korean President, and was divided into eleven departments administering all maritime affairs in the country through ten district authorities or District Maritime and Port Administrations.

The main responsibilities of the KMPA were described as follows (KMPA, 1979):

- to control the planning, design, construction and maintenance of all port facilities in the major ports within its jurisdiction;

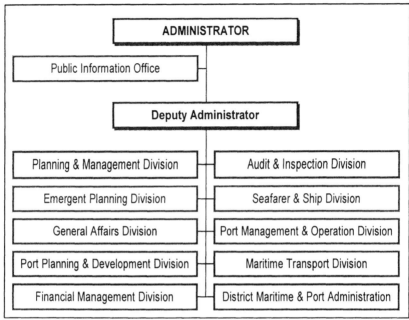

Source: Derived from KMPA (1979).

Figure 3.4 Organisation Chart of the KMPA

- to establish an appropriate form and structure of administration, organisation and management complying with government regulations at the port level;
- to ensure a sound financial system with public accounting methods and a reasonable level of port dues;
- to co-operate in the development of the port cities and related commercial services;
- to co-operate with other agencies, whether governmental or private, in developing the national economy; and
- to achieve efficient port operations.

In particular, the Divisions of 'Port Management and Operation' and 'Port Planning and Development' played an important role in the country's port industry. The former was in charge of aspects such as overall planning of port operations and management, traffic policy on port facilities, the control of public waterways within the harbour, supervision of companies associated with ports, and the maintenance of port statistics. The latter, on the other hand, was in charge of activities such as overall planning for construction of ports and inland navigational waterways, budgeting for port construction investment and maintenance, general supervision of port construction, engineering research, and selection and procurement of port equipment.

In early 1996, the Korean government announced it would merge three maritime-related agencies into a new Ministry of Maritime Affairs and Fisheries (MMAF) to help the country become a maritime superpower. The ministry was finally launched in August 1996 by merging the three existing maritime-related organisations; the KMPA, the Fisheries Administration, and the Maritime Police Administration. The MMAF has a remit to control and manage its seaports and other related activities and to improve management efficiency in the maritime area. The KMPA now constitutes one branch of the MMAF under the assistant minister of the shipping and ports division (see Appendix 1).

As Hong (1995) points out, since the 1950s logical consolidation in Korea's maritime administration has been supported by maritime interests but has received no political propulsion. The major motive for establishing the MMAF comes from a change in the administrative environment. This is an important issue in a country like Korea, where traditions of centralised government are strong and where planning decisions are usually made at the national level. The contemporary vision incorporates an integrated policy aimed at putting in place a single, unifying concept to draw together the interests involved. Underdal (1980, p. 167) explores the major option of creating a new institution as follows:

"This [creating a new institution] could be done by merging two or more existing institutions, creating a new agency to promote certain values and policy perspectives through bargaining with other agencies, or by establishing a new superagency to co-ordinate work done by other specialised agencies. . . . . The common denominator for these measures is that they seek to achieve policy integration by reorganising the institutional structure so that it better reflects the policy perspective desires."

With a single government organisation responsible for maritime affairs, the case of France may be a good example and provide object lessons for the Korean government. France integrated the government organisations related to maritime and ocean industries under the auspices of the Ministry of the Sea in order to more effectively operate maritime related policies (Aquarone, 1988). There were arguments for and against the plan for establishing the Ministry. In spite of several drawbacks such as the costs of the integration effort, the main motives for establishing a single government organisation responsible for maritime policy and management were (i) an attractive and simple solution for increasing the importance of the maritime sector, (ii) policy coherence and consistency, (iii) the avoidance of duplicated effort, (iv) consolidation of information, and (v) clarity of command (Aquarone, 1988). These motivations are equally relevant to the Korean case.

Administration and Operation of the Container Terminals

As far as the administration of container terminals in Korea is concerned, the Korea Container Terminal Authority (KCTA) has played a central role in the management and operation of the country's container terminals. All the container terminals in Korea are controlled, managed, operated, and supervised by the KCTA which is a public organisation set up in 1990. Before the KCTA was established, the development and operation of ports in Korea was entirely dependent upon government funds. This system caused problems because of the inflexibility of the budget and the bureaucratic procedures for obtaining funds necessary for port development and maintenance, thus resulting in a situation where the required financing had not been provided at the right level or at the right time.

In order to avoid these delays in financing, the government launched the KCTA Act in December 1989 and, finally, established the KCTA on the basis of the Act. One of the main aims for creating the KCTA was that profits accruing from operation, management, and development of a container terminal should be reinvested into the development and maintenance of that container terminal, and that financial sources should be diversified to efficiently develop and operate the terminal. The objectives of the KCTA can be described as (i) the timely development, effective operation and management of the container terminals in Korea; (ii) the promotion of a smooth flow of container cargo traffic; and (iii) promoting national economic development. The duties can be defined as (i) the development of new container terminals, their management and operation; (ii) the establishment and management of Inland Container Depots and approach roads to container terminals; and (iii) the carrying on of terminal stevedoring services.

In order to carry out these tasks the KCTA can, if necessary, engage in such business as (i) purchasing and selling land and any properties on it; (ii) investment in other businesses; (iii) borrowing money from commercial banks including foreign loans; (iv) issuing the Container Terminal Development Bonds; and (v) charging fees for using the container terminal facilities.

The KCTA currently controls and supervises the Jasungdae, Shinsundae, Gamman and Uam terminals in Pusan together with the Kwangyang terminal located in the country's south west. These terminals are all leased without payment from the government in the form of the MMAF (the KMPA prior to 1996). The KCTA then rents these terminals out to each terminal operator in return for payment: the Jasungdae terminal to the BCTOC, the Shinsundae terminal to the PECT, the Uam Terminal to the UTC, and the others to private companies, mainly shipping and transportation companies. The locations of each container terminal in the port of Pusan can be seen in Appendix 2.

As shown in Figure 3.5, the Jasungdae container terminal is operated by the BCTOC, which was founded in March 1978 as a non-profit making public organisation and was the first to introduce the idea of a container terminal into Korea. The aim of establishing the BCTOC was to contribute to the national economy through the efficient operation and modernisation of the container terminal, and thus to cope with customers' needs in the rapidly changing environment of international trade.

On the other hand, a limited company (the PECT) operates the Shinsundae container terminal, the construction of which was finished in June 1991. In setting up the PECT, the total capital injected was 18 billion won, which had risen to 47 billion won as of 1995 after continuously increasing the capital. The KCTA holds 25% of the total shares, thus having control over the PECT, and another 11 stevedoring companies hold the remaining 75% (Korea Maritime Institute, 1996a).

Figure 3.5 shows that there are three different entities controlling the container terminals in Korea; the terminal operators (i.e. BCTOC, PECT, UTC) and other private companies, are subject to the supervision of the KCTA, and in turn the KCTA is under the control of the MMAF (the KMPA prior to 1996). This hierarchy gives much power to the MMAF acting on behalf of the government, indicating that the government has heavily influenced the processes of management, operation, and development of the container terminals in Korea.

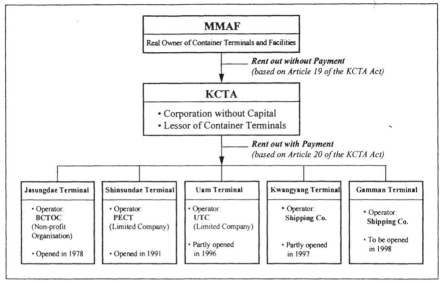

Figure 3.5 Korea's Container Terminal Administration and Operation
Source: Derived from the KCTA Act.

NEW TERMINAL DEVELOPMENT PLANS

Korea, neatly positioned between Japan and China, should be the ideal place to tranship the growing volume of container traffic emanating from the northern and central parts of China, currently emerging as one of the fastest growing economies in the world. The country continues to lose out, however, for want of sufficient port facilities. Although the existing port infrastructure is far from undeveloped, it has been hard pressed in recent years just to keep pace with the growing export and import traffic generated within the country itself.

The consensus is that the recent policy and actions of the state-controlled port industry has done little to ease the problem (Fairplay, 1995). The governmental port authority, embodied in the MMAF (the KMPA prior to 1996) could, on the surface, be applauded for the way it has restructured its operation to allow a greater participation by the private sector in the area of terminal funding and management. In reality, this process is proving very tortuous and has markedly slowed the construction and opening of new terminal sites. It could be argued that, because of its drive to shift the cost burden of port development away from the government, and onto the commercial transport sector, the MMAF (the KMPA prior to 1996) has singularly failed to match new container port development with that required by the shipping lines, shippers and the national economy.

In order to modernise and expand the country's port facilities as a means of solving the problem of serious congestion at the port of Pusan and of meeting the expected increase in container throughput into the next century, the public port authority has launched a 15-year port development programme that could boost cargo handling capacity by more than 500 million tonnes per year. The KMPA has stated that the need for extra handling capacity became essential as trade with China began to flourish and new routes were being planned that would substantially increase the number of container shipments between the two countries (Lloyd's List, 1995). The plan hopes to result in large-scale local port development that is funded and managed by both foreign and domestic companies. To alleviate Korea's port congestion and keep pace with ever-increasing container cargo, the programme comprises the following new projects that are either under construction or being considered.

Gamman Container Terminal (The Fourth Phase Development at Pusan)

As the existing container terminals are working to capacity, much attention has been paid to Pusan's fourth phase development. To release the enormous burden on the port of Pusan, the fourth phase development plan was launched near the existing Shinsundae terminal. The planned facilities include a new 1,400 metre quay capable of accommodating four post-Panamax containerships with a total handling capacity of 1.2 million TEU per year. It is expected to cost US$ 500 million and 30% of this total has been funded by private companies. The rest will be funded by the government, which will raise the money through bond issues to which shipping companies such as Hyundai Merchant Marine, Hanjin and Cho Yang are expected to subscribe. The terminal commenced operation in

1998. Table 3.8 shows the forecast cargo handling capacity at the port of Pusan after the opening of the Fourth Phase terminal, which will be able to solve the current congestion problem.

Table 3.8 Forecast of Cargo Handling Capacity at the Port of Pusan (Unit: Million TEU)

Year	1996	2001	2005	2011
Estimated Container Traffic	2.95	3.20	3.77	4.47
Estimated Cargo Handling Capacity	2.88	3.62	4.23	4.52
Jasungdae	0.90	0.90	0.90	0.90
Shinsundae	0.96	0.96	0.96	0.96
Conventional Berths	0.36	-	-	-
4th Container Terminal	0.66	1.20	1.20	1.20
Multipurpose Berths	-	0.56	1.17	1.46
Surplus Capacity (Shortage)	**(0.07)**	**0.42**	**0.46**	**0.05**

Source: Lim and Shin (1993).

Uam Container Terminal

Even after the completion of the Gamman Container Terminal by 1998, there will still be a long-term shortage of container handling capacity. The development plan for additional container terminal capacity at Pusan includes the Uam terminal. The plans consist of four phases which are expected to be completed by 1999. In the middle of 1996, the Phase One terminal began partial operation. The terminal is managed and operated by the newly established Uam Terminal Company (UTC), whose shares are jointly held by two transportation companies: the Korea Container Terminal Company and the Dongsung Silup Company. The former company holds 60% of the shares and the latter 40%.

Kwangyang Container Terminal

As a way of encouraging a two-port system in Korea and thus of dispersing the container traffic currently concentrated in the port of Pusan, the government is keen to see the development of a new container terminal at Kwangyang in the south-west of the country (Nah, 1994). The development project consists of Phase One and Two as well as further development plans. Four berths on 1,400 metres of quay are now being constructed under Phase One of the plan. Each berth is capable of accommodating a 50,000 dwt container ship with 350 metres of quay per berth and 14.5 metres of water depth. They are expected to be in operation in 1998, and have a designed handling capacity of 960,000 TEU per year, and a terminal area of 840,000 square metres with 600 metres of depth from the apron. The terminal will also have a container railway yard for transporting containers from the terminal to the hinterland. Phase Two is planned to be completed between 1996 and 2001, creating six berths. Four 50,000 and two 20,000 dwt container ships can berth alongside simultaneously when it is completed. The construction of the rest of the ten berths planned will be carried out in the future. Table 3.9 shows the overall cargo handling capacity in Korea after the completion of the Kwangyang terminal.

Table 3.9 Forecast of Cargo Handling Capacity in Korea (Million TEU)

Year	1996	2001	2005	2011
Estimated Container Traffic	4.62	6.48	8.59	11.46
Estimated Cargo Handling Capacity	4.23	6.62	8.42	10.02
Pusan Port	2.82	3.62	4.22	4.52
Kwangyang Port	0.96	2.40	3.60	4.80
Other Ports	0.45	0.60	0.60	0.70
Surplus Capacity (Shortage)	**(0.39)**	**0.14**	**(0.17)**	**(1.44)**

Source: Lim and Shin (1993).

Gaduk Island Container Terminal (New Pusan Port)

As can be seen in Table 3.9, even when the new facilities at Pusan and Kwangyang are completed, the expected long-term demand for container port facilities in Korea will not be met. For this reason, there are plans to develop the Gaduk Island terminal off the southern tip of the country into a major port facility with container berths. After setting up a master plan and carrying out a feasibility study in early 1996, the project is currently underway. Plans are for a 25-berth port to form part of a larger redevelopment project to be completed in 2011, and designed to have a mix of general cargo and container wharves, with an annual capacity of approximately 4.6 million TEU (90 million tonnes). The Gaduk Island scheme will also be built in two phases with the first stage due for completion by 2005 and the second phase by 2011 (Fossey, 1997). The main infrastructure work will be carried out by the government and includes a breakwater, railway systems, container depots and marshalling yards. It is expected, however, that there will be a major involvement from the private sector. The 'New Pusan Port Corporation' was recently established as a form of 29 member consortium to accelerate the process of constructing the terminal as planned (Lee, 1998).

All of the above development plans should be finished around 2011, at which time the port of Pusan should have sufficient capacity for handling an ever-growing container traffic. As a consequence, it is hoped that congestion will become a thing of the past. In addition, the future of Pusan as a cargo hub depends on the successful implementation of these long range development programmes.

PRIVATE SECTOR PARTICIPATION IN PORTS

Under the New FYP, the government has released ambitious plans for expanding social overhead capital in order to build up an efficient overall transport system throughout the country. The ultimate objective is to promote the efficient distribution of export and import goods in an effort to accelerate economic growth. Port development was one element of this plan. Given the enormity of the capital requirement, a major problem hindering the process of Korean port development was recognised to be the question of how such projects should be financed. The government has regarded the participation of the private sector as an important method of reducing its financial burden in all spheres of activity and has encouraged private sector participation in numerous investment projects in all sectors. The port industry is no exception.

As the government implements its plan to bring private capital into both existing and new port facilities, new policies are opening up Korean ports to competition. In addition, a degree of privatisation is sought whereby the costs and returns to port operation can be shared between government and private sectors.

Building Dedicated Terminals by Private Shipping Companies

Private companies are already heavily involved in the port projects mentioned in the previous section and their participation is increasing. Shipping lines themselves are setting up dedicated facilities and thereby, for the first time, engaging in competition with the two existing container terminals in Pusan. Hanjin Shipping Company, the biggest container liner company in Korea, for example, is planning a dedicated terminal at Gamchun, close to Pusan. A container yard and berthing for ships of up to 3,000 TEU will be built as part of its global strategy to develop its logistics and intermodal operations. At the new Kwangyang terminal, the Cho Yang Shipping Company, the third biggest liner shipping company in Korea, has set up a task force to evaluate the potential of building a private berth of 210,000 square metres on a greenfield site with a 350 metre quay which, once the terminal is in operation in 1998, will be capable of handling 300,000 TEU annually. Cho Yang considers that a dedicated terminal will be cheaper than using public berths and will improve their ships' ability to keep to schedule. The company is also planning a terminal of similar capacity in Pusan, on a greenfield site occupying 148,750 square metres.

At present, Hanjin uses the Jasungdae terminal operated by the BCTOC. The Director of BCTOC's operations department has commented that finding replacement business when Hanjin moves away will be a new experience. Currently, existing container berths in Korea are all operated on a common user basis and are publicly controlled. Some concessions, however, on port facilities in Pusan and Inchon are due to be handed over in 1998, and more than half of the investment necessary for port construction up to 2011 is expected to come from the private sector (Lloyd's List, 1997). After 1998, therefore, Korean port operators will have to worry about the competition, and they are working towards that (Fairplay, 1996). Obviously, this will be a new experience and terminal operators should prepare for the fact that this business environment is changing.

Financing New Terminal Development from the Private Sector

The port industry, in general, requires huge amounts of capital for its development. In particular, as Slack *et al.* (1996) point out, recent technology changes in the shipping industry and the trend towards larger ships has had a major impact on the ports in the world. Having already invested heavily in container facilities, ports are now being called upon to provide extra facilities such as deeper channels, larger cranes, on-dock rail connections, and more extensive storage facilities. Ports, therefore, are being compelled to invest heavily, or lose their competitive edge. As a consequence, port financing has become a major issue in many countries, and there are severe financial pressures on ports everywhere.

The KCTA, which is in charge of the development, management and operation of Korean container terminals, issues 'Container Terminal Development Bonds' in accordance with the provision of Article 25 of the KCTA Act in order to partly provide funds required to develop and modernise port facilities. The participants selected for taking part in this financing scheme purchase the Bonds in accordance with specific procedures. As at the end of 1996, the total amount of bonds either issued and about to be issued is 200 billion won (US$ 258 million), with the KCTA issuing 50 billion won (US$ 65 million) of bonds each year.

To encourage private participation in this funding scheme for the development of container terminals, the KCTA gives exclusive use rights of the terminal to selected participants. The period of exclusive use is ten years and may be renewed if agreed between the KCTA and the participants prior to the expiration of the period. This exclusivity of use has currently been agreed on two berths: one from the Kwangyang first phase development terminal and the other from the Pusan fourth phase development terminal (Gamman Terminal). Details of the exclusive use rights are as follows (KCTA, 1993):

- They are related to overall terminal operational rights such as the participants' vessels berthing and leaving the quay, container loading and unloading, transit, storage, delivery and receiving etc., in relation to the container ship operation.
- The participants may entrust the whole operation of the terminals to a third party who holds a stevedoring service license issued by the government in accordance with the relevant provisions of the Port Stevedoring Services Business Act.
- The participants may handle the container cargoes of the other container liner operators using the berths.
- The participants shall co-operate by allowing other container liner operators to use the berths upon the order from the

Regional Maritime and Port Authority in cases where the Authority decides it is necessary to allow other liners to use the berth for the efficient management of the port concerned (in this case, the participants may collect use charges from the other liner operators).

• The details of the exclusive use rights of the container terminals (berths) shall be provided by the Agreement to be concluded between the KCTA and the participants, and the Agreement shall be concluded three months prior to the starting of the actual operation of the terminals.

In addition, the government launched the 'Promotion Act of Private Capital Inducement' in August 1994 for attracting private finance into social infrastructure investments including roads, distribution centres and port facilities. The Act has encouraged the private sector to take a financial stake in infrastructure development as a strategic option so that they are able to reduce logistics-related costs (Yoo, 1997).

To keep in step with this movement towards private sector participation in port development and operation as a form of privatisation policy, Korea Maritime Institute (1996b) conducted a feasibility study of privatising the BCTOC, the public sector operator of the Jasungdae container terminal at Pusan. The study was carried out under the assumption that the centralised and government-controlled port administration and operation could not properly cope with the changing port industry environment which has become a much more customer-oriented business, i.e., necessitating the provision of port user services on time and with higher quality and thereby satisfying their major needs.

In conclusion, the MMAF is keen to attract investment from domestic and overseas private sectors for achieving its ambitious plan of making the national port the hub of Northeast Asia in the 21st century (Sohn, 1998). The basic policy for achieving this objective is a form of port privatisation whereby the MMAF owns national ports while private companies are in charge of port operations. In other words, the Korean government pursues the privatisation policy on ports of 'public ownership and private operation'.

REFERENCES

Aquarone, M.C. (1988), French Marine Policy in the 1970s and 1980s, *Ocean Development and International Law*, Vol. 19, pp. 267-285.

Baird, A. (1996), Containerisation and the Decline of the Upstream Urban Port in Europe, *Maritime Policy and Management*, Vol. 23, No. 2, pp. 145-156.

Bang, H.S. (1984), *Factors Affecting Container Terminal Development: A Critique of the Approach Applied in Korean Port*, PhD Thesis, UWIST.

Beth, H. (1985), Economic Effects of Port Congestion, in Beth, H. (ed.), *Port Management Textbook: Containerisation*, Institute of Shipping Economic and Logistics, Bremen.

Canna, E. (1995), Japanese Cargo Shifts to Korea, *American Shipper*, Vol. 37, No. 10, p. 34.

Cargo Systems (1996), *Top 100 Container Ports*, March, Supplement.

Chung, B.M. (1995), Estimation of Congestion Costs in Container Traffic in Pusan Port, *Korea Maritime Review*, Vol. 129, pp. 7-17.

Containerisation International (1996), Congestion: the Carrier's Three-Pronged Defence, April, pp. 56-59.

Containerisation International (1997), Post-Panamax Passion, February, pp. 44-46.

Containerisation International Yearbook (several years), Emap Business Communications, Ltd., London.

Cullinane, K. and Khanna, M. (1997), Large Containerships and the Concentration of Load Centres, *Proceedings of Port Strategy and Development II*, 23-25 February, Port Training Institute, Egypt.

De Salvo, J. (1994), Measuring the Direct Impacts of a Port, *Transportation Journal*, Vol. 30, No. 4, pp. 33-42.

Drewry Shipping Consultants (1996), *Global Container Markets: Prospects and Profitability in a High Growth Era*, Drewry Shipping Consultants, London.

Fairplay (1995), Pusan Takes Action to Relieve Pressure, 10 August, p. 25.

Fairplay (1996), Port Policies Open Up, 8 August, p. 30.

Fleming, D. (1997), World Container Port Rankings, *Maritime Policy and Management*, Vol. 24, No. 2, pp. 175-181.

Fossey, J. (1997), Regional Focus - South Korea: Boxes Galore, *Containerisation International*, January, p. 71.

Frankel, E. (1987), *Port Planning and Development*, John Wiley & Sons, New York.

Gilman, S. (1983), *The Competitive Dynamics of Container Shipping*, Gower Publishing Company, Aldershot.

Goss, R. (1990), Economic Policies and Seaports 2: The Diversity of Port Policies, *Maritime Policy and Management*, Vol. 17, No. 3, pp. 221-234.

Haralambides, H. and Veenstra, A. (1996), Ports as Trade Facilitators in the Export-led Growth Strategies of Developing Countries, in Valleri, M. (ed.), *L'industria Portuale Per Uno Sviluppo Sostenibile Dei Porti*, Cacucci Editore, Bari.

Haynes, K., Hsing, Y. and Stough, R. (1997), Regional Port Dynamics in the Global Economy: The Case of Kaohsiung, Taiwan, *Maritime Policy and Management*, Vol. 24, No. 1, pp. 93-113.

Hong, S.Y. (1995), Marine Policy in the Republic of Korea, *Marine Policy*, Vol. 19, No. 2, pp. 97-113.

Imakita, J. (1978), *A Techno-Economic Analysis of the Port Transport System*, Saxon House Teakfield Limited, Westmead.

Korea Container Terminal Authority (1993), *Public Notice on the Scheme for Financing from Private Sector for the Development of Container Terminals*, KCTA, Pusan.

Korea Container Terminal Authority (1996), *Report on Operations*, KCTA Internal Document, KCTA, Pusan.

Korea Maritime Institute (1996a), *A Study on Privatisation Schemes of the BCTOC* (An Interim Report), KMI, Seoul.

Korea Maritime Institute (1996b), *A Study on Privatisation Schemes of the BCTOC* (The Final Report), KMI, Seoul.

Korea Maritime and Port Administration (1979), *Introduction to Functions of Korea Maritime and Port Administration*, KMPA, Seoul.

Korea Maritime and Port Administration (1989), *Report on Basic Plan for Development of Pusan Port* (Vol. 3), KMPA, Seoul.

Korea Maritime and Port Administration (1992a), *Report on the 3rd Phase Container Terminal Development in Pusan*, KMPA, Seoul.

Korea Maritime and Port Administration (1992b), *The Calculation of Optimum Port Capacity and Basic Development Plan*, KMPA, Seoul.

Korea Maritime and Port Administration (1993), *Statistical Yearbook of Shipping and Ports*, KMPA, Seoul.

Korea Maritime and Port Administration (1996), *Statistical Yearbook of Shipping and Ports*, KMPA, Seoul.

Korean National Statistical Office (1996), *Major Statistics of Korean Economy*, Seoul.

Lee, T.W. (1998), Keeping the Maritime Sector Afloat, *Lloyd's List*, 6 January.

Lim, J.S. and Shin, S.J. (1993), *A Study on the Cargo Handling System of the Container Terminal*, KMI Working Paper No. 85, Seoul.

Lloyd's List (1995), South Korean Ports Development Plan Launched, 25 October.

Lloyd's List (1997), Korean Shipping Firms Slump, 14 March.

Lloyd's List Maritime Asia (1995), Unlimited Capacity?, June.

Moon, S.H. (1992), *The Economic Impact of the Korean Port Industry on the National Economy: A Port Planning and Development Perspective*, PhD Thesis, University of Wales College of Cardiff.

Moon, S.H. (1995), Port Economic Impact Model (PIM) and Its Planning Applications, *Maritime Policy and Management*, Vol. 22, No. 4, pp. 363-387.

Nah, H.-J. (1994), KCTA Puts Its Case, *Containerisation International*, December, pp. 92-94.

Nagorski, B. (1972), *Port Problems in Developing Countries: Principles of Port Planning and Organisation*, International Association of Ports and Harbours, Tokyo.

Park, M.D. (1995), *The Development of the New Kwangyang Container Terminal in Korea*, MSc thesis, University of Plymouth.

Pearson, R. (1988), *Container Ships and Shipping*, Fairplay Publications, London.

Port Development International (1995), Bursting Pusan, September, pp. 59-61.

Raven, J. (1982), *Ports and Politics*, Paper presented at the International Association of Ports and Harbours, Nagoya.

Robinson, R. (1998), Asian Hub/Feeder Nets: the Dynamics of Restructuring, *Maritime Policy and Management*, Vol. 25, No. 1, pp. 21-40.

Slack, B., Comtois, C. and Sletmo, G. (1996), Shipping Lines as Agents of Change in the Port Industry, *Maritime Policy and Management*, Vol. 23, No. 3, pp. 289-300.

Sohn, T.S. (1998), Korea to Emerge as Marine Superpower in the 21st Century, *Korea Herald*, 1 June.

Suykens, F. (1989), The City and its Port: An Economic Appraisal, *Geoforum*, Vol. 20, No. 4, pp. 437-445.

Thomas, B. (1976), Port Administration (I): A Review of the Different Forms of Port Ownership and the Numerous Functions Undertaken within Ports, in *Manual on Port Management*, Part I, UNCTAD, pp. 95-102.

UNCTAD (1985), *Port Development: A Handbook for Planners in Developing Countries*, TD/B/C.4/175/Rev.1, New York.

UNCTAD (1992), *Port Marketing and the Challenge of the Third Generation Port*, TD/B/C.4/AC.7/14, Geneva.

Underdal, A. (1980), Integrated Marine Policy - What? Why? How?, *Marine Policy*, Vol. 4, No. 3, pp. 159-169.

Vogel, R. (1994), The Future Role of Ports, *Proceedings of the Future Role of Ports in the G.C.C.*, 3-5 December, Kuwait Ports Authority.

Yoo, C.M. (1997), Heavy Logistic Costs eat into Exports, *Korea Herald*, 20 June.

4 Privatisation Theory and Evidence

INTRODUCTION

Privatisation is a relatively new word. The word made no significant appearance in political and economic literature before 1979, when the UK Conservative Party was elected. Since then, the term 'privatisation' has rapidly become one of the most important facts of the 1980s and 1990s, with the concept spreading beyond boundaries of the UK to be adopted throughout the world. The Financial Times (1986) states that if political ideas could be copyrighted, Thatcher's government would be well on the way to achieving a runaway international best-seller.

In simple terms, to privatise is to place a state activity or industry in the private sector, *or* to transfer the ownership of an asset to private ownership. The privatisation programme of the UK Conservative government transferred a large number of public-owned enterprises to the private sector, thereby withdrawing the government from the production of goods and services. In the UK, it is an economic policy that has been pursued further and faster than in any other country. Privatisation has also led to what amounts to a political contradiction. Veljanovski (1987) mentions that whatever the final assessment of UK's affair with privatisation, it is clear that the Conservative Party has altered not only the nature of the state's role in the British economy but also the terms of the political debate about industrial policy for the next decade.

In this chapter, relevant issues and theories associated with privatisation will be discussed. These include the economic and political background to privatisation, the objectives and methods of privatisation, incentive structures under public and private ownership, and performance comparison under the two different forms of ownership in order to find out which factors are pivotal to the implementation of a successful privatisation policy.

THE PRIVATISATION CONTEXT

In the *Wealth of Nations*, Smith (1776) argued that:

"In every great monarchy in Europe the sale of the crown lands would produce a very large sum of money, which, if applied to the payment of the public debts, would deliver from mortgage a much greater revenue than any which those lands have ever afforded to the crown . . . . . When the crown lands had become private property, they would, in the course of a few years, become well improved and well cultivated."

Adam Smith's perspective was that private ownership improves productivity and efficiency, hence enhancing economic performance. While advocating only a limited role for government, he attempted to show how competition and the profit motive would lead individuals, in pursuing their own private interests, to serve the public interest. The profit motive would lead individuals to supply the goods other individuals wanted. Through competing against one another, only firms that produced what was wanted, and at as low a price as possible, would survive. Smith (1776) argued that the economy was led, as if by an *invisible hand*, to produce what was desired and in the best possible way.

This argument has not gone without a great debate. Several studies, e.g., Vickers and Yarrow (1988), claim that in many contexts public management will do better in terms of economic efficiency than its private counterpart. Again, they maintain that it would be wrong to conclude that the issue of ownership has occupied a central place in the development of economic analysis, and that the economic theory has, in fact, tended to bypass the issue. In other words, they suggest that there has been little or no discussion of positive theories of public enterprises. This tendency may have resulted from the idea that public policy on this particular issue is influenced much more by political philosophy and convenience than by the rigours of economic analysis.

Privatisation Defined

According to the Oxford English Dictionary (1993), 'privatisation' is taken to mean (i) to assign a business, service, etc. to private as distinct from state control or ownership and (ii) to transfer from ownership by the state to private ownership, which is synonymous with 'denationalisation'. The meaning of 'deregulation' is to free from regulations or control, while that of 'liberalisation' is to remove restrictions imposed on businesses.

In the context of economics, 'privatisation', or 'denationalisation', is generally taken to mean the sale of publicly owned assets, thus transferring their ownership from public to private sectors. Definitions of the other two terms, however, are inconsistently used. For example, Yarrow (1986) defines 'deregulation' as a removal of market restrictions and 'liberalisation' as a measure to increase competition. Bishop and Kay (1988), however, define 'deregulation' and 'liberalisation' to mean the same, i.e., a removal of statutory restrictions on competition. For Parker (1991), the privatisation programme has had two main components: the sale of state assets (denationalisation) and the introduction of competition into areas previously monopolised by state owned suppliers (liberalisation).

Wiltshire (1988, p. 1) points out that there are no clear concepts or definitions of privatisation as follows:

"In the world of government, it is often the policies that are accompanied by the least public fuss and fanfare that have the greatest and most lasting impact. This certainly holds true for privatisation in the UK. There was no green paper, no white paper, no definitive piece of legislation, no second-reading speech, and the concept was not even contained in the manifesto.... Even today there is no distinct policy document.... defining and justifying privatisation, outlining its objectives, or spelling out its future applications."

In the UK, a government-controlled or -owned firm is privatised if a large proportion of its equity, usually in excess of 50%, is sold (Veljanovski, 1987; Beesley and Littlechild, 1988). In this sense, the policy of privatisation is the opposite of nationalisation. Thus, it is clear that official sources do not provide a definition of privatisation, but rather describe its aims, scope, methods and results. It may be worth mentioning here how others have defined it. The following are some of them:

"There are four principal strands in the policy of the Thatcher government towards the institutions and enterprises of the public sector as a whole: (i) to transfer them to private ownership, wherever that is possible; (ii) to open up their activities to competition, which has become known as liberalisation; (iii) to eliminate certain functions carried out by the public sector altogether or to sub-contract them to the private sector where this can be achieved at lower cost; and (iv) to charge the public for public sector services currently provided free." (Clementi, 1985, p. 171)

"The idea involves transferring the production of goods and services from the public sector to the private sector. At its lowest common denominator, it means having done privately that which was done publicly.... it is not a policy but an approach. It is an *approach* which recognises that the regulation which the market imposes on economic activity is superior to any regulation which men can devise and operate by law." (Pirie, 1988, pp. 2-3)

"By privatisation, I mean strictly the permanent transferring of service or goods production activities previously carried out by public service bureaucracies to private firms or to other firms of non-public organisation, such as voluntary groups." (Dunleavy, 1986, p. 1)

"Privatisation is a term which is used to cover several distinct, and possibly alternative, means of changing the relationships between the government and the private sector. Among the most important of these are denationalisation (the sale of publicly owned assets), deregulation (the introduction of competition into statutory monopolies) and contracting out (the franchising to private firms of the production of state financed goods and services)." (Kay and Tompson, 1986, p. 18)

From the above definitions, the following four separate elements can be drawn to provide an all-encompassing definition of privatisation in its various guises: (i) 'privatisation' of the financing of a service that continues to be produced by the public sector, (ii) 'privatisation' of the production of a service that continues to be financed by the public sector (usually through taxation), (iii) 'liberalisation', meaning relaxation of any statutory monopolies or licensing arrangements that prevent private sectors from entering markets previously exclusively supplied by the public sector, and (iv) 'denationalisation' and 'load-shedding', meaning selling of public enterprises and transfer of state functions to the private sector, respectively.

Political Background to Privatisation

With most political transformations it is essential to know a little of their history to gain an understanding of their meaning and impact. The historical origins of privatisation policy comes from the UK, a country that initiated the concept and has been implementing it faster and more comprehensively than any other country. A brief review of the UK policy of nationalisation as exercised in the early post-war period up to 1979 is a necessary precursor, therefore, to the analysis of UK privatisation which follows it.

After World War II, the nationalisation of industry was much more prominent than ever before. One of the momentous changes after the Second World War was the increasing demand from both sides of the political spectrum, as well as the general public, for government intervention in the economy. The ideology for nationalisation is based on the concept of 'the common ownership of the means of production' (Dunkerley and Hare, 1991) and on the belief that under public, rather than private, ownership various large and strategic industries would serve the public interest better because of their accountability to the people through a board appointed by the government which would be accountable to the minister and, in turn, to parliament (Wiltshire, 1988). In addition, the fact that the private sector had failed to invest sufficiently in the coal and rail industries in the period prior to the Second World War also provided some impetus for nationalisation in the post-war period, especially since it was felt that an enormous investment was necessary to allow such capital-intensive industries to compete effectively with continental rivals. Since this was not an attractive proposition for the private sector, nationalisation seemed to provide the only feasible way forward.

In consequence, the public sector grew substantially after the mid-1940s and the nationalised industries became responsible for a large part of economic growth. The impact of public sector industry upon the economy was even further exaggerated since the coal, gas, steel, transport and other nationalised infrastructure industries were in a position to significantly affect the cost structure of other industries, even in the private sector. Table 4.1 shows the share of the public sector in Gross Domestic Product (GDP) and employment over the period between the 1940s and the 1970s.

Table 4.1 Public Sector Contribution to the UK Economy (1948-1979)

Year	1948	1951	1956	1961	1971	1977	1978	1979
Gross Domestic Product (£billion)								
Public Sector (A)	0.8	1.2	-	2.4	4.9	14.5	16.5	18.1
Total Industry (B)	10.3	12.6	-	24.2	49.4	129.0	148.1	172.1
(A/B)	7.8	9.5	-	9.9	9.9	11.2	11.1	10.5
Employment (thousands)								
Public Sector (A)	-	-	2084	2196	2009	2089	2061	2065
Total Industry (B)	-	-	24509	25057	24398	24865	25134	25393
(A/B)	-	-	8.5	8.8	8.2	8.4	8.2	8.1

Source: Derived from Dunkerley and Hare (1991, p. 405).

In the 1960s and 1970s, when serious industrial disputes broke out in many of the nationalised industries, their continued existence as national entities became seriously compromised, especially since this was a period when the overall economic performance of the UK was falling well below that of its Western counterparts. Successive governments had to grapple with these problems. Conservative governments had taken some limited action, including the partial privatisation of the iron and steel industries between 1951 and 1955. Even Labour governments became involved in the same way by selling off and contracting-out, including the sale of some British Petroleum shares.

The mixed economy, however, remained at the nucleus of the country's economic life in spite of a lot of political rhetoric aimed at changing things. All post-war British governments seem to have focused their attention on establishing appropriate methods of control over various parts of the public sector. There were successive white papers, the net result of which was to generate greater direct government involvement in the affairs of nationalised industries.

In the 1970s there was considerable debate on public sector industries, with the main focus being on their economic performance. With a few exceptions, on the basis of indicators such as return on capital, growth and labour productivity, the nationalised or public sector industries were compared unfavourably with the private sector (Wiltshire, 1988). Due to a lack of surpluses earned and the continued enormous demand for capital, one factor very relevant to government was the drain that the economic activities of nationalised industries were having on the Public Sector Borrowing Requirement (PSBR).

In 1979, when the Conservative Party was elected into government, the concept of privatisation gradually made its appearance. Taylor (1983) states the reason for the elements of privatisation being downplayed in the run up to the 1979 election was that the Thatcher faction had to compromise their basic objectives in the interest of wider party unity; a missionary zeal to privatise was not that widely shared in the shadow cabinet of the time. The 1979 Conservative election manifesto included, therefore, only a vague declaration of faith in the long term aim to reduce the preponderance of state ownership and to widen the basis of ownership in the country. This is the political background to the origins of the privatisation policy, a policy that emerged and evolved incrementally rather than being planned rationally as an element of political strategy (Brittan, 1984).

The following description of the British experience of privatisation policy is suggested by Bishop and Kay (1988, p. 1):

"Privatisation is a policy which was adopted almost by accident, but has become politically central; a policy which has no clear-cut objectives, but has become almost an end in itself, and which has certainly acquired a momentum of its own; a policy which has at once changed the agenda of British politics, but yet closed off options for more radical reform; and a policy which has been contemporaneous with significant improvements are no greater than those in publicly owned companies which have not been privatised."

Economic Background to Privatisation

The question of which entity, the market or the government, should control economic activities has been the subject of heated debate amongst economists for several decades. An interesting asymmetry emerges when comparing the sources and types of support for the pro-market (or anti-government intervention) views with the pro-government (or anti-market) views. The argument between the pro-market and pro-government positions tends to be unbalanced, because, as a counterpart to the existing theory of market failures, a comprehensive theory of government *or* nonmarket failures is lacking. This asymmetry is shown by the shaded rectangle in Table 4.2.

Table 4.2 Markets versus Governments: Sources of Support and Opposition

	Markets	**Governments (Nonmarket)**
Pro	Theory of *competitive markets*, supported by examples and country experience	Theory of *planning and welfare economics*, supported by examples and country experience
Anti	Theory of *market failures*, supported by examples and country experience	**Examples and country experience**

Source: Wolf (1993, p. 5).

A more fully developed theory of government failure would help to provide better balance in Table 4.2, as well as a better guide to public policy (Wolf, 1993). A brief discussion of each failure as a way of understanding the economic background to privatisation now follows.

During the period between the 1930s and the 1960s, economists became aware of a large number of ways in which the free-market economy seemed to fail to meet certain social needs. In response to this failure, the government took a more active role in attempting to stabilise the level of economic activity. Furthermore, whether or not competitive markets do lead to economic efficiency has been a question at the heart of theoretical research in economics during the last few decades. The principal results can be summarised by a fundamental theorem of welfare economics; that is, under certain conditions, competitive markets lead to an allocation of resources with the special property that there is no rearrangement of resources, or no possible change in production and consumption, such that someone can be made better off without, at the same time, making someone else worse off. Resource allocations with this property are termed *Pareto-efficient* or *Pareto-optimal* (Begg *et al.*, 1991), which is a concept based on the assumption of perfectly competitive markets.

There are, however, several important circumstances under which the market is not Pareto efficient. These are referred to as *market failures*, where the conditions necessary to achieve the market-efficient solution fail to exist or are contravened in one way or another (Brown and Jackson, 1990) and provide a justification for government involvement.

Several researchers, e.g., Stiglitz (1988), Cullis and Jones (1989) and Wolf (1993), point out the following as factors which bring about the failures in achieving efficient outcomes:

- externalities and public goods;
- imperfect competition or increasing returns;
- market imperfection or incomplete information;
- distributional inequality;
- uncertainty;
- unemployment, inflation and disequilibrium.

While market failures led to government intervention during the period between the 1930s and the 1960s, in the 1970s the shortcomings of government involvement led economists to investigate *government failures*. The basic implication of government failure is that too many public sector activities are provided. The literature centres on the inefficiencies and/or inequities that can be traced to collective decision-making and public sector provision (Cullis and Jones, 1989). The primary issue is that government intervention in an economy introduces its own costs, which may outweigh the costs of simply living with an imperfect market.

Stiglitz (1988) suggests four limitations as the major reasons for the systematic failures of the government to achieve its objectives, i.e., limited information, limited control over private market responses, limited control over bureaucracy, and limitations imposed by political processes. In addition, Jackson and Price (1994) state that government failure arises from the problems of securing appropriate incentives to pursue the public interest and appropriate information to determine what it is. Brown and Jackson (1990, pp. 57-58) identify the following as sources of government failure:

- Government intervention results in changes that are often unpredictable;
- It is often difficult to state clearly the ends of government

policy. Concepts such as serving the public interest are vague. Knowledge about means and ends relationship in the policy sphere is often weak or unknown;

- Implementation failures exist. Implementation often requires complex systems and involves bargaining, both of which can break down. Government often lacks adequate control over agencies and processes that it uses to implement policies;
- Government intervention is not a free good. Government is served by a bureaucracy that is expensive to administer; and
- The public choice literature draws attention to rent-seeking behaviour on the part of politicians and bureaucrats. Individuals seek to influence the state in order to transfer welfare to themselves. Hence lobby groups will invest resources to influence the form, structure and incidence of regulations, licensing laws, tariffs and quotas.

Among these sources of government failure, a further discussion of rent-seeking behaviour may be worthwhile. The rent-seeking approach studies the competition of groups for scarce resources rather than through the market system. In return for their contribution to the group's effort, individuals are entitled to a share of its expected rent (*or* profit). One issue is whether or not such behaviour is efficient. Competition amongst rent-seekers will tend, however, to reduce the expected utility of per-member rent to the individual's reserve level of utility (Tullock, 1967; Posner, 1975). Suppose a situation exists where more than one shipping line could serve a certain route but a single shipping line obtains the monopoly right (rent) over the route by successfully inducing a governmental authority to grant this right. In this case, the monopoly rent is a kind of prize to be awarded to the shipping line. Other lines will invest their efforts and resources to increase the probability of achieving the rent. These investments constitute a social cost of monopoly as well as a loss of consumer surplus. Buchanan (1980, pp. 12-14) identifies the following three types of rent-seeking expenditure as sources of government failure:

- efforts and expenditures of the potential recipients of the monopoly;
- efforts of the civil servants to obtain the expenditures; and
- third-party distortions induced by the monopoly itself or the government as a consequence of the rent-seeking activity.

The theory of market failure provides a useful corrective to the basic tenet of the theory of perfectly functioning markets in that they lead to outcomes which are both efficient and socially equitable. Equally, the theory of government failure provides a corrective to the implicit theory of perfectly functioning governments also leading to efficient and equitable outcomes, or at least to ones that are more efficient and equitable than market outcomes. In fact, both markets and governments are prone to several shortcomings. It is, therefore, extremely difficult to make a fair comparison between market and government alternatives. Wolf (1993) argues that the reason for this difficulty is that there is no generally applicable formula for choosing between them; the results of such a comparison often depend more upon the predisposition of the evaluators than upon their objective analyses. Overall, however, government failure can be seen as a motive for privatisation (Jasinski and Yarrow, 1996).

PROBLEMS OF THE PUBLIC SECTOR

In general, the situation of government-controlled and -owned enterprises is quite different from that of their private sector counterparts in the statutory monopoly power that many of them have and in the fact that, as their owner, the government inevitably stands behind their borrowing and makes up for any losses (Brittan, 1984). At the same time, however, the public sector is itself plagued by a number of serious economic and institutional problems which are mainly due to a difference from private enterprises in their underlying attributes. Pirie (1988) identifies the following problem areas emerging from a study of the public sector and its activities.

Higher Production and Labour Costs

Private business has costs of production that are, on average, between 20% and 40% lower than those of its public sector counterpart. It appears that market-driven pressures to keep costs down and profits up provides greater discipline on the private sector than does the desire for economy in the public sector. In addition, public sector activities are likely to be more vulnerable to the pressures which increase labour costs. The main factor seems to be the ability in the public sector, often because of the monopoly power enjoyed, to pass on the results of wage agreements directly to the taxpayers who finance its activities. In the private sector, in contrast, there is a greater tendency to negotiate wage agreements with more concern for their effect on costs.

Lower Efficiency

Public businesses tend to employ a higher level of manpower for identical business activities, thus making less effective use of their labour resource. The lower costs in private operations have their basis in the more efficient utilisation of both labourers and equipment. The implication seems to be that market competition and profit-seeking keep private enterprises more efficient than their public counterparts. If a private enterprise fails to keep up with the competition, it will be forced out of business; a public enterprise hardly ever faces the same fate under similar circumstances.

Lower Capital Expenditure and the Poor Condition of Equipment

The level of capital investment in the public sector depends on the funds available to government which, in turn, relies on the national economy, on the level of taxation, and on the demands of the public. Political control over the activities of public sector businesses has had an effect on their ability to raise the capital required for this operation and production. In addition, capital spending tends to be cut in favour of expanding more immediate current spending. This environment which surrounds publicly run businesses frequently causes the public sector to make products with outmoded equipment and old technology, thus losing the opportunity to reduce production costs by using more high technology equipment. As a result, the supply of improved, innovative and added value services is delayed and existing capital stock is made to last much longer than its plan for lifetime. In addition, publicly owned equipment is not owned by one particular person and, therefore, few people will treat it with the same care and consideration that they would give to their own property.

Lack of Consumer Input

In order to make profits through meeting customers' needs, products and services have to be oriented towards inducing customer satisfaction. In fact, the consumer is able to exercise a certain degree of control on private firms by deciding whether to shop with them or elsewhere. In the case where the public has no choice but to pay and take what is provided, as is usual in the public sector, this degree of control over the public enterprise is limited or absent. In this context, the primary aim of a public sector business is sometimes shifted from the production of goods for consumers to the provision of jobs for workers. Ironically, therefore, in this way the general public tends to exert greater control over private businesses rather than the public ones which they nominally own. This is because the former can be influenced directly by consumer decisions, while the latter can only be influenced, if at all, by the ballot box and, thus, only in a very indirect and ad hoc manner.

Slower Innovation and Inflexibility

When a number of competing firms exist in the market, consumers are more keen to find goods and services satisfying their individual needs. Private firms are constantly seeking new products and ways to give them a competitive edge; they adapt swiftly to a changing environment, with an apprehension that failure to do so may result in bankruptcy. On the other hand, where goods and services are produced under government control, it is necessary to deal with the problem of control, i.e., to solve a bureaucratic problem. Consequently, the rate of innovation in public operations is much lower, and public services appear to change relatively slowly over time. During a period of time when private sector goods and services may change in an effort to satisfy the wants of customers, the public sector is likely to make the same products year after year. A noticeable reason for this is that the absence of rewards for entrepreneurial innovation makes the public sector slow to adopt new ideas and technology and to be less adaptable to the changing environment which surrounds them.

Political, Rather than Economic, Decision Making

As part of every day business, firms have to deal with the level of demand, given the price and availability of capital, and with other relevant activities. Decisions on these economic activities in the private sector are made on the basis of economic reasoning. Many of the important decisions in the public sector, in contrast, are made on political grounds. In other words, private business exists in the economic world, while government business in the political world and is influenced and controlled accordingly. Overall decision-making in the public sector is separated from the realities of supply and demand, thus resulting in a situation where the public sector does not operate with the same degree of efficiency achieved by the more market-driven private business.

More Vulnerable to Interruption of Service

Public sector products and services are usually supplied by a public monopoly with no alternative source of supply permitted. This means that any interruption can shut down all sources of supply to consumers. Whilst, in the private sector, a labour dispute in one firm threatens only its own customers, a labour dispute in a public monopoly, on the other hand, threatens the whole economy.

Lack of Responsiveness to Cost Control

Costs incurred in the private sector are controlled competitively and are not, in any case, financed out of taxation. If an increase in the costs of private goods or services is reflected in a price rise, the consumer may decide to turn to cheaper alternatives, to take up substitutes, or to spend less money. The public sector, in contrast, with a budget which is nominally under the control of government, and thus heavily influenced by political decisions, shows an immunity against cost controls. What matters is that costs in the public sector consist of various factors, many of which are outside government control through its legislative domain. In general, civil servants make little effort to reduce costs. Furthermore, the savings realised by cutting costs hardly benefit those governmental officers; those who ultimately pay for public programmes are neither as self-conscious nor as visible as those who benefit from them. All of these circumstances make costs incurred in the public sector hard to control.

Not one of these problem areas of public sector activity is in any sense coincidental. All the problems arise from the structure and organisation of the public sector itself and from the pressures and forces that are brought to bear on it in the political realm. In response to these problems, much attention has been paid to various ways in which their effect could be reduced or eliminated. Several approaches, including privatisation, have been implemented in order to impose outside controls upon the public sector to make it conform to government requirements, or to set forces to work within it which can bring about an improvement in its performance.

OBJECTIVES OF PRIVATISATION

In an important speech by the UK Minister John Moore (1986), it was stated that privatisation was a key element in the UK government's economic strategy. It would lead to a fundamental shift in the balance between the public and private sectors, bring about a profound change in attitudes within the state industries, open up exciting possibilities for the consumer, better pay and conditions for employees, and a new freedom for the managers of the industries concerned.

However, several studies, e.g., Heald (1982), Yarrow (1986), Vickers and Yarrow (1988), and Jasinski and Yarrow (1996), argue that the UK privatisation programme did not start with a coherent set of objectives and that a comprehensive list of goals ranked by priority or weight has never been defined. In fact, the objectives of privatisation programmes are as numerous and diverse as the agendas of politicians and bureaucrats and will tend to vary over time and from country to country. The comprehensive and principal aims of privatisation programmes can be summarised as follows (Vickers and Yarrow, 1988; Jasinski and Yarrow, 1996).

Improving Economic Efficiency

Privatisation improves economic efficiency if it provides incentives to cut costs and set prices in line with costs, i.e., managing business according to economic disciplines. The achievement of such efficiency improvement is, however, much dependent on the scheme of competition and regulation in which the privatised company operates. This objective can also be achieved by allowing firms to borrow freely from the capital markets without having to obey the borrowing constraints faced in the public sector.

Reducing the PSBR

Once a firm has been privatised and therefore is no longer a drain on the public sector borrowing requirement (PSBR), the government is able to reduce the PSBR through privatisation.

Reducing Government Involvement

Privatisation is also a direct and immediate way of reducing government intervention in the decision making of a company. As mentioned in the previous section, a major weakness in operating nationalised enterprises is this vulnerability to political whim, whereas privatisation provides a plausible method of giving management more independence to develop their business strategies based not on political decisions but on economic decisions.

Lessening Union Power

Privatisation can also be considered as a way of promoting government objectives regarding the labour market: vis a vis the lessening union power. Nationalisation has increased the monopoly power of unions if public sector managers and their supervising ministers have weak incentives to cut labour costs and limited power to negotiate wage settlements. Government can reduce, to some extent, the power of unions by privatisation.

Widening Company Ownership

Privatisation presents an excellent vehicle for encouraging the wider ownership of economic assets. Although the programme by itself does not necessarily facilitate this objective, it gives a rare opportunity to offer shares to the general public at a discount and with additional bonuses for the small shareholder.

Encouraging Employee Share Ownership

As far as the UK Conservative party is concerned, its privatisation policy has yielded important political benefits: millions of new small shareholders possess portfolios that are typically made up of privatisation stocks, such as BT and British Gas.

Gaining Political Advantage

This objective has been an implied one, but it has influenced several critical policy decisions.

In addition to these objectives of the privatisation programme, Veljanovski (1987) put forward two more objectives: (i) creating an enterprise culture and (ii) replacing ownership and financial controls with a more effective system of economic regulation designed to ensure that the benefits accruing from greater efficiency are passed on to consumers.

From the above discussion, three common objectives can be identified. These are (i) to increase economic efficiency at the level of individual firms and industries (*efficiency objectives*), (ii) to raise revenue for government activities (*fiscal objectives*) and (iii) to seek political advantage by means of income distribution (*distributional objectives*).

METHODS OF PRIVATISATION

Public enterprises must, ultimately, be disposed of one-by-one and each case must be examined on its own merits in terms of deciding upon an appropriate method of privatisation. Vuylsteke (1988) categorises seven methods of privatisation which are the most commonly observed. These methods also constitute the main options or alternative approaches available to governments. Several of these methods can bring about total denationalisation or can be implemented partially or gradually. Several combinations of these methods exist as well.

Public Offering of Shares (Full or Partial)

Under this method, the state sells to the general public all or large blocks of stock it holds in a wholly or partly owned public enterprise which, it is assumed, will be a going concern as a public limited company. Technically, this transaction amounts to a secondary distribution of shares. When a government decides to sell only a portion of its holding, the result is joint state and private ownership of the enterprise. The government may pursue such an approach either as a deliberate policy to maintain its presence or as a first step towards full privatisation. Where a private shareholding already exists, the transaction may simply be a further privatisation.

Public offerings require that (i) the enterprise be a sizeable going concern with a reasonable earning record or potential, or that it can be made ready to become so; (ii) a full body of financial, management and other information is available or can be prepared for disclosure to the investing market; (iii) there is discernible liquidity in the local market; and (iv) either the equity markets are developed or there is some structured mechanism including a regulatory body that can be made to function to reach, inform and attract as well as protect the general investing public. This method conforms to the government objective of encouraging widespread share ownership.

Private Sale of Shares (Full or Partial)

In this case, the state sells all or part of its shareholding in a wholly or partly owned public enterprise to a pre-identified single purchaser or group of purchasers. It is assumed that the public enterprise in question is a going concern in the form of a corporation represented by shares. The transaction can take various forms, such as a direct acquisition by another corporate entity, or a private placement targeting a specific group, for example institutional investors. The privatisation can be full or partial, the latter resulting in mixed ownership enterprises. A private sale of shares may also be carried out before, or sometimes simultaneously with, a public offering.

Thanks to their flexibility, private sales are preferred for weakly performing public enterprises or public enterprises in need of strong owners with relevant industrial, financial, commercial and other experience and a high financial stake in the success of the firm. It may also be the only feasible alternative in the absence of developed equity markets, where no mechanism exists or is possible for reaching the general investing public, and where the size of the enterprise may not justify a public offering.

One of the main advantages of the private sale of shares is that the prospective owner is known in advance and can be evaluated, in terms of their ability to bring a number of benefits such as management, technology, market access and so on. In many cases, the future success of the operation may be as important to the government as are the proceeds from the sale. In some cases, a partial private sale may be a necessary first step to full privatisation, as it brings in a leveraged party who is able to turn the company around so that it becomes attractive to investors. The private sale also permits the required flexibility to conclude special arrangements with a suitable purchaser as dictated by the condition of the public enterprise. For example, a public enterprise with a negative present worth may be attractive to an investor with whom a special synergy exists, such as market share, technology, etc.

Sale of Government or Public Enterprise Assets

Under the previous two methods of privatisation, the private sector purchased shares in a public enterprise that was a going concern. This method, on the other hand, consists basically of the sale of the assets, rather than shares, in a going concern. A government may sell the assets directly or the public enterprise may dispose of major assets. In general, while the purpose may be to hive off separate assets representing distinct activities, the sale of separate assets may be a means of selling the enterprise as a whole. Thus, the assets may be sold individually or together as a new corporate entity. Assets can only be sold privately unless the government embodies the assets and activities into a new company established for the purpose of privatisation, in which case a public offering or private sale of shares is possible.

By definition, a sale of assets involves a known party and, in that sense, it may have the same advantages as a direct sale of shares. In addition, it offers the additional flexibility that it may be more feasible to sell individual assets rather than the whole public enterprise, or it may permit the sale of a public enterprise that might be extremely difficult to sell as a going concern. It should be borne in mind, however, that often this approach may result in residual liabilities for the government. In many cases of public enterprises that are not saleable as going concerns, the sale of assets is the preferred method, if not the only alternative. This method is possible because the enterprise's products and assets may be of relevance to a buyer in the private sector. In such cases, the government may decide to dissolve or dismantle the public enterprise and liquidate it by selling its assets and writing off its uncovered liabilities. The entity can then emerge as a private company. This method is also appropriate in some cases involving the privatisation of public enterprises that are not set up under company law (unless a public offering is planned, in which case conversion to a public limited company is necessary).

Reorganisation into Component Parts (or Fragmentation)

This approach involves the breaking-up or reorganisation of a public enterprise into several separate entities or into a holding company and several subsidiaries. In some sense, this technique can be regarded simply as a form of restructuring prior to privatisation. This method permits piecemeal privatisation, and further different methods of privatisation to be applied to different component parts, thereby possibly facilitating the overall process. If a public enterprise incorporates too many activities that, in aggregate, are not attractive to potential investors, whereas individual units would be, fragmentation is a possible alternative. Sometimes, a state wishes to sell only certain components of the public enterprise, while retaining others. Some port authorities that embody many different operations (general port services, stevedoring, transit, towing etc.) have found that certain activities are better handled by a private sector which may find them attractive, whereas the global operation might not be. Another reason for the fragmentation of a public enterprise may be that it is a monopoly and the government would like to be break up it into separate enterprises to create competition, as in the case of British Rail.

New Private Investment in Public Enterprises

A government may wish to inject more capital into a public enterprise (mostly for rehabilitation and for expansion) and to achieve this by opening equity ownership to the private sector. The main characteristic of such a privatisation method is that the state is not disposing of any of its existing equity in the public enterprise. Instead, it increases the equity and causes a dilution of the government's equity position. This will result in joint private and government ownership of the enterprise (often referred to as a *joint venture*). If the public enterprises are not wholly state-owned, but majority-owned, then the new capital subscription will simply result in a further dilution of the government's interest, possibly resulting in a private majority holding. In a large number of cases, the government has brought in the assets of a public enterprise (with or without accompanying liabilities) as a contribution in kind to the capital of a new corporation, while the cash contribution to the capital of the new corporation by new private investors will permit necessary rehabilitation, restoration of working capital, or an expansion of operations. Normally, a new equity issue does not result in sales proceeds for the state.

In summary, this will be the preferred method if a government's objective is both to reduce its proportionate shareholding or to change the state and private mix in the public enterprise and if the enterprise is in need of capital.

Management and Employee Buy-out

Generally, the term management buy-out (MBO) refers to the acquisition of a controlling shareholding in a company by a small group of managers. It often also designates a similar transaction where employees, or management and employees, acquire a controlling interest. This approach focuses particularly on the acquisition by management and work force. For simplicity, this transaction is referred to here as a management and employee buy-out (MEBO).[1] Wright and Coyne (1985) and Blackstone and Franks (1986) explain:

---

(1)   Reference is sometimes made to employee buy-outs (EBOs) and leveraged management buy-outs (LMBOs). EBOs are buy-outs where, apart from the management team investing in shares in the buy-out company, a significant number of employees also invest in shares. This arrangement carries particular tax problems. LMBOs are leveraged (or geared) buy-outs where the management team has a controlling number of shares. Generally they would, however, be termed MBOs (Krieger, 1990, p. 3).

"The special characteristic of the financing arrangements for management buy-outs is that the financiers provide the bulk of the funds but take a disproportionately small proportion of equity; on the other hand, the buy-out team obtains a large share of the equity but provides a small proportion of the funding. High gearing ratios, where borrowings can be initially as much as five times the amount of share capital in the company, are not unusual and in some cases may even be higher than this. In such cases it is naturally important that the projected cash flow is sufficient to allow for the payment of large sums of interest and capital repayments without placing the viability of the business in jeopardy."

Management and employee buy-outs can be a relevant means of transferring ownership to management and employees with little wealth or knowledge of share ownership and may be a solution for public enterprises not otherwise saleable. These methods also constitute an enormous incentive to productivity. Clearly this can provide a solution to the employment issue where the alternative is liquidation; the management and employee buy-out should minimise lay-offs and other substantial costs of closing a public enterprise. This method, however, requires the presence of competent and skilled management and a committed and stable work force. A strong cash flow potential is usually a precondition for obtaining credit to finance a buy-out.

Lease and Management Contract

Both leases and management contracts are arrangements whereby private sector management, technology and/or skills are provided under contract to a public enterprise or, in respect of state-owned assets, for an agreed period and compensation. While there is normally no transfer of ownership and, therefore, no divestiture of state assets, these arrangements can be used to privatise management and operations and, thereby, possibly increase the efficiency and effective use of state assets. While there are many variations, the basic difference between a lease and a management contract can be summarised as follows.

Lease

The private operator leases assets or facilities owned by the state and uses them to conduct business on its own account. The lease sets forth the terms and conditions under which the lessee may operate these assets and facilities, the compensation that must be paid to the state, and the respective responsibilities of the parties. The key feature of a lease arrangement is that the lessee assumes the full commercial risk for operating the assets. In addition to the lease payment, the lessee is normally obliged to maintain and repair the assets in use or to share in that cost in accordance with an agreed schedule. Unlike the management contractor, who assumes no financial responsibility for the enterprise's operation, the lessee suffers from direct financial repercussions if it fails to use the leased assets or facilities in an efficient manner and to ensure effective management.

Management Contract

The management contract involves assuming responsibility for managing the enterprise for compensation. Unlike other arrangements providing for management services or technical assistance, the management group is given full management control and the authority to manage. The contractor derives its authority from this control and must manage the operation within that confine. Whereas a lessee pays the state for the use of assets or facilities, a management contractor is paid by the state for its management or other skills. While the contractor might be given extensive management powers and operational control, it has no financial exposure and receives its fee regardless of the profitability of the enterprise. (Where performance or incentive payments are part of the overall compensation package, these are forfeited if the level of performance or other criteria are not met.) The public enterprise continues to bear the full commercial risk and is responsible for all working capital and debt financing. To this extent, the state is not relieved of any financial burden and, in fact, takes on a higher short-term burden in the form of the management fee. The advantage of this method, however, is that ownership is retained, a defined degree of control is maintained, and a high level of management and other skills is injected into the enterprise, thus enhancing its overall efficiency and profitability.

Leases and management contracts are the principal method of privatisation of an activity in situations where the privatisation of the ownership of the assets or public enterprise is not appropriate. Both, however, offer advantages that may in certain cases make their application preferable to other methods of privatisation. The lease may also be used as an intermediate solution aimed at making a subsequent sale possible. Similarly, the management contract may also be an intermediate solution in turning an enterprise around for subsequent privatisation of ownership.

When selecting a method of privatisation, several factors should be normally taken into consideration. These include the objectives of the privatisation programme, the size of the public enterprise to be privatised, the share of the public sector in the national economy, and the like. Vuylsteke (1988) lists seven factors influencing the methods and procedures for privatisation: (i) the objectives of the government, (ii) the current organisational form of the public enterprise, (iii) the financial condition and record of performance of the public enterprise, (iv) the sector of activity of the public enterprise, (v) the ability to mobilise private sector resources, (vi) the degree of development of the capital market, and (vii) socio-political factors. In fact, no generalisation can be made as to the relative weight of these elements in choosing how to privatise. Regarding this matter, UNCTAD (1995) recommends that given the strong links between privatisation objectives and the method of privatisation, it is clear that a consensus on the objectives to be achieved must first be reached and that this should have been done as part of developing a strategy to guide the privatisation programme.

OWNERSHIP AND INCENTIVE STRUCTURES

The effect of privatisation is to substitute shareholder for governmental monitoring and control of the firm's management and operation. Under private ownership, management is directly responsible to shareholders, although it might be constrained in its actions by a regulatory agency. Under public ownership, management is monitored by government which, in turn, can be regarded as an agent of the voting population. As a result of the change in property rights, there exists a different structure of incentives for management and hence to changes in both managerial behaviour and company performance (Vickers and Yarrow, 1988).

Hartley and Parker (1991) suggest a theoretical framework for analysing the effects of privatisation with particular emphasis on the differences in incentives between public and private organisations. Incentive problems arise as a result of a lesser ability of owners to monitor managers. This is a problem that arises when the objectives of principal and agents diverge. The property rights and public choice literature give insights into this problem.

According to *property rights theory* (Alchian, 1965; De Alessi, 1980; Barzel, 1989), an organisation may be considered a team of factor suppliers with contracts established and monitored by management. Where management prevents 'slacking' in the team, the result is higher productivity and lower costs. To perform this task well, however, management requires an incentive. The main argument here is that private organisations, in which rights to profits are clearly defined, will perform better than public organisations, where the rights are diffused and uncertain. In this theory the source of inefficiency in public firms lies in the attenuation of property rights. In the archetypal capitalist firm the entrepreneur has a direct interest in the most efficient use of the firm's resources because his or her income is the residual after production costs are deducted from revenues.

This view is supported by *public choice theory* (Niskanen, 1971; Dunsire *et al.*, 1988; Borooah, 1996), which is concerned with the nature of decision-making within government. Politicians and government bureaucrats pursue their own self-interest rather than the public interest or social welfare. Policies are arranged to maximise votes and departmental budgets are expanded so that bureaucrats benefit from better jobs and higher salaries. Since bureaucrats tend to have more information than taxpayers on the consequences of budgetary changes, this asymmetry of information inhibits public monitoring of spending and provides fertile ground for public sector trade unions to inflate wage demands and protect over-manning.

Although there are different nuances to the property rights and public choice theories, they obviously complement each other. A common element in property rights and public choice literature is that, in the absence of the profit motive, government departments will tend to pursue goals such as budget maximisation, risk aversion, over-manning and non-optimal pricing, employment and investment (Hartley and Parker, 1991). In contrast to this argument, Posner (1984) states that politicians and bureaucrats do indeed pursue the public interest, and that, like their private sector counterparts, government employees may find satisfaction 'in a job well done'.

Although some distinctions can be drawn between private and public sector organisations as in the above arguments, such a simple framework runs the risk of overlooking significant differences between organisational forms of enterprises within each sector. It could be important to highlight such differences when classifying enterprises for performance comparison.

. Discussion on the differences between public and private sectors can start simply with the point that the objectives of the owners are different in the two cases. In private ownership, it is generally assumed that owners are interested in the financial performance of the firm such as profit maximisation. In respect of public ownership, in contrast, the appropriate specification of objectives is less clear. The assumption generally made is that the objective will be to maximise social welfare, but this assumption leads to the problem of how social welfare should be defined and measured, but is usually represented as the sum of consumer and producer surpluses.

In addition, except where the scale of operation is very small, typical commercial enterprises, whether private or public, tend to be characterised by the delegation of decisions to managers and other employees. Although privatisation changes the objectives of owners, it does not in any immediate way alter the objectives of those to whom decisions are delegated (Jasinski and Yarrow, 1996). The owners of both public and private enterprises, therefore, face a similar agency problem: how managers and other employees can be encouraged to act in ways that contribute to the owners' objectives. This is the problem of incentives *or* of monitoring.

Private Ownership and Incentives

The *principal-agent problem* arises wherever one person (the principal) hires another person (the agent) to make decisions. Since the agent may make different decisions from those of the principal, the motivation of this agent must be taken into account. The principal (shareholders) then needs to provide incentives to the agent (managers) to ensure that the agents do, in fact, act in the principal's interests. There are, however, two main problems at this point (Yarrow, 1986). First, monitoring activities by one owner confer external benefits on others, and thus there is a tendency towards sub-optimal levels of monitoring, which gives rise to a free rider problem with regard to shareholder monitoring. Second, the arrangement gives rise to asymmetric information, i.e., managers typically know more about the firm's opportunities than owners. Although shareholders could formulate and impose optimal profit-related incentive schemes, these are unlikely to reward a manager with the full incremental benefits of extra effort.

Adam Smith (1776) understood the basic conflict between owners (principal) and managers (agent) in his book the *Wealth of Nations* as follows:

"The directors of such [joint-stock] companies, however, being the managers rather of other people's money than their own, it cannot well be expected, that they should watch over it with the same anxious vigilance with which the partners in a private copartnery frequently watch over their own. Like the stewards of a rich man, they are apt to consider attention to small matters as not for their master's honour, and very easily give themselves a dispensation from having it. Negligence and profusion, therefore, must always prevail, more or less, in the management of the affairs of such a company."

By using the Royal African Company, the Hudson Bay Company, and the East India Company as examples, Smith (1776) mentioned some of the consequences of management by non-owners, which provide an important starting point for the principal-agent problem. The incentive characteristics under two different ownership structures are suggested by Vickers and Yarrow (1988) who developed two versions of the basic principal-agent model. Bishop and Thompson (1992) explored this model further.

Let a and 6 be the agent's action, which may represent his level of effort, and the state of the world, let $x(a, 6)$ represent the outcome of the agent's action given 6, and let y and $y(x)$ be a function of the observed outcomes (the principal's action to the agent) and the incentive scheme for the agent respectively. The principal cannot observe a or 6 individually, but he or she can observe the outcome $x(a, 6)$, thus conducting his or her own action accordingly, e.g., a remuneration to the agent as an incentive. In this circumstance, a salient decision to be made by the principal is to choose $y(x)$, which indicates the *incentive scheme* for the agent. The principal, however, faces two constraints when choosing the scheme: (i) the agent tends to behave in a self-interested way given the incentive scheme, (ii) the incentive scheme must be an appealing reward for the agent to be willing to participate in the project with the principal. The two different models are developed by the distinction of whether the agent is able or unable to observe 6 at the time when he or she chooses an action.

In the *first* model, where the agent cannot observe 6, thus selecting a to maximise his or her expected utility given $y(x)$ the agent's attitude toward risk is involved in decision making. If the agent is risk-neutral, the principal receives a flat amount from the agent whatever happens. In other words, the agent bears all the risk, but being risk-neutral, he does not mind that, incentives are perfect, and there is no monitoring problem. If the agent has a risk aversion, an optimal condition will be achieved when the principal offers the agent an insurance against adverse circumstances. This diminishes the incentives for the agent, since he or she gains only part of the benefit which arises from his extra efforts. Consequently, the asymmetry of information between the principal and the agent can cause a surplus.

The *second* model imposes that the agent is able to observe 6 before making up his or her mind on an action. The strategy available to the agent given the incentive scheme $y(x)$ will be a function $a(6)$, since the most rewarding action will depend on 6. As is the case of the first model, the principal must also guarantee that the incentive provision is attractive enough to the agent to want to take part in a project.

Several applications of principal-agent theory can be made (e.g. Rees, 1985; Sappington, 1991). These include relationships between regulators and firm managers, employers and employees, lenders and borrowers, landlords and tenants, insurers and the insured, and tax authorities and households.

Alchian and Demsetz (1972) mention that changes in the number of principals and in the distribution of shareholding can rapidly take place in a conventional large company. The shares of the company are held by a number of shareholders, each of whom possesses a relatively small portion of the total equity of the company. The shares are marketable as well, and thus the property right of a shareholder can be changed at any time by transferring his shares to others, hence closing his relationship with the company. Under these circumstances, the management of the company will be restricted by the following three participants in capital markets (Vickers and Yarrow, 1988, p. 11):

- the firm's shareholders;

- other investors or their agents (e.g. managers of other companies); and
- the firm's creditors (including lenders at fixed interest).

These three groups have their impact on managerial incentives: (i) the shareholders of a firm are seeking contractual arrangements with the management to maximise their own payoffs, which results in problems of shareholder monitoring, (ii) other investors purchase the firm's shares as an overture to an effort for reshaping contractual arrangements in existence, thus causing the threat of takeovers and (iii) the creditors want to change managerial status in the case of threatened or actual default, which can create the threat of bankruptcy.

In respect of private ownership, the threats of takeover and bankruptcy become obviously crucial to management since these generate incentives for managers to act in the interests of owners. By purchasing shares on the market, an individual or firm can quickly concentrate ownership and wrest control of the target company from its incumbent management. This possibility gives rise to a potentially powerful incentive effect. If the performance of a management is poor then the share price of the firm will drop and the returns from a takeover raid designed to introduce a new management will increase. The threat of replacement, as a consequence, serves as a disciplining factor on incumbent managements. Unfortunately, however, there are strong grounds for believing that the market for company control exhibits a number of significant imperfections. The marketability of property rights does not correct the market failure arising from dispersed shareholdings. For instance, a small shareholder can neglect the consequences of his or her selling and holding decision on the outcome of a takeover, and, if the bid is expected to succeed, will prefer to hold in order to take part in the profit gains accruing from the change in control. If enough shareholders behave in this way, the takeover will fail. Singh (1975) conducted extensive empirical research to find the relationship between company performance and takeover, and found evidence that the threat of involuntary takeover is not strongly related to a given management's relative profit performance.

In summary, private enterprises may be subject to a variety of capital market pressures not faced by public counterparts, and these pressures will, in turn, be dependent on the nature of the financial institutions in the economy. The privatisation of industrial enterprises might mean very little, therefore, if the government continued to dominate the economy's financial system (Jasinski and Yarrow, 1996). In countries which do not have a sophisticated stock market and banking system, one of the objectives of privatisation may be to strengthen private capital market institutions. What is crucial, on the other hand, is a case-by-case approach to the incentive problem that allows for some quantification of the various factors that are relevant to the principal-agent relationships.

Public Ownership and Incentives

According to the argument of Stiglitz (1988), the main difference between public and private enterprises is concerned with incentives, both organisational and individual. In terms of the organisational incentives, public enterprises differ from private enterprises in two important ways: (i) they do not need to worry about bankruptcy, and (ii) they usually do not have to worry about competition. In terms of individual incentives, on the other hand, the differences come from the incentive structures facing government employees, that is, (i) managers in public enterprises seldom have pay structures that are as closely related to profit as managers in private ones, (ii) it is generally very difficult to fire government employees, and this attribute of security is often cited by potential employees as one of the more desirable features of government employment.

Vickers and Yarrow (1988) identify the most obvious differences in the relationships between managers and their immediate principals, by comparing public ownership with private. The differences arise from the fact that (i) the principals do not typically seek to maximise profits, (ii) there are no marketable ordinary shares in the firm, and hence no market for company control, and (iii) there is no direct equivalent to the bankruptcy constraint on financial performance.

The politicians and bureaucrats responsible for monitoring public enterprises can themselves be viewed as agents of the wider public (the principals). The incentives for politicians to act in the best interests of the public will depend on factors such as the nature of the relevant political system, which varies over time and from place to place. More importantly, incentives to act in the public interest can be expected to be generally weak. In addition to the difficulty of defining the underlying objectives, there exist very severe free rider problems in monitoring politicians and bureaucrats. Elections only occur at long intervals, and when the opportunity to vote comes, it usually involves casting a single vote on a whole bundle of issues in an election where the performance of particular public enterprises is likely to be only a minor factor. Moreover, even where more sophisticated procedures are available to reveal public preferences, voters may have only sketchy information on the performance of public enterprises.

Under public ownership, the agency problem may lead to political discretion (Jasinski and Yarrow, 1996). Political decision makers will be able to introduce their own agendas into the process. For example, bureaucrats may pursue the goal of expanding their own departments, while politicians will be much more concerned about their political careers and their individual and party electoral prospects. This phenomenon implies that the objectives of political decision makers can be expected to deviate significantly from social welfare objectives, with the extent of the deviation being influenced by certain social and political contexts. While the mechanism of the 'invisible hand' indicates that, in the absence of major externalities, competition will tend to bring profit objectives into alignment with social objectives, there is no equivalent mechanism to bring political objectives into a similar alignment. The divergence between political and social welfare objectives reinforces earlier results suggesting that private enterprises can be characterised as superior (in terms of economic efficiency) in conditions of competition where major externalities are absent (De Alessi, 1980; Fare *et al.*, 1985; Jasinski and Yarrow, 1996).

In appropriate circumstances, however, hierarchical arrangements can lead to more efficient monitoring than that of the capital markets. Government monitoring has two potential advantages over the market one (Yarrow, 1986); (i) it does not encounter the public goods problem associated with dispersed shareholding, and (ii) it can take immediate account of deviations between social and private returns in products and factor markets. In other words, public ownership provides an instrument for correcting failures in the markets for products, factors and corporate control. This view frequently underpins the case for public ownership.

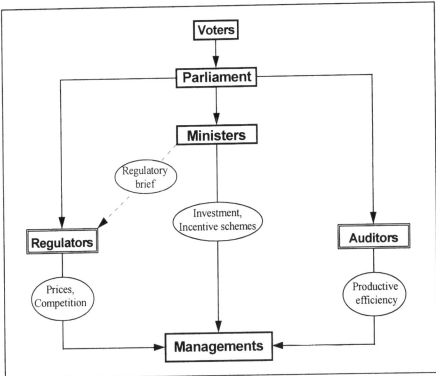

Figure 4.1 A Public Sector Monitoring Hierarchy
Source: Vickers and Yarrow (1988, p. 152).

Vickers and Yarrow (1988) point to four developments in public policy which have provided a means for enhancing the performance of the public sector. These include (i) the introduction of greater competitive pressure on public enterprises that have enjoyed protected market positions, (ii) the creation of specialised regulatory agencies entrusted by government with duties in respect of price controls and the promotion of competition similar to, but stronger than, those afforded to the regulatory bodies that were later established as part of the privatisation programme, (iii) the creation of a specialised agency for the sole purpose of conducting efficiency audits on the nationalised industries and responsible directly to parliament rather than to the government, and (iv) the more widespread use of performance-related incentive schemes for the management of public enterprises. Figure 4.1 illustrates the type of monitoring hierarchy which might result from these changes.

COMPARATIVE PERFORMANCE UNDER PUBLIC AND PRIVATE OWNERSHIP

Performance Indicators

Despite the widespread adoption of privatisation measures in recent years, knowledge on the impact is rather limited. To some extent, this reflects a failure on the part of policy makers to specify clearly the objectives of privatisation before implementation. It also reflects a paucity of performance indicators which can be applied systematically across enterprises and industries to allow a comparative analysis of performance to be undertaken. It is essential, therefore, to have a system of impact evaluation which is widely applied and to provide a systematic and practical analytical framework to assess the results of privatisation.

The analysis of the effects of privatisation encounters several methodological constraints. The basic question is simple enough: '*is the economy better or worse off after privatisation?*' A comprehensive answer to this question, however, requires answers to the following sub-questions: (i) what variables should be used to assess the impact of privatisation on the economy?, (ii) what changes occur as a result of privatisation? and (iii) how are different changes to be ranked and valued? Each of these questions raises serious methodological difficulties (UNCTAD, 1995).

In general, performance can be defined in terms of success in achieving stated objectives. The case where multiple objectives are set for privatisation requires a range of performance indicators for assessment. UNCTAD (1995, pp. 262-264) suggests that these indicators can be grouped into two broad categories, covering macro and micro level performance. *Macro* indicators measure impacts on the economy-level variables, while *micro* ones measure the input and output results at the enterprise level. The impact of privatisation on the macro economy can be measured, amongst other things, by the following:

- an increased share of the private sector in the economy, or alternatively, a decline in the government's share;
- a reduction in fiscal imbalance through increased revenue and the reduction of the government's budget deficit;
- the development of domestic capital markets;
- improvement in the external trade balance; and
- changes in the level of employment.

These impacts can be measured and their relative importance depend mainly on the primary objectives of the privatisation programme set by the government concerned. Moreover, there are methodological difficulties in distinguishing the effects of privatisation from other factors influencing the variables.

In the case of micro performance indicators, there are four types to be categorised:

- productive efficiency;
- cost efficiency;
- financial profitability; and
- real prices.

Productive Efficiency

Productive efficiency is concerned with efficiency in input use. Two approaches have been used to compute productive efficiency. The first approach estimates a production function for the 'best practice' firm, and then this estimation is used to calculate a productive efficiency index which compares the efficiency of each firm to that of the best practice firm (a more detailed discussion of production functions follows in Chapter 6). The other approach makes use of productivity ratios, including total factor productivity, which is the ratio of total output to total factor input, as well as partial productivity ratios for the measurement of output as a ratio of a single factor input. Whichever approach is used, the assessment of the impact of privatisation will require the comparison of productive efficiency pre- and post-privatisation.

Cost Efficiency

Cost efficiency also has two main methods for its measurement. The first method estimates a cost function for the firm in the industry, then attempts to determine whether there is a difference in cost efficiency after privatisation. The second calculates cost per unit of output directly, then compares cost per unit of output under public and private ownership. The main limitation of cost efficiency measures is that differences in cost will reflect differences in input prices, as well as differences in efficiency.

Differences in cost may also reflect the influence of changes in the scale of activity, if ratios to scale are not constant.

Financial Profitability

Financial profitability is a commonly used measure of performance. Despite its wide use, it is important to note that profitability does not necessarily imply efficiency. If it has market power or if it benefits from preferential arrangements such as subsidised inputs or exemptions from duties on imported inputs it is possible for an inefficient firm to be profitable. On the other hand, efficient firms may exhibit low profitability due to controls on the prices of their outputs. Another problem is that differences in profitability can arise from differences in accounting conventions, particularly the treatment of items such as depreciation, inflation and subsidies, which are all subject to variation.

Real Prices

Real prices charged for the output of the privatised enterprises can be compared pre- and post-privatisation as a micro performance indicator of the impact on consumers.

Any attempt to judge privatisation programmes is confronted by the methodological problem of determining how much of any change is attributable to the programme and how much to exogenous changes in market conditions and institutions. These problems are compounded by the problems of data availability and measurement.

The Central Hypothesis

Hartley *et al.* (1991) and Parker (1994) attempt to set up a framework for testing the importance of ownership under the central hypothesis, illustrated in Figure 4.2.

Point A represents the position of a firm which is directly controlled by a government department. It is politically controlled and there are no tradable shares, hence we would expect from the public choice and property rights theories that efficiency will be low. Point B represents an activity undertaken by a government agency which has some, if limited, autonomy from the political process. Public corporations can be placed at point C. They have more autonomy than quasi-governmental agencies.

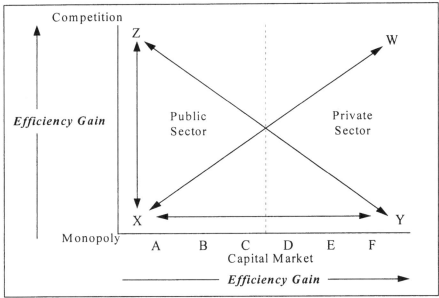

Figure 4.2 A Conceptual Mapping of Efficiency Improvements
Source: Parker (1994, p. 153).

Points D, E and F correspond to forms of ownership in the private sector. Point D includes those private sector firms which are close to the public sector because of government funding or a reliance on government contracts. This might diminish incentives to be efficient. Point E is a joint stock company, while point F represents private ownership where property rights are least attenuated, particularly the owner-manager company.

With regard to the vertical axis, movement upwards corresponds to a shift away from monopoly towards competition and, thus, greater product market pressure to be efficient. Figure 4.3, therefore, provides a mapping of the expected relationship between ownership and performance, drawn from the theories of public choice and property rights, and competition and performance. The schema implies the following:

- Changes in ownership involving movement away from political control towards private ownership, but with no change in competition, will be associated with improved efficiency due to a change in the capital market (X to Y).

Table 4.3 Ownership Status and Performance

Organisa-tions	Types of Change	Date	LP	TFP	EF	FR
British Airways	Public corporation to public limited company	1987-88	O	O	O	O
London Transport (1984)	Local government to public corporation	June 1984	O	O	O	O
National Freight	Public corporation to public limited company	Feb 1982	O	O	O	O
Royal Mint	Government department to trading fund	April 1975	O	O	O	NA
British Aerospace (privatisa-tion)	Public corporation to public limited company	Feb 1981	O	O?	O?	O?
HMSO	Government department to trading fund	April 1980	O	X	O	O?
Post Office Telecomm-unications	Government department to public corporation	April 1969	O	Unclear	O?	O?
Post Office Postal	Government department to public corporation	April 1969	O	Unclear	X	O
British Aerospace	Public limited company to public ownership	Feb 1981	O	Unclear	O?	X
Royal Ordnance Factories	Government department to trading fund	July 1974	X	X?	X	O
London Transport (1970)	Public corporation to (local) government	Jan 1970	X	O	X	X
Rolls-Royce	Public limited company to public ownership	Feb 1971	X	X	X	X

Notes: (1) *LP*-Labour Productivity; *TFP*-Total Factor Productivity; *EF*-Employment Function; *FR*-Financial Ratios; (2) O means 'improved' while X 'reduced', and *NA* no data available; (3) A question mark after the result indicates that the result was not entirely clear.
Source: Derived from Parker (1994, pp. 155 and 165).

- Increased competition in the absence of a change in ownership will be associated with improved efficiency due to a change in the product market (X to Z).
- Changes in ownership involving a movement away from private ownership towards public ownership will be associated with reduced efficiency due to a change in the capital market (Y to X).
- Less competition, even where there is no change in ownership, will lead to a reduction in efficiency (Z to X).

The largest efficiency gains are likely to be associated with movements from X to W; that is, towards private ownership and more competition. A movement from W to X, involving greater political control and less competition, is likely to lead to a significant deterioration in efficiency. Movements either way between Z and Y imply an ambiguous result caused by the conflict between changes in the product and capital market constraints on managerial behaviour. From this discussion the *central hypothesis* of Parker (1994) can be derived that changes in ownership away from political control and towards private ownership, especially when also associated with increased competition, will lead to an appreciable improvement in efficiency.

Empirical Evidence

To test the hypothesis that ownership affects economic performance, Parker (1994) selects twelve relevant ownership status to analyse. After testing 12 organisations by using several performance indicators, Parker (1994) produces Table 4.3 with the conclusion as follows:

> "It is always dangerous to draw firm conclusions from what was clearly a small sample. However, the results do not contradict the view that privatisation improves performance and they provide some support for the argument that political intervention in an organisation's operations damages efficiency."

Moreover, Pryke (1982) concludes that, whatever the reason may be, the record of the activities being investigated suggests that public ownership leads to performance which is relatively poor by the standards of private enterprises. In contrast, Hutchinson (1991), by applying regression analysis to the labour productivity and profitability of the aerospace and electronics and electrical industries, reveals that the empirical evidence gives mixed results as to the effects of ownership on the performance of firms in the UK. That is, public ownership was found to correspond with higher levels of growth in labour productivity, while private ownership gave rise to higher levels of profits. This result suggests that the privatisation of public enterprises is likely to have a positive effect on the profitability performance of the affected firm, and a negative impact on the firm's labour productivity. /

By surveying the empirical literature up to around 1980, Millward (1982) concludes that there appear to be no general grounds for believing that managerial (*or* productive) efficiency was lower in public firms. Vickers and Yarrow (1988), after a close examination of the material on which Millward (1982) based his article, suggest the slightly different conclusion that privately owned firms tend, on average, to be the more internally (*or* productively) efficient when competition in product markets is effective. Millward and Parker (1983), after testing several industries in several countries, draw the conclusion that there is no systematic evidence that public enterprises are less cost effective than private firms. The poorer performance in this respect, exhibited in the studies of refuse collection and water supply, has to be balanced against the absence of any significant difference in Canadian railways and Australian airlines and the superior performance in US electric power. With respect to electricity supply, in fact, several economists (e.g. Meyer, 1975; Fare *et al.*, 1985) have concluded that publicly owned utilities typically have lower unit costs than privately owned ones.

Table 4.4 provides a summary of the empirical evidence on the relative performance of different ownership types. Although the table suggests an 'edge' for the private sector, the results vary considerably across the sectors.

From the above discussion, the evidence does not establish a clear-cut superiority of private ownership over its public counterpart. A large number of studies, e.g., Yarrow (1986), Vickers and Yarrow (1988, 1991), Bishop and Kay (1988, 1989), Bishop and Thompson (1992), Rowthorn and Chang (1993), Parker (1994), and Jackson and Price (1994), conclude that competitive environment, regulatory policy and organisational reforms can be more important determinants of economic performance than ownership *per se*.

Table 4.4 Results on Relative Efficiency of Public and Private Enterprises

Sectors	Public Company More Efficient	No Difference or Ambiguous Results	Private Company More Efficient
Electric Utilities	3	5	6
Refuse Collection	1	3	5
Water Supply	2	1	4
Health-related Services	-	1	11
Airlines	-	3	2
Railroads	-	2	-
Financial Institutions	-	1	1
Fire Services	-	-	1
Nonrail Transit	-	-	3
Total No.	6	16	33

Note: Figures in cells indicate the number of empirical results in each industry sector.
Source: Derived from Boardman and Vining (1989, p. 6).

With regard to this matter, it might be worth quoting the following two comments:

"Competition, which is conceptually distinct from ownership, can greatly improve monitoring possibilities, and hence incentives for productive efficiency....But product market competition, or even the threat of it, does not always exist....Regulation for competition may then be a desirable complement to privatisation." (Vickers and Yarrow, 1991)

"Economists are now generally agreed that simply changing the ownership of assets is not sufficient, and indeed is not even necessary, to improve efficiency. What is important is the threat of competition and, therefore, market conditions and perhaps the regulatory regime." (Bishop and Thompson, 1992)

In summary, privatisation is a controversial policy. Its supporters and critics base their cases on a mixture of ideological, political and economic arguments. The highly political nature of privatisation makes it difficult to assess the truth of many claims made for and against it. Political bargaining in the process of privatisation, to some extent, seems to work against the results we expect to achieve: efficiency improvement (Antal-Mokos, 1998). As Liu (1995) points out, the problem of determining the relative efficiencies of alternative forms of ownership is, therefore, solved through empirical analysis.

REFERENCES

Alchian, A. (1965), Some Economics of Property Rights, *Il Politico*, Vol. 30, No. 4, pp. 816-829.

Alchian, A. and Demsetz, H. (1972), Production, Information Costs and Economic Organisation, *American Economic Review*, Vol. 62, pp. 777-795.

Antal-Mokos, Z. (1998), *Privatisation, Politics and Economic Performance in Hungary*, Cambridge University Press, Cambridge.

Barzel, Y. (1989), *Economics Analysis of Property Rights*, Cambridge University Press, New York.

Beesley, M. and Littlechild, S. (1988), Privatisation: Principles, Problems and Priorities, in Johnson, C. (ed.), *Lloyds Bank Annual Review: Privatisation and Ownership*, Printer Publisher Ltd., London, pp. 1-29.

Begg, D., Fisher, S. and Dornbusch, R. (1991), *Economics* (3rd ed.), McGraw-Hill International UK Ltd., London.

Bishop, M. and Kay, J. (1988), *Does Privatisation Work?: Lessons from the UK*, London Business School, London.

Bishop, M. and Kay, J. (1989), Privatisation in the United Kingdom: Lessons for Experience, *World Development*, Vol. 17, No. 5, pp. 643-657.

Bishop, M. and Thompson, D. (1992), Regulatory Reform and Productivity Growth in the UK's Public Utilities, *Applied Economics*, Vol. 24, No. 11, pp. 1181-1190.

Blackstone, L. and Franks, D. (1986), *Guide to Management Buy-outs*, Economist Publications Ltd., London.

Boardman, A. and Vining, A. (1989), Ownership and Performance in Competitive Environments: A Comparison of the Performance of Private, Mixed and State-Owned Enterprises, *Journal of Law and Economics*, Vol. 32, pp. 1-33.

Borooah, V. (1996), Widening Public Choice, in Pardo, J. and Schneider, F. (eds.), *Current Issues in Public Choice*, Edward Elgar, Cheltenham, pp. 43-50.

Brittan, S. (1984), The Politics and Economics of Privatisation, *Political Quarterly*, Vol. 55, pp. 109-128.

Brown, C. and Jackson, P. (1990), *Public Sector Economics* (4th ed.), Basil Blackwell Ltd., Oxford.

Buchanan, J. (1980), Rent Seeking and Profit Seeking, in Buchanan, J. and Tollison, D. and Tullock, G. (eds.), *Toward a Theory of the Rent-Seeking Society*, A&M Press, Texas, pp. 3-15.

Clementi, D. (1985), The Experience of the United Kingdom, in Asian Development Bank, *Privatisation*, pp. 167-182.

Cullis, J. and Jones, P. (1989), *Microeconomics and the Public Economy: A Defence of Leviathan*, Basil Blackwell, Oxford.

De Alessi, L. (1980), The Economics of Property Rights: A Review of the Evidence, *Research in Law and Economics*, Vol. 2, pp. 1-47.

Dunkerley, J. and Hare, P. (1991), Nationalised Industries, in Crafts, N. and Woodward, N. (eds.), *The British Economy Since 1945*, Clarendon Press, Oxford.

Dunleavy, P. (1986), Explaining the Privatisation Boom: Public Choice versus Radical Approaches, *Public Administration*, Vol. 64, No. 1, pp. 13-34.

Dunsire, A., Hartley, K., Parker, D. and Dimitriou, B. (1988), Organisational Status and Performance: A Conceptual Framework for Testing Public Choice Theories, *Public Administration*, Vol. 66, No. 4, pp. 363-388.

Fare, R., Grosskopf, S. and Logan, J. (1985), The Relative Performance of Publicly Owned and Privately Owned Electric Utilities, *Journal of Public Economics*, Vol. 26, pp. 89-106.

Financial Times (1986), Best-seller with a Choice of Ending, 10th December.

Hartley, K. and Parker, D. (1991), Privatisation: A Conceptual Framework, in Ott, A. and Hartley, K. (eds.), *Privatisation and Economic Efficiency: A Comparative Analysis of Developed and Developing Countries*, Edward Elgar Publishing Ltd., Aldershot, pp. 11-25.

Hartley, K., Parker, D. and Martin, S. (1991), Organisational Status, Ownership and Productivity, *Fiscal Studies*, Vol. 12, No. 2, pp. 46-60.

Heald, D. (1982), Privatising Public Enterprises: An Analysis of the Government's Case, *Political Quarterly*, Vol. 53, pp. 333-340.

Hutchinson, G. (1991), Efficiency Gains through Privatisation of UK Industries, in Ott, A. and Hartley, K. (eds.), *Privatisation and Economic Efficiency: A Comparative Analysis of Developed and Developing Countries*, Edward Elgar Publishing Ltd., Aldershot, pp. 87-107.

Jackson, P. and Price, C. (1994), Privatisation and Regulation: A Review of the Issues, in Jackson, P. and Price, C. (eds.), *Privatisation and Regulation: A Review of the Issues*, Longman Group Ltd., Essex, pp. 1-34.

Jasinski, P. and Yarrow, G. (1996), Privatisation: An Overview of the Issues, in Yarrow, G. and Jasinski, P. (eds.), *Privatisation: Critical Perspectives on the World Economy*, Routledge, London, pp. 1-46.

Kay, J. and Tompson, D. (1986), Privatisation: A Policy in Search of a Rationale, *Economic Journal*, Vol. 96, pp. 18-32.

Krieger, I. (1990), *Management Buy-Outs*, Butterworths, London.

Liu, Z. (1995), The Comparative Performance of Public and Private Enterprises: The Case of British Ports, *Journal of Transport Economics and Policy*, Vol. 29, No. 3, pp. 263-274.

Meyer, R. (1975), Publicly Owned versus Privately Owned Utilities: a Policy Choice, *Review of Economics and Statistics*, Vol. 57, pp. 391-399.

Millward, R. (1982), The Comparative Performance of Public and Private Ownership, in Roll, E. (ed.), *The Mixed Economy*, Macmillan Press, London, pp. 58-93.

Millward, R. and Parker, D. (1983), Public and Private Enterprise: Comparative Behaviour and Relative Efficiency, in Millward, R., Parker, D., Rosenthal, L., Sumnar, M. and Topham, N. (eds.), *Public Sector Economics*, Longman Group Ltd., New York, pp. 199-274.

Moore, J. (1986), *Why Privatise?*, in Kay, J., Mayer, C. and Thompson, D. (eds.), *Privatisation and Regulation: The UK Experience*, Clarendon Press, Oxford, pp. 78-93.

Niskanen, W. (1971), *Bureaucracy and Representative Government*, Aldine-Altherton, New York.

Oxford English Dictionary (1993), Clarendon Press, Oxford.

Parker, D. (1991), Privatisation Ten Years on: A Critical Analysis of its Rationale and Results, *Economics*, Vol. 27, Part 4, No. 116, pp. 154-163.

Parker, D. (1994), Nationalisation, Privatisation, and Agency Status within Government: Testing for the Importance of Ownership, in Jackson, P. and Price, C. (eds.), *Privatisation and Regulation: A Review of the Issues*, Longman Group Ltd., Essex, pp. 149-169.

Pirie, M. (1988), *Privatisation*, Adam Smith Institute, London.

Posner, M. (1984), Privatisation: the Frontier between Public and Private, *Policy Studies*, Vol. 5, pp. 22-23.

Posner, R. (1975), The Social Costs of Monopoly and Regulation, *Journal of Political Economy*, Vol. 83, pp. 807-827.

Pryke, R. (1982), The Comparative Performance of Public and Private Enterprise, *Fiscal Studies*, Vol. 3, No. 2, pp. 68-81.

Rees, R. (1985), The Theory of Principal and Agent, *Bulletin of Economic Research*, Vol. 37, pp. 3-26.

Rowthorn, B. and Chang, H.J. (1993), Public Ownership and the Theory of the State, in Clarke, T. and Pitelis, C. (eds.), *The Political Economy of Privatisation*, Routledge, London, pp. 51-69.

Sappington, D. (1991), Incentives in Principal-Agent Relationships, *Journal of Economic Perspectives*, Vol. 5, No. 2, pp. 45-66.

Singh, A. (1975), Takeovers, Economic Natural Selection and the Theory of the Firm, *Economic Journal*, Vol. 85, pp. 497-515.

Smith, A. (1776), *An Inquiry into the Nature and Causes of the Wealth of Nations*, edited by Sutherland, K. (1993), Oxford University Press, Oxford.

Stiglitz, J. E. (1988), *Economics of the Public Sector* (2nd ed.), W.W. Norton and Company, New York.

Taylor, R. (1983), Thatcher's Public Putsch, *Management Today*, May, pp. 54-59.

Tullock, G. (1967), The Welfare Costs of Tariffs, Monopolies and Theft, *Western Economic Journal*, Vol. 5, pp. 224-232.

UNCTAD (1995), *Comparative Experiences with Privatisation: Policy Insights and Lessons Learned*, UNCTAD/DTCI/23, New York.

Veljanovski, C. (1987), *Selling the State: Privatisation in Britain*, Butler and Tanner Ltd., London.

Vickers, J. and Yarrow, G. (1988), *Privatisation: An Economic Analysis*, MIT Press, Cambridge, Massachusetts.

Vickers, J. and Yarrow, G. (1991), Economic Perspectives on Privatisation, *Journal of Economic Perspectives*, Vol. 5, No. 2, pp. 111-132.

Vuylsteke, C. (1988), *Techniques of Privatisation of State-Owned Enterprises: Methods and Implementation* (Volume I), World Bank, Washington, D.C.

Wiltshire, K. (1988), *Privatisation: The British Experience*, Longman Cheshire Pty Ltd., Melbourne.

Wolf, C. Jr. (1993), *Markets or Governments: Choosing between Imperfect Alternatives* (2nd ed.), MIT Press, Cambridge, Massachusetts.

Wright, M. and Coyne, J. (1985), *Management Buy-Outs*, Croom Helm, London.

Yarrow, G. (1986), Privatisation in Theory and Practice, *Economic Policy*, April, pp. 323-377.

5 Port Privatisation: Theory and Practice

INTRODUCTION

In the past decade, a number of countries have undertaken or considered institutional reform in the port industry in an effort to improve efficiency and performance and to reduce the government's financial and administrative responsibility for the industry. Institutional restructuring in the port sector can consist of various methods, but it should have a single overall objective: i.e., to make the port responsive to the market and thus satisfy client needs (UNCTAD, 1995). Organisational changes have been introduced through measures such as commercialisation, deregulation and privatisation so that the role of government and the public sector has been significantly reduced. At the same time, the private sector has been encouraged to take part in port activities more actively than ever before.

The participation of the private sector in port management and operation has become the norm rather than the exception (Fairplay, 1996). The expansion of the private sector's role in the ownership, management and operation of ports is one of the major issues in today's port industry. A report by Port Development International (1993) surveys 31 countries where some form of port privatisation has taken place. Those countries which still have a state controlled port sector are facing a new wave in port administration and operation. This new wave can be considered a revolution in port operations and a development yielding benefits to a national economy.

Following the review of privatisation theory earlier, this chapter critically analyses the privatisation principles applicable to, and practices taking place in, the port industry. The context of port privatisation is evaluated following an analysis of its motivation and rationale, current patterns of port administration and ownership are addressed, and the arguments presented for and against port privatisation in principle and practice. The discussion moves on to the several functions of ports and models of port administration, which are represented in a 'port function

117

matrix'. The role of the port authority in this era of privatisation is assessed and is then followed by an analysis of the privatisation methods applicable to the port industry. Finally, this chapter contains a review of how such privatisation programmes have worked in practice, placing particular attention on the UK experience.

THE PORT PRIVATISATION CONTEXT

Before going into the main theme of port privatisation any further, it might be helpful to understand the basic functions of a port. In general, a port can be regarded as acting as a gateway through which goods and passengers are transferred between ships and the shore (Goss, 1990a). In other words, a port exists to provide terminal facilities and services for ships, and transfer facilities and services for water-borne goods and passengers. Flere (1967, p. 9) describes the fundamental characteristics of a port as follows:

> "It [a port] should be able to accommodate ships on the one hand and inland transport vehicles on the other. That is why every port is equipped to look two ways - outwards over the sea or the waterway and inwards over its economic hinterland."

From the above note, it can be said that the most important function of a port is to ensure the transfer of goods from inland transport to maritime transport and vice versa. Jansson and Shneerson (1982, pp. 9-10) provide a schematic of the entire process in a port subdivided into seven major processes as follows:

- passage of ship through approach channel up to quay;
- discharge of cargo from ship's hold to quay;
- moving cargo from quay to transit storage;
- transit storage;
- moving cargo from transit storage to the loading platform;
- loading cargo on to inland transport vehicle; and
- departure of land vehicle from port area

From the above processes, as Suykens (1983) suggests, the traditional economic functions of a port can be classified into three types: the *commercial* function which is increasingly developing into a storage and physical distribution function, the *cargo-handling* function which can be seen as the very basic function of a port, and the *industrial* function which has mainly influenced the Continental European ports.

Ports constitute a critical link in the overall trading chain. Thus, their level of efficiency and performance determines, to a large extent, a country's competitiveness. To achieve and maintain a competitive edge in the international markets, however, the country needs to understand, above all, the underlying factors influencing port competitiveness and continually assess the performance of its own port sector in comparison to other ports in the world. Tongzon (1995) identifies the various determinants of port performance and efficiency by using multiple linear regression of a sample of 23 international ports. His research supports the argument that port performance is influenced by several factors, some of which are beyond the control of port authorities, such as the level of economic activity and geographical location. There are, however, two variables which ports are able to control: port charges and terminal efficiency. Finally, he concludes that the single most significant contributor to port performance is terminal efficiency. This finding supports the view that port and terminal efficiency has a considerable bearing on the success of a country's imports and exports, and that higher port efficiency might result in lower prices, and should certainly help to ensure a nation's products are more competitive in international markets.

As a means of improving port and terminal efficiency and hence increasing overall performance, a number of countries worldwide have implemented and considered, amongst other measures, the policy of port privatisation.

Port Administration, Ownership and Privatisation

The administration of a port, its form and structure are obviously of importance to all aspects of organisation. The selection of an appropriate form of port administration is a matter of port policy. The basic system of port administration, whether it is to be an autonomous or a centrally controlled administration, should be determined by the public or national port authority (UNCTAD, 1985). There are, however, some organisational elements of the port administration responsible to the local port authority, as listed in Table 5.1.

The main duty of port administration is to organise in a proper and efficient way the complicated and diversified flow of traffic through the port (Nagorski, 1972). There are a number of alternative forms of port administration and ownership. Stehli (1978) and Goss (1986) note that although most of the physical methods used within ports (e.g. loading and discharging) vary little between ports, the systems of administration and ownership vary considerably. Some countries have port systems which are managed and operated under the control of their central governments; others have a more decentralised system such as those under the control of regional governments and municipal bodies. Still others have mixed systems with no clear pattern.

Table 5.1 Check List of Organisational Elements for a Port Administration

1.	Organisational structure;
2.	Administrative procedures;
3.	Cost analysis and control;
4.	Traffic structure;
5.	Consignment documentation and customs procedures;
6.	Electronic data processing and telecommunications systems;
7.	Data collection, analysis and dissemination procedures;
8.	Staffing and manning policies;
9.	Staffing selection procedures;
10.	Training programmes; and
11.	Marketing and public relations (including the education of potential users of a proposed new facility).

Source: UNCTAD (1985, p. 17).

It can be said, therefore, that there is no standard model for the best possible form of ownership and organisational structure, and ports adopt a variety of different administrative systems, management and operational styles. Diversity, rather than similarity, prevails in terms of port administration and ownership.

Another difference which can be observed among port administrative systems is the extent to which port authorities responsible for controlling ports are actually directly involved in port management and operations. The management and operation of most ports in the world, as Thomas (1976) points out, is vested in a port authority. Focusing on the UK, Douglas and Geen (1993) describe several different types of port or harbour authorities,[1] highlighting the main difference between their functions. Generally speaking, in the UK, in addition to national (or publicly owned and operated) ports, there are three main types of port ownership (Thomas, 1994a). These are *trust ports* administered by self-governing statutory bodies, *municipal ports* owned by local authorities, and *company ports* which are effectively privately owned statutory companies.

This diversity in the form of ownership and administration is largely due to the fact that ports have been developed in different ways in which social, political, cultural, geographical, commercial and military influences have played a significant part (Thomas, 1994b). This variation in the styles of port administration and ownership, therefore, is not surprising. Regarding different ownership styles and administration in ports, the following comment by Suykens (1985, p. 181) is salient:

"Every administrative system which favours the prosperity of a port and the expansion of traffic is good, provided that its administration is also efficient. This means in fact that the application of principles is more important than the principles themselves since very efficient ports have been found to have many different systems of administration."

This argument implies that there is no single optimum category for the management, operation or administration of ports, and that ports should be able to seek ways to improve their efficiency in given circumstances in order to contribute to the national economy through the efficient transportation of imports and exports goods.

Whatever form ownership takes, as Cass (1996) notes, a port is ultimately in either public or private ownership unless it is in some form of joint ownership between the two basic forms. This ownership structure, however, does not establish which activities are undertaken by the private or public sector within ports. With reference to this issue, it might be useful to review the way in which ports have been organised by examining the types of ports.

Prior to any discussion of port types, however, an examination of the various activities in ports should be carried out. The list of facilities and

---

(1)   The words 'port' and 'harbour' seem to be synonymous for most purposes in that a port *or* harbour is a place where a vessel can lie in a position of more or less shelter from the elements, with a view to the loading and discharge of cargo (Douglas and Geen, 1993, p. 1).

services provided by ports for ships and cargo is shown in Table 5.2. According to which entity (private, public or joint) owns and provides the facilities and services listed in Table 5.2, ports can be categorised into two distinct types: the comprehensive and the landlord port.[2]

Table 5.2 List of Port Facilities and Services

Infrastructure	Approach channel, Breakwater, Locks, and Berths
Superstructure	Surfacing, Storage (transit sheds, silos, warehouses), Workshops, Offices
Equipment	Fixed (ship-to-shore crane, conveyor belts, etc.) Mobile (straddle carriers, forklifts, tractors, etc.)
Services to Ships	Harbour Masters office (radio, VTS*, etc.), Navigational aids, Pilotage, Towage, Berthing/unberthing, Supplies, Waste reception and disposal, Security
Services to Cargo	Handling, Storage, Delivery/reception, Cargo processing, Security

Note: (*) Vessel Traffic System.
Source: UNCTAD (1995, p. 27).

In the *comprehensive port*, the public port authority provides all facilities and services within the port, thus having direct responsibility for the management and operation of port services and facilities. Independent (private) operators are prohibited from undertaking any port activity. This kind of port, therefore, can be said to be the 'totally integrated port'. On the other hand, in the *landlord port*, the activities of the port authority are limited simply to providing and maintaining the basic infrastructure and essential services (e.g. fire service, security etc.), while all the other facilities and services such as the superstructure and stevedoring labour are provided by independent private (or public) companies. This port can be called the 'purely regulatory port'.

Cass (1996) describes more specific characteristics of each port along

---

(2)　Some maritime economists, e.g., Baudelaire (1997), Liu (1995a) and Baird (1995a, 1995b), divide ports into three different types with a different terminology such as *service ports*, *tool ports* and *landlord ports*. In general, however, ports are grouped into two types as suggested by the majority of maritime economists such as Goss (1986, 1990b), Thomas (1994b), Heaver (1995) and De Monie (1996). In definition, service ports have the same functions as comprehensive ports. Tool ports exist somewhere between comprehensive and landlord ports, and can be regarded as a variant of the landlord ports.

with ownership structures. The *comprehensive port* is publicly owned and open to all, but infrastructure, superstructure and equipment are financed by the port entity, sometimes with government involvement in investment and loans. Facilities and operations are placed under the direct control of the port authority, which employs dock labour, owns cranes, superstructure and infrastructure, and for which the private sector is, at most, simply a client. The comprehensive port generally prohibits intra-port competition and is a monopolistic port.

The *landlord port* is also publicly owned and open to all. The port authority may or may not be the ultimate owner of land on which the port is established. Part or all of the superstructure is financed and operated by independent private companies, which employ dock labour or by a franchised government-owned corporation under a monopoly. There are also specialised terminals financed by private operators (e.g. dedicated terminals).

Although it is not difficult to find examples of the above extreme positions, most ports lie somewhere between comprehensive and landlord ports and operate within a wide range of different types of port organisation which vary from country to country and sometimes even within the same country (Goss, 1990b). Although the port applying the landlord concept is the most common type, it is not possible to identify one extreme as better than the other. For example, both the port of Hong Kong, which can be considered representative of landlord ports, and the port of Singapore, which can be considered a comprehensive port, are well known for their efficient management and operation.

In simple terms, *port ownership* can be defined in terms of who provides the port facilities and services, and *port privatisation* can be defined as the actual transfer of ownership of port properties from the public to the private sector *or* the actual application of private capital to fund investment in port development and maintenance as well as port activities. With respect to port ownership and privatisation, Cass (1996, p. 36) notes:

"If privatisation means the transfer of ownership of state assets to the private sector, then clearly, in the many instances where port ownership still remains with the state, a new definition of port privatisation is required. The different forms of port ownership, between and within countries, particularly public but also private, does lead to some confusion. But, ultimately, a port will either be in public or private sector ownership, unless of course it is jointly owned by both."

Reasons for and Objectives of Port Privatisation

During the last decade, there has been a worldwide trend of institutional restructuring of the public sector. In the past, political decisions transferred economic activities to the public sector. Now, however, markets are increasingly acting as a driving force for the national and international economy. This trend requires some institutional changes: i.e., movement away from economies where the public sector plays a pivotal role. In line with this changing environment, institutional and organisational reforms in ports are taking place in a number of countries.

In addition, there is another factor requiring changes. The economic characteristics of the port industry itself have recently altered. Heaver (1995) points out changes in technologies as the main factor influencing the structure and competitiveness of the port industry today. On the one hand, the industry has moved away from the state where public capital was predominantly used to provide common user facilities to the state where more private funds have been involved in the development and maintenance of ports and terminals which are designed to serve the logistics requirements of more narrowly defined groups of shippers. On the other hand, the efficiency of port cargo handling and of ocean and inland transport services has increased. The development of more specialised facilities has had the direct result of increasing the effectiveness of competition in the industry.

The technological developments in ports and in the transport industries have had an impact on the market power of ports as well. Heaver (1995, p. 126) lists the following major trends as a consequence:

- ships and terminals have become more specialised;
- the efficiency of inland transport systems has increased;
- terminals have been effective in the development of more efficient throughput capacity;
- terminals are more likely to serve one or a few logistics systems;
- terminals are becoming more capital intensive; and
- private investment in terminals is increasing.

Of these developments, the private sector has actively and increasingly been involved in supplementing and replacing their public counterparts. Frankel (1992, p. 201) notes:

"Port privatisation is not a new concept. Increasing capital intensity in shipping and related port facility requirements, greater integration of shipping, port and inland feeder transport, and a higher degree of concentration in the international transport industry, has caused many ship or transport operations or cargo owners to get involved in port and terminal ownership and operations."

Several studies, e.g., Nagorski (1972), Heggie (1974) and Eyre (1990), argue that ports operated directly by governments or public agencies and owned by the public sector are more expensive and less efficient, thus leading to less satisfactory results. In general, public ports appear to set rates on a basis which fails to cover full costs, thus subsidies are common (Wilder and Pender, 1979).

To overcome such drawbacks of publicly owned and operated ports together with the recent trends in the port industry, the policy of port privatisation has been implemented and taken into consideration. Haarymeyer and Yorke (1993) regard 'private sector participation' as a solution to the many problems faced by US public ports such as the lack of exposure to full commercial competitive pressures, inefficient operation and working under undue political interference. Eyre (1990, p. 113) argues that privatisation of a port is a philosophical cousin to the concepts of deregulation, free trade, laissez-faire and user pays.

A variety of forces can influence decisions to privatise public ports. Sherman (1995), UNCTAD (1995) and Frankel (1992) note the principal objectives for port reforms including privatisation. Some of these are (i) to enhance the efficiency of port services, (ii) to find new financial resources for development and maintenance, (iii) to strengthen entrepreneurial and managerial capacity, (iv) to relieve government's financial and administrative burden, and (v) to eliminate and/or minimise bureaucratic and political influence over port management and operation. In addition, economic benefits can be obtained from introducing more competition into port operations. Based on these objectives, the most obvious motivations can be categorised into two forces: improvement in port efficiency and reduction in public expenditure and responsibility.

Arguments For and Against Port Privatisation

While many argue for the benefits and advantages of privatisation mentioned in the previous section, it is equally obvious that there is a strong argument for giving careful consideration to whether to privatise or not.

Bassett (1993) and Baird (1995a) suggest various reasons in support of port privatisation. Since public ports could not pledge their assets to raise capital, they were consequently constrained in terms of expansion. Privatising the ports could enable them to broaden their capital base, allowing them to seek and obtain capital from the most appropriate source, and to invest in new facilities. In addition to this benefit, losing the public status of ports could allow them to diversify their activities and increase the level of competition in the industry.

In contrast, there are a number of drawbacks related to port privatisation programmes. De Monie (1996) points out four serious deficiencies which such a policy could cause. These are: (i) privatisation greatly increases the risk of a port administration disregarding statutory 'public service' functions that have been entrusted to it. Private investors and/or operators tend to favour profit maximisation and cost minimisation. As a result, they may be inclined to abandon facilities and services which, although socially or environmentally essential, are less rewarding or that incur expenditure rather than earn revenues, (ii) where no or only a limited degree of competition exists (e.g. because of the narrow traffic base, the limited scale of the operations, the port's geographical location, or the lack of an adequate inland transport network), there is a strong probability that a public monopoly will be turned into a private one, (iii) a division of responsibilities between a public port authority and private sector operators may well result in poor co-ordination of investments, services and operations and lead to reduced efficiency of operations at sea-to-land and land-to-land interfaces, and (iv) as their priority, private operators may favour the business interests of their beneficial owners; thus privatisation could lead to discriminatory treatment of the port's clientele and common users could find themselves in a weaker negotiating position than those users who are controlled by, associated with or part of the beneficial owners of the private operating company.

Of these four shortcomings, the first relates to debates on whether services provided by ports are public or private. Public goods (and services) are defined as those unlikely to be provided sufficiently, satisfactorily or even at all, by competitive industries; in other words, that there is a market failure (Goss, 1990c). Evans (1969) argues that it is in the common interest that a port, as a public utility, is economically protected because of its importance to the economy. In general, it is difficult to find a private company which provides public goods (e.g. national defence) if they cannot be allowed to earn financial revenues from them.

There are, however, some arguments against the above discussion: i.e., a port can be partly a public service and partly a commercial activity. Hershman (1988) mentions that ports are 'public' in that the government owns them, statutes set them up and dictates their objectives, and public subsidies are often provided. Ports, in contrast, are 'private' in that their management often operates independently, money can be raised from private sources, revenues can be retained and reinvested, and often there is no dependence on tax revenues. The private character of public ports derives from the competitive marketplace within which they operate.

Although port productivity has dramatically improved in UK ports over recent years, this cannot be attributed directly to privatisation itself. Thomas (1994a), for instance, has found that after privatisation any increase in profits was mainly due to property developments rather than port operations. Iheduru (1993) supports the findings that the advocates of privatisation policies have failed to make a distinction between ownership and management, and that they also equate private ownership with efficiency. Again, Thomas (1994b) argues that changing the management culture of a port authority can be achieved by modifying the organisation within the existing institutional framework and the key to reform lies in changing people's beliefs and values and ensuring that these are compatible and in harmony with the corporation's objectives. From this argument, a conclusion can be drawn that port privatisation should be considered and implemented only against the whole background of the country, culture, economic and political situation concerned, and that its constitution and general way of doing things should also be considered.

PORT PRIVATISATION OPTIONS

Although ports are fundamentally owned and operated by either the public or the private sector or even as a joint venture by both sectors, and can be classified as being either comprehensive or landlord ports (Goss, 1981; De Monie, 1996), there are few completely privatised ports or even fully public ones. Furthermore, there is great variation in the jurisdictional forms between the two different types of ports. This makes it difficult to identify the extent of involvement of both the public and private sectors in any port. This situation does, however, make it necessary to distinguish between the alternative approaches to port privatisation.

Three Key Functions of Ports

Baird (1995b, 1997) proposes a framework called a *port function matrix*, as a model for port administration. The starting point of this framework is that, regardless of whether a port in question is in private or public hands, within the port area there will generally be three essential functions the port must fulfil and provide:

- a regulatory function;
- a landowner function;
- an operator function.

Firstly, the *regulatory function* of a port can involve substantial powers being given to the port's management which is public or private, the majority of which will be of a statutory nature. This function, in general, may be regarded as the primary role of a port authority. These powers and responsibilities will be likely to include:

- to maintain the conservancy function;
- to provide vessel traffic management;
- to enforce applicable laws and regulations;
- to license port works; and
- to safeguard port users' interests against the risk of monopoly formation, and to control natural monopolies.

Secondly, in the *landowner function*, ports control significant land areas. Irrespective of whether the land area of a port is large or small, however, the essential tasks a port landowner will be required to undertake include the following:

- to manage and develop the port estate;
- to implement port policies and development strategies;

- to supervise major civil engineering works;
- to co-ordinate port marketing and promotion activities;
- to provide and maintain channels, fairways, breakwaters etc.;
- to provide and maintain locks, turning basins, berths, piers and wharves; and
- to provide or arrange road and rail access to the port facilities.

Thirdly, the *operator function* is concerned with the physical transfer of goods and passengers between sea and land. In a comprehensive port, for example, the cargo-handling activity will be controlled by state-owned organisations, in a landlord port, private companies will undertake this activity, while a mix of private and public companies may be involved as well.

According to which of these three functions are the responsibility of public or private organisations, the matrix, presented in Table 5.3, makes it possible to ascertain the extent of the influence public and private sectors have within a given port. The matrix presented in Table 5.3 also suggests the four main patterns in terms of port administration, ownership, management and operation, in which a government is able to organise its port industry.

Table 5.3 Port Function Matrix

Port Models	Port Functions		
	Regulator	**Landowner**	**Operator**
PUBLIC	Public	Public	Public
PUBLIC/private	Public	Public	Private
PRIVATE/public	Public	Private	Private
PRIVATE	Private	Private	Private

Source: Baird (1995b, 1997).

Port Administration Models

The models are divided into four types of port administration: the *PUBLIC port*, the *PUBLIC/private port* with the public sector dominant, the *PRIVATE/public port* with the private sector dominant, and the *PRIVATE port*.

Firstly, a *PUBLIC port*, which can be also referred to as a comprehensive port, is a port in which all three functions are controlled by the government or public authority. While the *PUBLIC port* model is perhaps the most inefficient of the four alternatives as claimed by advocates for port privatisation, it has also paradoxically proved to be one of the most efficient approaches as can be seen in the case of the port of Singapore. In fact, while still preferred by some countries, the *PUBLIC port* seems no longer to be regarded as a realistic option for most governments, particularly where major new capital investment projects are under consideration. As a vivid illustration of this, the organisational restructuring, or corporatisation, of the port of Singapore is currently being considered (Port Development International, 1997).[3]

Secondly, in the *PUBLIC/private port*, the operator function is controlled by the private sector, with both the regulatory and landowner functions remaining in the hands of the government. This type of port, therefore, can be called a variant of the landlord port and is common in Continental Europe and North America. The port of Rotterdam is a typical example, where terminals are leased out to private terminal operators. Similarly, Pusan's Shinsundae container terminal falls into this type of port administration structure. The popularity of *PUBLIC/private ports* or the landlord ports is likely to continue increasing because of their ability to allow the benefits of private sector management in the efficient handling of cargo to be combined with public and common user interests (Saundry and Turnbull, 1997). In Far East Asia, several private companies (e.g., International Container Terminal Services Inc., which manages and operates the Manila international container terminal under a 25-year contract) have obtained concessions for terminal operations (Fairplay, 1996). This arrangement means that the port in question is still in public ownership, but individual terminals are leased to independent private companies.

Thirdly, in the *PRIVATE/public port*, both the landowner and operator functions are in private hands, while the regulatory function remains in the public sector. A classic example of this type is the port of Hong Kong, where private companies build their own terminals but the government

---

(3) The Port of Singapore Authority is no longer the statutory body in charge of controlling the port; on 1 October 1997, the Singapore government established the PSA Corporation Ltd., which is a wholly owned subsidiary of state-owned Temasek Holdings (Lloyd's List, 1998; SingaPort '98, 1998). This reform of port administration can be seen as the first step towards privatisation.

retains responsibility for vessel traffic management and other regulatory policies, as well as the planning of new port and terminal development.

Finally, in the *PRIVATE port*, all three essential functions are controlled by the private sector. There are currently many *PRIVATE ports* in the UK, including all 23 ports owned by Associated British Ports, and the ports of Liverpool, Manchester and Felixstowe.

In the second and third models (i.e. the *PUBLIC/private* and *PRIVATE/public ports*), a port can be viewed as a public enterprise (Olson, 1988). The public enterprise generally represents a mix of government agencies and private enterprises. The *public* character involves three primary features such as its creation by the government, the statutory assignment of powers, and ownership by the public. The *enterprise* character provides its market orientation and includes the four features of expectations of market efficiencies in operations, commercially defined performance goals, reliance upon user fees for operating revenue and capital markets for construction funds rather than general government appropriations, and the absence of partisan intervention in its operations. Each of these characteristics necessitates structural independence and autonomy from government.

From the discussion until now, it can be said that the role of the private sector in the port industry has consistently increased. There are still many instances, however, in which the significant role of the public sector is required. Of the four models mentioned in this section, the second alternative (the *PUBLIC/private port* or the landlord port) is extensively preferred throughout the countries of North America, Europe and Asia (see Appendix 3). This type of port also seems to be popularly pursued by countries such as those in Latin America and Eastern Europe. Although still preferred by certain countries, the PUBLIC port is unlikely to continue as a realistic policy option and the UK ports present a number of examples of the *PRIVATE port* model.

Baird (1997) concludes that the UK approach toward port privatisation could be considered as real privatisation while other options such as *PUBLIC/private ports* merely as private sector participation in the industry. Everett and Robinson (1998) note that the privatisation of ports is viewed not simply in terms of transfer of ownership but the transition of port authorities from statutory bodies providing the public services to corporations being in quest of competitiveness in unconstrained competitive markets.

THE ROLE OF THE PORT AUTHORITY

As several changes, economic and technological, have affected the characteristics of the port industry, today's port authorities find themselves less and less in control of their destinies. With respect to port authorities' decreasing power, Slack (1993, p. 580) notes:

"Clients of long standing are demonstrating little loyalty in maintaining their business activities in the port. Ports are becoming pawns in an game of commerce that is global in scale, and on a board where the major players are private corporations whose interests rarely coincide with the local concerns of the port administrations."

In addition, as privatisation gains worldwide impetus, questions of whether public port authorities are still necessary in this changing environment are seriously raised. In fact, different opinions are voiced as to whether there remains a need for port authorities in a situation where the private sector is increasingly taking over the previously publicly-run activities of port operations.

At one end of the spectrum, some private sector entities argue that public organisations, such as port authorities, constitute an additional layer of port management and operation, hence causing problems of bureaucracy, and, ultimately, inefficiency. This argument suggests that port authorities should be replaced by landlord companies, driven by the profit motive and coupled with limited liability status.

At the other end of the spectrum, others support the comprehensive role of a port authority even in conditions where the actual operational activities such as cargo and ship handling, towage and mooring have been entrusted to private hands. In general, management and operations in respect of port development still require a certain role for commanding as well as controlling, along with a long term plan, which is said to be a widely recognised advantage of a public port authority. An increasing involvement in ports by the private sector, therefore, does not mean the redundancy of port authorities.

Goss (1990c) argues conceptually on the issues of whether or not port authorities are necessary, with suggestions for and against having public port authorities. As discussed in Chapter 4, property rights, the need for planning, the significance of public goods, dealing with externalities and promoting efficiency are claimed as advantages. In contrast, bureaucratic systems, absence of response to market forces and other problems in general public organisations are regarded as disadvantages. Finally, Goss (1990c, p. 269) concludes:

> "There are likely to be many instances of *market failure* in seaports, e.g., in the processes of planning, controlling externalities and promoting competition if these were left wholly to the private sector; but there are also many opportunities for *government failure*, whether in port authorities or in other official bodies, including government departments supervising the port authorities."

As Sherman (1995) recommends, when making a decision on privatising port activities, determination must be made as to what, if any, role should be retained by the public sector or public port authority, what restrictions or limits should be placed on private operators, and what safeguards are needed to prevent abuses.

According to Agerschou *et al.* (1983, p. 257) and Douglas and Geen (1993, p. 11), the main functions of a port authority may, in general terms, include:

- providing and maintaining port facilities such as navigational channels, quays, wharves, and anchorage etc.;
- conservancy functions, including lighting and buoying the port, the removal of wrecks and other obstructions and maintenance dredging;
- regulating the activities of other persons or organisations at the port, including the movement and berthing of ships;
- the provision of a pilotage service;
- carrying out port operations such as cargo handling activities, shore handling and storage of cargo; and
- providing bunker fuel, water and other supplies for ships.

The port authority itself may manage and operate all of these functions, although it may be practical to let other organisations, private or public, handle some. Traditionally, the port authority provides the facilities required to undertake the first three functions, which involve heavy investment expenditure. Other functions can be handled by one or more specialised companies under relatively long term contracts.

Fundamentally, however, port privatisation alters several missions and functions of the traditional port authority. Instead of acting as a body responsible for everything but ineffective in most of its efforts, a modern port authority is required to take a role in which it is required to act in close co-operation with private sectors and to efficiently concentrate its efforts on the performance of a number of fundamental functions as seen in the following (De Monie, 1994):

- the landlord and performance monitoring function;
- the policy-making, planning and development function;
- the traffic control, regulatory and surveillance function;
- the marketing, public relations and promotion function; and
- the human resources development function.

Irrespective of whether a port acts in a landlord or a comprehensive role, of these newly demanded missions for port authorities, the most important would seem to be the second function: i.e., policy-making, planning and development. In addition to this function, the port authority is required to ensure that efficiency is enhanced through competition and fair play. This can be referred to as a monitoring function, aimed at smoothing the operations of ports since the port is a significant contributor to the national economy.

Juhel (1998) refers to these functions that are required to be undertaken by public authorities or bodies: (i) the *catalyst* mission - financing facilities which it is unlikely to gain access to private or alternative sources of funds and the completion of which appears on the critical path of national or regional development programmes, (ii) the *statutory* mission - dealing with navigational safety, environmental protection and fostering common development policies between ports and adjacent cities, and (iii) the *facilitator* mission - strengthening public governance (improving institutional ability to monitor new public and private partnerships and oversee operations without interfering in commercial activities) and spearheading initiatives conducive to trade integration (assisting design and implementation of development initiatives to induce value added activities to settle in port areas).

METHODS OF PORT PRIVATISATION

The port function matrix discussed in section 5.3 gives an idea of the balance, extent and mixture of public and private options according to the way in which port activities are controlled and operated. It is now necessary to examine the various methods by which private sector participation in port activities can be brought about. In addition to the methods mentioned in Chapter 4, which are applicable to broader industries, this section will be focusing on the methods typically applicable and adaptable to the port industry, taking into account some of the characteristics of the industry.

A variety of alternative methods for port privatisation have been suggested and implemented and certain variations on them exist. To put it simply, one or more of the following forms are chosen when port privatisation takes place (Frankel, 1992, p. 205):

- private management of port facilities, individual terminals or operations without ownership transfer in any form;
- private management of ports in total or part with temporary transfer of ownership control by leasing of facilities, equipment, etc.;
- private management of ports in total or part with partial or total transfer of assets; and
- complete divestiture of ownership and management of the port.

De Monie (1996, pp. 277-278) specifically divides the privatisation of port facilities and services into the following three types:

- the management of the port in accordance with the landlord concept;
- the total transfer of ownership of both the infra- and superstructures and of the equipment; and
- the concept of the division of port activities.

Although they provide some insight into port privatisation, these 'methods' are so abstract that they cannot be used in practice. More practical and applicable methods are suggested by several maritime economists, e.g., Iheduru (1993), Baird (1995a), UNCTAD (1995) and Cass (1996). The following methods are those which can be comprehensively and universally applied to and implemented in the port industry.

Commercialisation (or Pseudo Privatisation)

The process of commercialisation involves dividing the principal activities of port authorities into separate operating units, each of which functions as an independent and commercial company. Each company is allowed to procure services from any other company according to market needs and at market rates, while paying a rent to the port authority for the premises it occupies. This method requires ports to follow economic objectives and to adapt the port organisation and management in line with commercial requirements and market needs.

Corporatisation (or Incremental Privatisation)

Corporatisation is a half-way arrangement, which attempts to gain most of the benefits from private sector involvement and privatisation while retaining a public interest. These objectives can be achieved by establishing a public sector landlord, e.g., a port corporation, while simultaneously providing more freedom in port operations through giving full autonomy to the port in question, with some powers being retained by ministers. In other words, corporatisation refers to the conversion of public sector activities to corporate companies, with a board and managers who are given commercial objectives and the powers to raise funds on private capital markets. Proprietorship, however, would reside with the government. Iheduru (1993) points out that the method of corporatisation is the most appropriate alternative for revitalising the maritime sector in the developing countries, such as in certain African nations.

Joint Ventures

In general, the main reason behind the launch of a joint venture is that neither party alone has at its disposal all the elements necessary to realise the objectives of the venture. Each party, therefore, relies upon the other to supply the missing elements. The joint venture generally involves being set up by two or more organisations and is undertaken for mutual interest, e.g., one side may gain technological expertise while the other gains access to different markets, or when a project is so expensive that a number of companies decide to pool their resources to share the risks.

Concessions (or Build-Operate-Transfer)

This method could be said to be the most unique to be found in the port industry. A concession could be defined as the granting of specific privileges by government. It can be interpreted as the equivalent of a lease but, strictly speaking, it is a kind of contract by which the grantor (e.g. the public port authority or government) grants to the grantee (e.g. the independent private company) the right to finance, build and operate facilities or equipment for private and/or public use, for a limited period of time after which the equipment will be transferred free of charge to the grantor. The concession is, therefore, obviously not a form of privatisation, but just a legal technique for creating, delivering and operating a public service.

In general, concessions or build-operate-transfer (BOT) schemes have been successful in the port industry. The main advantage is that they relieve the finances of the grantor. Either the grantee pre-finances the whole operation, operates, ensures and maintains the facilities and recovers their investment through tariffs or, alternatively, sets aside all reserves necessary for the replacement of facilities and equipment included in the concession. A second advantage is that they establish a strong legal relation between the grantor and the grantee. Candidates for concessions are carefully screened and preselected. The duration of the contract and its public character gives it special importance and prevents, within certain limits, shady operations. A further benefit is that the granting of a concession permits a country or a port authority to attract capital, especially from overseas, without losing long term control over its vital port facilities.

Concessions, however, also have drawbacks and have not always been popularly implemented. This is because of the dominant position of the grantor. This condition results in complaints that concessions lack transparency. The grantee is often subjected to pressure to employ staff designated by the government or the port authority, thus creating a breeding ground for corruption and patronage as well as easy means of securing full employment.

Although both concessions and BOT schemes have much in common, each method has its own unique characteristics. The concession involves the port authority giving certain rights over specified port land for a certain period of years, usually in return for an agreed fee. This may involve a single terminal or an entire port. In the BOT scheme, however, the private sector builds and operates the new port or terminal for an agreed period, for example 20 years, with ownership transferring to the government thereafter. Little change, therefore, exists in the regulatory functions and responsibilities of a port authority in respect to the BOT schemes, only a shift in emphasis from owner and operator to trade facilities and port marketer.

In addition to these, several other methods are available as discussed in Chapter 4. These include the sale of assets such as infrastructure, superstructure and equipment through various methods, and the application of a management contract.

PORT PRIVATISATION IN PRACTICE: THE UK EXPERIENCE

Port privatisation programmes have been, or are currently being, undertaken throughout the world, but privatisation models and methods applicable to the port industry have varied widely from country to country. This phenomenon undoubtedly springs from the different environment of each country in which the port is operated, such as their economic, political, geographic and cultural features. This variety has been reported in several studies, e.g., Newman (1980), Transport (1991), Port Development International (1993), Abbott (1995) and De Monie (1995). This section will be devoted to a brief discussion of what has happened in the UK port privatisation scene. The UK, in fact, initiated the policy of port privatisation and its effects are more advanced there than anywhere else in the world. Hence, it provides a great richness of port industry ownership structures (including private ports) which are hardly found anywhere else in the world.

Port Administration and Ownership in the UK

Due to geographic characteristics, such as an extensive coastline and several navigable rivers and waterways, the UK has a large number of ports, playing a crucial role in the national economy, especially in foreign trade. The UK, as an island country, provides a variety of types of port administration and operations. In the mid-1970s it had over 250 port authorities or public operators and approximately 1400 other entities engaged in various activities such as stevedoring, towage and warehousing (HMSO, 1974).

In the UK, there have been two contrasting approaches towards port administration and ownership (Liu, 1992). One is the 'intervention approach', which has been historically influential, and points to the deficiencies of port markets and insists on some form of public ownership with a certain degree of central control over port development. The other is the 'market approach', which was until recently very much the central theme of the Conservative government, and maintains that the efficient provision of port facilities and services should rely on the market mechanism.

The National Ports Council (1973) and Thomas (1994a) present four different main types of UK port ownership, although the importance of each type has changed significantly in recent years. These include (i) public or nationalised ports, (ii) trust ports, (iii) municipal ports and (iv) company ports.[4]

Public or Nationalised Ports

Public or nationalised bodies played a predominant role in the management and operations of UK ports from 1948 to the early 1980s, accounting for about a third of its ports. Until 1962 when it was abolished, these ports were controlled by the British Transport Commission (BTC). The Transport Act of 1962 distributed the assets of the BTC to a number of newly organised national agencies such as the British Transport Docks Board (BTDB), the British Waterways Board and the British Railways Board. The BTDB then owned many of the largest ports at the time. This is a model that has been adopted by a number of developing countries, especially at the early stage of development of their national ports.

---

(4) Adams (1973) adds one more type: ports that are subsidiaries of other companies [parent companies] and that are run privately for the purpose of dealing with the specialised cargoes of a particular company or group, though occasionally dealing with the cargoes of others.

Trust Ports

A trust port is a self-governing statutory body, which is sometimes referred to as a Board, Trust, Authority or Commission. Trust ports are established under individual Acts of Parliament. These trust ports were created mainly in the late 19th and early 20th centuries in order to take over private dock companies which were unable to develop and maintain their port facilities. The main advantage of this port system has been considered to be its ability to provide independent administration, free from political interference, with jurisdiction over an area that may cross local authority boundaries and with a constitution tailored to local conditions. Wild *et al.* (1995) argue that this type of port administration can best serve the needs of the local commercial interests using a port without any one interest being able to secure an advantage over another.

Municipal Ports

Some ports are owned and controlled by municipal authorities, generally a large city. These ports are administered under relevant local legislation and are ultimately responsible to taxpayers through their local councillors.

Company Ports

Company ports are those having share capital and whose shareholders participate in the appointment of their board members (Douglas and Geen, 1993). Relatively few ports were administered in this ownership style prior to 1979. Examples are the ports of Liverpool and Manchester, set up under local Acts of Parliament and the port of Felixstowe, incorporated as far as back as 1875 as a private enterprise (Thomas, 1994a).

Table 5.4 compares the main characteristics of alternative forms of port administration and ownership in the UK. Liu (1992) points out one striking characteristic in the British port administration; unlike their counterparts in the rest of the world, 'public ports' are financially independent and are required to cover costs with no financial assistance or subsidies from the government. UK public ports, therefore, are free to set their own operational objectives such as port charges, subject only to the right of appeal of port customers. Thus, they operate as commercial undertakings in the same way as private company ports.

Table 5.4 Main Features of Port Administration and Ownership in the UK

	Company Port	Trust Port	Municipal Port
Ownership	Shareholders	Public trusts	Local authorities
Management	Elected by shareholders	Appointed by the Ministry	Appointed by local authorities
Objectives	Profit making	Public interests	Local interests
Managerial Constraints	Shareholders, take overs and bankruptcy	Managerial changes	Managerial changes and intervention by local authorities
Pricing	No restriction	No restriction	No restriction
Financing	Share issuing and borrowing from markets	Fixed-interest loans[1]	Fixed-interest loans[2]
Activity Area	Free to diversify	Legislatively restricted to port activity[3]	Legislatively restricted to port activity
Taxation	National and regional tax	National and regional tax	National and regional tax[4]

Notes: (1) There is a borrowing limit imposed by the government; (2) There is a borrowing limit imposed by local authorities, which is tighter than the borrowing limit imposed on trust ports; (3) Recently the restriction on the trustports' diversification has been removed; and (4) Except the corporation tax.
Source: Derived from Liu (1992, pp. 20-21)

Two Phases of Port Privatisation

Poor financial performance was the main motivation for implementing a policy of port privatisation in the UK. In the early 1980s, when intermodalism and specialisation were developed in shipping and port industries, the problems the UK ports were facing were likely to become worse. This situation stimulated the government to force on its port industry the discipline of market forces by withdrawing from any control over port development and operations and by cutting off financial support to the industry. The port privatisation programme in the UK was carried out in two different phases.

The first phase commenced in 1982 under the Transport Act 1981, which established the framework for the privatisation of the BTDB. Under the Transport Act 1981, Associated British Ports (ABP) was set up as a holding company for the 19 ports in the group. ABP was controlled by a company, formed by the government and registered under the Companies Act 1985 in substantially the same way as if they were a wholly owned subsidiary of that company (Douglas and Geen, 1993). This company is known as Associated British Ports PLC and in 1983 the government offered 49% of its shares for sale to investors. A year later the rest of its shares were sold to become a public company floated on the stock market. In particular, the directors of ABP are appointed by Associated British Ports PLC for such a period as that company may determine. The directors have to pay Associated British Ports PLC such a sum that the directors deem to be justified according to the profits made by ABP. This mechanism corresponds to the dividends which a subsidiary pays its holding company. Associated British Ports PLC, however, has no power to give directions to the directors of ABP with respect to the exercising of their statutory powers and duties as a port authority.

A further step was taken to increase competition in the port industry in 1989 when the National Dock Labour Scheme (NDLS) was abolished. Initially designed to end the use of casual labour on the docks, the NDLS dated back to 1947 under the Dockworkers Act 1946. Port employers had long campaigned for its abolition claiming that it was an unsatisfactory arrangement that failed to allow the efficient use of labour or to foster viable industrial relations.

Early reports of the effects of abolition of the NDLS have pointed to a combination of job losses, increasing labour market flexibility, rapid restructuring of working practices, and increased productivity and profits (Turnbull, 1991). ABP is reported to have largely withdrawn from its stevedoring role, trimming a fully unionised workforce of 9,000 in 1989 down to 2,000 in 1993, with no union recognition (Fairplay, 1993). In spite of such public enthusiasm by port owners and managers, however, as Bassett (1993) points out, it is not yet clear whether these changes will solve the more fundamental problems of over-capacity and lack of competitiveness compared with the ports of other countries, particularly in respect of investment and service quality.

The second phase of port privatisation was initiated under the Ports Act 1991, which provides for the transfer of trust ports to companies limited by shares and registered under the Companies Act 1985 (HMSO, 1991). There were over 100 trust ports in 1991, administered and controlled by various constitutions. A trust port is described as an *ad hoc* body created by, or operated under, a statute for the purpose of managing a port and not having share capital (Douglas and Geen, 1993). They had no equity but were subject to public borrowing limits. This unusual position meant that they were neither strictly public nor private bodies and were not clearly accountable to either central government or the local community.

The trust ports do not trade for profit (Adams, 1973) and have no shareholders claiming payment of dividends from profits. As they are partly financed by public subscription bonds, however, they have a duty to pay interest to the people or organisations who have lent them money. A large proportion of their total debt is in fact owed to the government. Baird (1995a) notes two main functions of the trust ports, both as publicly owned ports and as navigation authorities. In the former, ports provide cargo and passenger handling facilities within designated port areas, and constitute the maritime regulatory body for a large area within and around their ports. In the latter, the ports hold responsibility for estuarial safety, pilotage and conservancy and are in overall control of defined areas of jurisdiction.

The Ports Act 1991 was not a compulsory measure for most trust ports. If a port had a turnover of more than £5 million per annum at 1991 prices, the government could require the port trust to come forward with a plan for privatisation within two years. This affected 14 ports. Other ports could bring forward privatisation proposals voluntarily if they so wished. Section 5(3) of the Act stated that any sale should pay particular regard to the desirability of encouraging the disposal of the equity to managers and staff on the whole, or a substantial part of it. The Act, therefore, provided for the privatisation of trust ports, and applied to the majority of port authorities. Port authorities were given the power to form a limited company which could assume all property rights, liabilities and functions previously held by the recognised authority (Comptroller and Auditor General, 1993). Appendix 4 illustrates the current ownership structure of major British ports.

Lessons from the UK Experience

In terms of improved efficiency and productivity after privatisation, the benefits are difficult to identify and quantify, particularly in the case of the ports which have recently been privatised and are influenced by various factors. Thomas (1994a) notes that it is too early to measure the commercial and operating benefits of privatisation although there is considerable evidence to suggest that the programme is proving successful. These benefits have occurred not directly from privatisation, however, but from other measures such as the abolition of the NDLS in 1989. Furthermore, John (1995) asserts that port productivity pre- and post-privatisation has not been as significant as the changes that took place after the abolition of the NDLS. The overall evidence points, however, to a significant improvement in the performance of the UK ports in recent years and to a turnround in the industry's fortunes (Thomas, 1994a).

On the other hand, in terms of the turnover of major British ports from 1980 to 1990, Bassett (1993) highlights substantial growth in the ports mainly located on the east and south coasts, thanks to increasing trade with Continental Europe. Liu (1995a, 1995b) argues that, after measuring the productive efficiency of major ports during 1985-1990, port efficiency can be explained by locational differences rather than diversity in the forms of port ownership. Suitable geographical and economic conditions favour the development of trade and ports at particular sites. Saundry and Turnbull (1997) proclaim that the financial and economic performance of UK private ports has failed to achieve what was expected: higher efficiency relative to public ports.

From the above discussion, it is possible to draw a conclusion that, in the case of British ports, ownership cannot be considered as a significant factor, although it does indirectly affect and influence improvements in port performance and efficiency. Instead, other factors, such as geographical location, seem to have a major impact on efficiency. As previously mentioned in Chapter 4, the matter of whether privatisation improves efficiency or not is still not clear in the case of British ports.

In summary, privatisation is only a partial cure for what ails the port industry, and cannot alone provide the panacea for the industry. When privatising, possible risks should be completely understood and controlled in order to avoid unnecessary wasting of economic resources. What is needed here is further consideration of the variations in port administration and ownership forms taken against the whole background of the country including its cultural, constitutional and historical circumstances, as well as the peculiarities of outside pressures. Taking into consideration the special characteristics of ports, as Goss (1998) points out, a specifically tailored port privatisation policy should be implemented, rather than merely employing policies directly that have been applied in other industries. Finally, more important than ownership, as Nagorski (1972) mentions, is the fact that a port is a vital instrument of national economic policy. Close co-operation of the port with the national economic planning department is essential and the entire port system should be flexible enough so as to permit modification in accordance with the changing business environment.

REFERENCES

Abbott, P. (1995), Privatisation: Enhancing Efficiency of Ports of Latin America, *World Wide Shipping*, Vol. 58, No. 4, pp. 14-16.

Adams, G. (1973), *Organisation of the British Port Transport Industry*, National Ports Council, London.

Agerschou, H., Lundgren, H. and Sorensen, T. (1983), *Planning and Design of Ports and Marine Terminals*, John Wiley and Sons, Chichester.

Baird, A. (1995a), Privatisation of Trust Ports in the United Kingdom: Review and Analysis of the First Sales, *Transport Policy*, Vol. 2, No. 2, pp. 135-143.

Baird, A. (1995b), UK Port Privatisation: In Context, *Proceedings of UK Port Privatisation Conference*, Scottish Transport Studies Group, 21 September, Edinburgh.

Baird, A. (1997), Port Privatisation: An Analytical Framework, *Proceedings of International Association of Maritime Economist Conference*, 22-24 September, City University, London.

Bassett, K. (1993), British Port Privatisation and Its Impact on the Port of Bristol, *Journal of Transport Geography*, Vol. 1, No. 4, pp. 255-267.

Baudelaire, J. (1997), Some Thoughts about Port Privatisation, in *Essays in Honour and in Memory of Late Professor Emeritus of Maritime Economics Dr Basil Metaxas*, Piraeus, Greece, pp. 255-260.

Cass, S. (1996), *Port Privatisation: Process, Players and Progress*, Cargo Systems Report, London.

Comptroller and Auditor General (1993), *Department of Transport: The First Sales of Trust Ports*, National Audit Office, HMSO, London.

De Monie, G. (1994), The Combined Effects of Competition and Privatisation on Ports, *Proceedings of the Future Role of Ports in the G.C.C.*, 3-5 December, Kuwait Ports Authority.

De Monie, G. (1995), Restructuring the Indian Ports System, *Maritime Policy and Management*, in Special Issue for Privatisation of Indian Ports, Vol. 22, No. 3, pp. 255-260.

De Monie, G. (1996), Privatisation of Port Structures, in Bekemans, L. and Beckwith, S. (eds.), *Ports for Europe: Europe's Maritime Future in a Changing Environment*, European Interuniversity Press, Brussels, pp. 267-298.

Douglas, R. and Geen, G. (1993), *The Law of Harbours and Pilotage* (4th ed.), Lloyd's of London Press, London.

Evans, A. (1969), *Technical and Social Changes in the World's Ports*, International Labour Office, Geneva.

Everett, S. and Robinson, R. (1998), Port Reform in Austria: Issues in the Ownership Debate, *Maritime Policy and Management*, Vol. 25, No. 1, pp. 41-62.

Eyre, J. (1990), Maritime Privatisation, *Maritime Policy and Management*, Vol. 17, No. 2, pp. 113-121.

Fairplay (1993), World Ports: Free to Grow, 25 March, p. 16.

Fairplay (1996), A New Deal for Ports: Multi-national Operators Show Their Hand, 13 June, pp. 12-14.

Flere, W. (1967), *Port Economics* (2nd ed.), Foxlow Publications, London.

Frankel, E. (1992), Debt-Equity Conversion and Port Privatisation, *Maritime Policy and Management*, Vol. 19, No. 3, pp. 201-209.

Goss, R. (1981), Editorial: The Public and Private Sectors in Ports, *Maritime Policy and Management*, Vol. 8, No. 2, pp. 69-71.

Goss, R. (1986), Seaports Should Not Be Subsidised, *Maritime Policy and Management*, Vol. 13, No. 2, pp. 83-104.

Goss, R. (1990a), Economic Policies and Seaports: 1. The Economic Functions of Seaports, *Maritime Policy and Management*, Vol. 17, No. 3, pp. 207-219.

Goss, R. (1990b), Economic Policies and Seaports: 2. The Diversity of Port Policies, *Maritime Policy and Management*, Vol. 17, No. 3, pp. 221-234.

Goss, R. (1990c), Economic Policies and Seaports: 3. Are Port Authorities Necessary?, *Maritime Policy and Management*, Vol. 17, No. 4, pp. 257-271.

Goss, R. (1998), British Ports Policies Since 1945, *Journal of Transport Economics and Policy*, Vol. 32, No. 1, pp. 51-71.

Haarymeyer, D. and Yorke, P. (1993), *Port Privatisation: An International Perspective*, Reason Foundation, Los Angeles.

Heaver, T. (1995), The Implications of Increased Competition among Ports for Port Policy and Management, *Maritime Policy and Management*, Vol. 22, No. 2, pp. 125-133.

Heggie, I. (1974), Charging for Port Facilities, *Journal of Transport Economics and Policy*, Vol. 8, No. 1, pp. 3-25.

Hershman, M. (1988), Harbour Management: A New Role of the Public Port, in Hershman, M. (ed.), *Urban Ports and Harbour Management: Responding to Change along US Waterfronts*, Taylor and Francis, New York, pp. 3-25.

HMSO (1974), *British Industry Today - Ports*, HMSO, London.

HMSO (1991), *Ports Act 1991*, HMSO, London.

Iheduru, O. (1993), Rethinking Maritime Privatisation in Africa, *Maritime Policy and Management*, Vol. 20, No. 1, pp. 31-49.

Jansson, J. and Shneerson, D. (1982), *Port Economics*, MIT Press, Cambridge, Massachusetts.

John, M. (1995), Port Productivity: A User's View, *Proceedings of UK Port Privatisation Conference*, Scottish Transport Studies Group, 21 September, Edinburgh.

Juhel, M. (1998), Global Challenges for Ports and Terminals in the New Era, *Proceeding of SingaPort '98*, 24-27 March, Singapore.

Liu, Z. (1992), *Ownership and Productive Efficiency: with Reference to British Ports*, PhD Thesis, Queen Mary and Westfield College, University of London.

Liu, Z. (1995a), Ownership and Productive Efficiency: The Experience of British Ports, in McConville, J. and Sheldrake, J. (eds.), *Transport in Transition: Aspects of British and European Experience*, Avebury, Aldershot, pp. 163-182.

Liu, Z. (1995b), The Comparative Performance of Public and Private Enterprise: The Case of British Ports, *Journal of Transport Economics and Policy*, Vol. 29, No. 3, pp. 263-274.

Lloyd's List (1998), New-look PSA Gets Down to Business, 30 January, p. 9.

Nagorski, B. (1972), *Port Problems in Developing Countries: Principles of Port Planning and Organisation*, International Association of Ports and Harbours, Tokyo.

National Ports Council (1973), *Functions and Powers of the Council*, National Ports Council, London.

Newman, N. (1980), Denationalisation: Private Problem for Public Ports, *Management Today*, December, pp. 66-74.

Olson, D. (1988), Public Port Accountability: A Framework for Evaluation, in Hershman, M. (ed.), *Urban Ports and Harbour Management: Responding to Change along US Waterfronts*, Taylor and Francis, New York, pp. 307-333.

Port Development International (1993), Port Privatisation: Privates on Parade, December / January, pp. 33-55.

Port Development International (1997), Singapore: State of Independence, May, pp. 35-37.

Saundry, R. and Turnbull, P. (1997), Private Profit, Public Loss: the Financial and Economic Performance of UK Ports, *Maritime Policy and Management*, Vol. 24, No. 4, pp. 319-334.

Sherman, R. (1995), Privatisation of Seaports?, *Transportation Quarterly*, Vol. 49, No. 3, pp. 93-100.

SingaPort '98 (1998), First Step Towards Privatisation, p. 6.

Slack, B. (1993), Pawn in the Game: Ports in a Global Transportation System, *Growth and Change*, Vol. 24, pp. 579-588.

Stehli, H. (1978), Typology of Ports, in Beth, H. (ed.), *Port Management Textbook*, Institute of Shipping Economics, Bremen, pp. 25-35.

Suykens, F. (1983), A Few Observations on Productivity in Seaports, *Maritime Policy and Management*, Vol. 10, No. 1, pp. 17-40.

Suykens, F. (1985), Administration and Management at the Port of Antwerp, *Maritime Policy and Management*, Vol. 12, No. 3, pp. 181-194.

Thomas, B. (1976), Port Administration (I): A Review of the Different Forms of Port Ownership and the Numerous Functions undertaken within Ports, in *Manual on Port Management*, Part I, UNCTAD, pp. 95-102.

Thomas, B. (1994a), The Privatisation of United Kingdom Seaports, *Maritime Policy and Management*, Vol. 21, No. 2, pp. 135-148.

Thomas, B. (1994b), The Need for Organisational Change in Seaports, *Marine Policy*, Vol. 18, No. 1, pp. 69-78.

Tongzon, J. (1995), Determinants of Port Performance and Efficiency, *Transportation Research*, Vol. 29A, No. 3, pp. 245-252.

Transport (1991), Ports Industry Review: Privatisation Problems, Vol. 12, No. 2, pp. 39-43.

Turnbull, P. (1991), Labour Market De-regulation and Economic Performance: the Case of Britain's Docks, *Work, Employment and Society*, Vol. 5, No. 1, pp. 17-35.

UNCTAD (1985), *Port Development: A Handbook for Planners in Developing Countries*, TD/B/C.4/175/Rev.1, New York.

UNCTAD (1995), *Comparative Analysis of Deregulation, Commercialisation and Privatisation of Ports*, UNCTAD / SDD / PORT / 3, Geneva.

Wild, P., Fells, H. and Dearing, J. (1995), *International Ports*, Lloyd's Business Intelligence Centre, Lloyd's of London Press, London.

Wilder, R. and Pender, D. (1979), Economic Behaviour of Public Ports in the United Sates, *Journal of Transport Economics and Policy*, Vol. 13, No. 2, pp. 169-181.

6 A Theoretical Framework for Efficiency Measurement

INTRODUCTION

This chapter sets up a framework for measuring productive efficiency and establishes the *frontier production function model* as the basic analytical tool for underlying the empirical research. To do so requires an in-depth analysis and review of the model, and the basic concepts related to production functions and economic efficiency. Following this, the range of econometric or parametric frontier models that operationalise the conceptual model (such as the deterministic and stochastic frontier models) are analysed and several estimation techniques applicable to the frontier model are examined. Finally, this will be followed by the empirical application of a production function relevant for the port industry.

THE PRODUCTION FUNCTION CONCEPT

Performance is synonymous with the degree of success in achieving stated objectives (Devine *et al.*, 1985). One of the main types of performance measure is the *frontier approach* which is currently in widespread use (Bauer, 1990). The basic concept of the frontier model is derived from production function theory.

Production may be regarded as a transformation from one state of the world to another. More generally, production may be defined as any activity, the net result of which is to increase the degree of compliance between the quantity, quality and distribution of products and a given preference pattern. Productivity may vary, however, due to several differences such as (i) differences in production technology, (ii) differences in the efficiency of the production process, and (iii) differences in the environment in which production occurs (Lovell, 1993).

The production function is the core concept in production economics. Production processes are, as mentioned above, viewed as means of

150

transforming certain inputs into certain outputs. In other words, the production function describes the relationship between changes in the quantities of inputs and changes in outputs. It is, therefore, critical to know how much output can be produced with certain combinations of inputs.

According to Nicholson (1995), the basic definition of a production function for a particular product is that it shows the maximum amount of the product that can be produced using alternative combinations of inputs such as labour, capital and land. The concept of maximality is important. In other words, the term *frontier* may meaningfully be applied in this case because the function sets a limit to the range of possible observations. Thus, while any point below the production frontier may be observed, it is not possible to observe points above the frontier. The amounts by which a firm or an industry lies below its production frontier can be regarded as *inefficiency*. The measurement of levels of inefficiency has been the main motivation for the study of frontier production function models.

Before turning to detail, it is initially useful to concentrate on the basic underlying concepts of a production function such as production factors, aggregation problems, a typical form of production function, i.e., the Cobb-Douglas case, and returns to scale.

Production Factors

A traditional production function expresses the output (Y) of a firm as a function of two typical inputs: capital (K) and labour (L) like this:

$$Y = f(K, L) \tag{6.1}$$

The labour input (L) represents human effort and intelligence in bringing about a better state of the world. Labour, however, is not a free commodity and, hence, it is necessary to recompense those who forego leisure in a certain way. This payment, or reward, is called a *wage*. On the other hand, the capital input (K) is a factor which has provoked, and continues to provoke, a great deal of controversy (Intriligator *et al.*, 1996). According to the concept used by Thomas (1993), capital is the flow of services provided by the existing capital stock rather than the capital stock itself, thus depending not only on the size of the capital stock but also on the extent of its utilisation. Capital receives two different types of payment or reward: (i) *interest*, which goes to those who abstain from immediate consumption and (ii) *profit*, which goes to those who bear the risk

(Heathfield and Wibe, 1987).

These arguments for reward payments require certain assumptions to hold such as (i) people prefer enjoying leisure to working, (ii) people do not like waiting, but may be willing to defer instant satisfaction and (iii) people wish to avoid taking a risk (i.e. people are innately risk-averse). Although none of these assumptions are always correct, they do hold for economically rational individuals. In other words, most people dislike working, want immediate rewards and are risk averse. Thus, each of these characteristics requires financial compensation for their mitigation. These compensation payments take the form of wages, interest and profit.

The Aggregation Problem

For simplicity, labour and capital are generally expressed as one kind of labour and one kind of capital. This simplification clearly causes several problems. From the perspective of productive output and, therefore, compensatory payments or rewards to factors, one hour of an unskilled labourer is not the same thing as one hour of a skilled or trained employee. Referring to this issue, Heathfield and Wibe (1987, p. 5) note:

"Once the possibility of disaggregation is opened up it is difficult to see where it can logically end. The degree and nature of the disaggregation we choose to specify is once again a matter of judgement. Too much disaggregation leads to an infinitely long list of separate inputs and outputs. Too little masks significant differences between input."

To understand a given production process, therefore, some aggregated factors are required in certain broad categories. The different kinds of labour (e.g. wages paid, hours spent and number of labourers employed) have to be aggregated into one or two broader categories. The different kinds of assets or machines have to be aggregated into one or two capital input factors.

On the output side of production, the aggregation problem also exists. Generally, most production units are firms which produce not just one but several goods possessing a range of quality characteristics. Again, with regard to the problem of input and output aggregation, Heathfield and Wibe (1987, p. 5) mention the following:

"Suffice it to say that there is no clear principle as to how to disaggregate each factor of production into its relevant subsets. It is simply a matter of common sense with classification depending on the purposes of the study and the data available."

Types of Production Function

A production function can be expressed as an attempt at mathematically specifying the range of technical possibilities available to producers. In other words, it specifies the set of maximum output from given levels of input; it is the set of possible efficient relations between inputs and outputs in a given state of technology.

The Cobb-Douglas production function is the most frequently used and best known specification for the production function in theoretical as well as empirical studies. This function was first presented by Cobb and Douglas (1928) and afterwards widely adopted for empirical tests. The general form of the Cobb-Douglas production function is expressed as:

$$Y = AK^{a}L^{\beta} \qquad (6.2)$$

....where A is a positive constant, $0 < \alpha < 1$, $0 < \beta < 1$, and K and L are the amount of capital and labour, respectively, used to produce output Y.

Equation (6.2) has a number of convenient properties. The parameters, α and β, measure the elasticities of output with reference to capital and labour respectively. The parameter, A, may be considered as an efficiency parameter (Schotter, 1997) since for fixed inputs K and L, the larger the value of A, the greater is the maximum output obtained from such inputs. In other words, without any impact on returns to scale, higher values of A imply that larger amounts are produced with the same input combination.

A generalised form of the Cobb-Douglas case is the *translog production function*, which is short for 'transcendental logarithmic' function and first noted by Christensen *et al.* (1973). Since it has a flexible and convenient form, the translog function has been adopted for widespread use in empirical tests. For a two-input case the function takes the form:

$a = \ln A$

$$\ln Y = a + \alpha \ln K + \beta \ln L + \gamma \ln K \ln L + \delta (\ln K)^{2} + \varepsilon (\ln L)^{2} \qquad (6.3)$$

....where $a = \ln A$ (≥ 0) and γ, δ and ε are parameters with values between zero and unity. Equation (6.3) reduces to the Cobb-Douglas function if the parameters γ, δ and ε are zero. More generally, for the n-input case, the translog function is defined by:

$$\ln Y = \alpha_0 + \sum_{i=1}^{n} \alpha_i \ln x_i + \sum_{i=1}^{n} \sum_{j=1}^{n} \gamma_{ij} \ln x_i \ln x_j \qquad (6.4)$$

....where x_i is the ith input and $\gamma_{ij} = \gamma_{ji}$ for all values of i or j. The function is quite flexible in approximating arbitrary production technologies in terms of substitution possibilities, thus providing a local approximation to any production frontier (Intriligator *et al.*, 1996). In principle, a logarithmic function can be derived from any normal or algebraic production function since any point in (x_i, x_j) space can be mapped onto a point in $(\ln x_i, \ln x_j)$ space. For any algebraic function, therefore, there must exist a logarithmic version.

Returns to Scale

The returns to scale of a production function indicate what happens to output when all units are increased proportionately. Nicholson (1995) provides a simple definition of returns to scale. If all inputs are multiplied by the same positive constant λ (where λ is greater than unity and, hence, input factors of production are increased), the returns to scale of the production function can be classified as shown in Table 6.1.

Table 6.1 Returns to Scale from Factor Increases

Effect on Output	Returns to Scale
(i) $f(\lambda K, \lambda L) = \lambda f(K, L) = \lambda Y$	Constant
(ii) $f(\lambda K, \lambda L) < \lambda f(K, L) = \lambda Y$	Decreasing
(iii) $f(\lambda K, \lambda L) > \lambda f(K, L) = \lambda Y$	Increasing

Source: Nicholson (1995, p. 322).

If, in the function of $Y = f(K, L)$, a proportionate increase in inputs (K and L) increases the output (Y) by the same proportion, the production function exhibits *constant* returns to scale. If output increases less than proportionately, the function exhibits *decreasing* returns to scale. Finally, if output increases more than proportionately, there are *increasing* returns to scale.

For the Cobb-Douglas production function, returns to scale are simply equal to $(\alpha + \beta)$. The Cobb-Douglas production function is homogeneous of degree $(\alpha + \beta)$. For example, suppose that K is changed to λK and L to λL, then the new output will be:

$$A(\lambda K)^{\alpha}(\lambda L)^{\beta} = \lambda^{\alpha+\beta} AK^{\alpha}L^{\beta} = \lambda^{\alpha+\beta}Y \qquad (6.5)$$

If $\alpha + \beta > 1$, then the production function has increasing returns to scale, and if $\alpha + \beta < 1$, then it has decreasing returns to scale. When $\alpha + \beta = 1$, the production function has constant returns to scale, which is often called 'linearly homogeneous'. Further, when the production function has constant returns to scale, equation (6.2) can be expressed as:

$$Y = AK^{\alpha}L^{1-\alpha} \qquad (6.6)$$

ECONOMIC EFFICIENCY

The matter of economic efficiency has been of interest since Adam Smith's pin factory. An analytical approach to efficiency measurement in production was, however, initiated by Debreu (1951) and later utilised by Farrell (1957). In the Farrell framework, overall efficiency consists of two different components: allocative efficiency and productive efficiency.[1]

---

(1) As a matter of terminology, Farrell (1957) names this efficiency 'technical efficiency'. Some economists (e.g. Vickers and Yarrow, 1988), however, refer to this concept as 'internal efficiency' or 'managerial efficiency'; Leibenstein (1966) labels it 'X-efficiency'. In the frontier literature, 'technical efficiency' has been popularly used after Farrell (1957). Throughout this study and in common with Nicholson (1995), the term 'productive efficiency' will be used as being synonymous with the other terms. For reference, see Kalirajan (1990), Lovell (1993) and Ferrantino and Ferrier (1995).

Allocative and Productive Efficiency

> "Inputs are of course everywhere. It is my observation that for some reason there are far more inputs than there are outputs, which means that a large number of inputs are disappearing somewhere in the process. God knows where they will turn up."
> (Newman, 1975)

In economic theory, costs can exceed their minimum feasible level for one of two reasons (Barrow and Wagstaff, 1989). One is that inputs are being used in the wrong proportions, given their prices and marginal productivity. This phenomenon is known as *allocative inefficiency*. The other reason is that there is a failure to produce the maximum amount of output from a set of given inputs. This is known as *productive inefficiency*. Both sources of inefficiency can exist simultaneously or in isolation. These sources of inefficiency can be easily explained by using the concept of a production function. Figure 6.1 provides an example of a production function where two inputs, x_1 and x_2, are employed to produce a single output, Y.

The isoquant Y_A indicates all the possible combinations of x_1 and x_2 that give rise to the same level of output, Y. Clearly, given a fixed amount of input x_2, using more of x_1 will result in an increase in output. The slope of the isoquant is, therefore, negative because in order to maintain the same output Y_A, x_2 must be reduced to compensate for the increase in x_1. The amount by which x_2 has to be reduced to compensate for a one unit increase in x_1 is the slope of the isoquant and is known as the 'marginal rate of technical substitution' (MRTS) between x_1 and x_2. In fact, this is equal to the ratio of the marginal products of the two inputs: i.e.,

$$\text{MRTS} = -\frac{MPx_2}{MPx_1} \tag{6.7}$$

....where MPx_i denotes the marginal product of input x_i.

C_1 is an isocost line, indicating the combinations of x_1 and x_2 giving rise to the same level of expenditure, C_1. The slope of the isocost line is equal to the ratio of the two input prices, $(-) Px_2/Px_1$, where Px_i denotes the price of each input x_i. The allocative efficient input mix at any level of output will be the mix that minimises the cost of producing the level of output in question or, equivalently, the mix that maximises the level of output obtained from a fixed money outlay. In Figure 6.1, this occurs at point C, where the slopes of the isocost line and the isoquant are the same, so that *allocative efficiency* requires that:

$$\frac{MPx_2}{MPx_1} = \frac{Px_2}{Px_1} \tag{6.8}$$

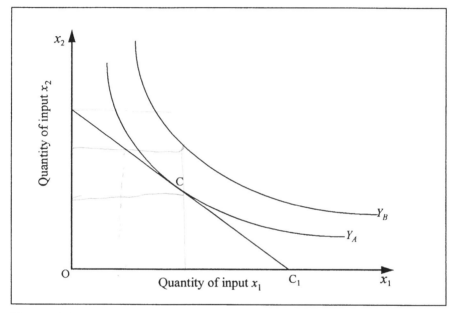

Figure 6.1 Allocative Efficiency and Productive Efficiency

Thus, if the unit cost of x_1 is twice that of x_2, then x_1 must be twice as productive as x_2.

Productive efficiency can also be illustrated by using the isoquant shown in Figure 6.1, which assumes that there is one isoquant associated with each level of output determined only by technology. Some firms, however, may be more efficient at transforming inputs into outputs than others. The isoquants Y_A and Y_B are both associated with the same level of output, but the isoquant of the less efficient firm (Y_B) lies further away from the origin than that of the relatively efficient firm (Y_A). The less efficient firm (B) ends up using more of both inputs to produce the same level of output as the more efficient firm (A). Productive inefficiency thus involves excessive usage of all inputs.

Measuring Efficiency

Suppose that a firm's frontier production function, as depicted in Figure 6.2, is $Y = f(x_1, x_2)$, where two inputs (x_1 and x_2) are used to produce one output (Y) and that the function is characterised by constant returns to scale. The isoquants Y_A and Y_B indicate all possible combinations of x_1 and x_2 which give rise to the same level of output.

Assume that the firm's efficiency is observed at point A, rather than C. This position is neither allocatively nor productively efficient. Its level of productive efficiency is defined as the ratio of OB/OA. Therefore, *productive inefficiency* is defined as 1-(OB/OA) and can be interpreted as the proportion by which the cost of producing the level of output could be reduced given the assumption that the input ratio (x_1/x_2) is held constant. Under the assumption of constant returns to scale, productive inefficiency can also be interpreted as the proportion by which output could be increased by becoming 100% productively efficient. The level of allocative efficiency is measured as OD/OB (or C_1/C_2). Thus *allocative inefficiency* is defined as 1-(OD/OB) and measures the proportional increase in costs due to allocative inefficiency.

Consider position B. At this point, the firm is allocatively inefficient since it can maintain output at Y_A but reduce total costs by changing the input mix to that which exists at point C. At point B, however, the firm is productively efficient since it cannot increase output with this input combination of x_1 and x_2 but, given a suboptimal input mix (i.e. allocative inefficiency), the firm has minimised the cost of producing this level of output.

ALTERNATIVE APPROACHES TO MODELLING FRONTIER PRODUCTION FUNCTIONS

Over the last decade a number of methods for measuring efficiency have been proposed, all of which have in common the concept of the frontier: efficient units are those operating on the cost or production frontier, while inefficient ones operate either below the frontier (in the case of the production frontier) or above the frontier (in the case of the cost frontier).

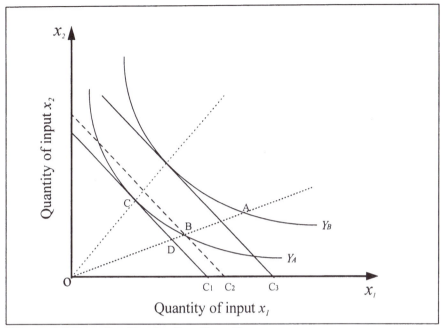

Figure 6.2 Frontier Production Function

There is one difference to be noted concerning the interpretation of the term 'frontier'. Some methods aim to uncover the *absolute* frontier, indicating what could be achieved if the available technology were used to full advantage; others aim to uncover the *best-practice* frontier, reflecting the achievements of the firm or industry in the sample (Barrow and Wagstaff, 1989). As Forsund *et al.* (1980) noted, however, the distinction is unlikely to be of much significance in practice, since the two different concepts of the frontier converge as sample size tends to infinity.

Bauer (1990, p. 39) pointed out the following reasons why the use of frontier models is becoming increasingly widespread:

- the notion of a frontier is consistent with the underlying economic theory of optimising behaviour;
- deviations from a frontier have a natural interpretation as a measure of the efficiency with which economic units pursue their technical or behavioural objectives; and
- information about the structure of the frontier and about the relative efficiency of economic units has many policy applications.

The literature on frontier production function models begins with Farrell (1957), who suggested a useful framework for analysing economic efficiency in terms of realised deviations from an idealised frontier isoquant. These and other frontier models are motivated in part by an interest in the structure of efficient production technology, in part by an interest in the divergence between observed and frontier operation and also in economic efficiency.

A distinction exists between the methods employed to derive the specification of the frontier model: either *statistical* or *non-statistical* methods may be used. The former technique makes assumptions about the stochastic properties of the data, while the latter does not. Another difference concerns whether the chosen method is *parametric* or *non-parametric*. While the former imposes a particular functional form, the latter approach does not. In a survey of empirically derived production frontiers and their relationship to efficiency measurement, Forsund *et al.* (1980, pp. 7-8) classify studies using the frontier approach according to the way the frontier is specified and estimated as follows:

- the frontier may or may not be specified as a parametric function of inputs;
- an explicit statistical model of the relationship between observed output and the frontier may or may not be specified; and
- the frontier itself may be specified to be either deterministic or stochastic.

According to this basis for classification, frontier models may be divided into *non-parametric* and *parametric* approaches. Again, the parametric approach can be divided into deterministic and stochastic frontier models. Both mathematical programming (*or* non-parametric) and econometric (*or* parametric) approaches were proposed by Farrell (1957) and have been developed separately in terms of how to construct frontiers. While the non-parametric approach revolves around mathematical (or linear) programming techniques, the parametric approach employs econometric techniques where efficiency is measured relative to a frontier production function which is statistically estimated.

The Programming Approach

Farell's non-parametric approach specifies linear programming techniques. Following this, many contributions have aimed to construct a less restrictive linear technology in order to enhance and promulgate non-parametric approaches. Work using linear programming techniques involves the application of a technique known as Data Envelopment Analysis (Fare *et al.*, 1994; Mansson, 1996). This form of analysis, initially developed by Charnes *et al.* (1978), revolves around an axiomatic formulation from which a series of efficiency measures relative to piece-wise linear technologies are constructed. Such applications are more often found in the literature of Operations Research and Management Science.

The Econometric Approach

This approach is founded on the econometric concept that a process can be adequately described by examining its inputs and its outputs. It is not necessary to know anything about the technologies involved in the production process; all that is needed is a set of reliable observations of what goes in and what comes out (Heathfield and Wibe, 1987). The parameter values are then statistically inferred from these observations.

Thus, this approach involves the specification of a parametric representation of technology which itself can be divided into two different models; either *deterministic* or *stochastic* frontiers may be specified according to whether or not certain assumptions are made concerning the underlying data.

The Deterministic Frontier Model

Aigner and Chu (1968) suggest a homogeneous Cobb-Douglas frontier production function which requires that all observations are on or beneath the frontier. Their model can be expressed as:

$$Y = f(X; \beta) - u, \qquad (6.9)$$

....where Y denotes the output, X a vector of inputs, β the input coefficients and u (≥ 0) is a one-sided error term which ensures that Y $\leq$

$f(X; \beta)$. Although Aigner and Chu (1968) did not do so, the productive efficiency of each observation can be computed directly from the vector of residuals, since u represents 'productive inefficiency'. It is labelled as 'deterministic' because, according to Greene (1993), the stochastic component of the model is contained entirely in the inefficiency term, u.

The main advantage of this approach as compared to the programming approach is its ability to characterise frontier technology in a simple mathematical form. As pointed out in both Forsund *et al.* (1980) and in Bauer (1990), however, the disadvantages of the frontier model represented in equation (6.9) are (i) the mathematical form may be too simple, (ii) the model imposes structure on the frontier that may not be guaranteed, (iii) the approach often imposes a limitation on the number of possible efficient observations, (iv) the estimated frontier is supported by a subset of the data and is thus extremely sensitive to outliers, and (v) the estimated results have no statistical properties; since no statistical assumptions are made about the disturbance term u in the model represented in (6.9), inferences cannot be reliably obtained from the results.

Since no efficiency differences between economic units are assumed to be generated by an explicit efficiency distribution, as Aigner and Chu (1968) admit, the estimation potential of the deterministic model (6.9) is reduced to some extent by this lack of available statistical procedures for the drawing of inferences. In an attempt to overcome this major drawback, namely no statistical basis, Afriat (1972) amended the frontier model to facilitate statistical analysis by making some assumptions about it. The equation in (6.9) can be rewritten as:

$$Y = f(X; \beta) \exp(-u), \qquad\qquad (6.10)$$

or

$$\ln Y = \ln f(X; \beta) - u \qquad\qquad (6.11)$$

….where $u \geq 0$ (and thus $0 \leq \exp(-u) \leq 1$), and where $\ln f(X; \beta)$ is linear in the Cobb-Douglas case exhibited in (6.9). The question that has to be asked is what to assume about X and u. One possible answer that has been most frequently used is to assume that observations on u are identically and independently distributed, and that X is exogenous and thus independent of u. Any number of distributions (e.g. normal, half-normal and exponential distributions) for u or $\exp(-u)$ could be specified.

The early parametric frontier models are deterministic in the sense that all economic units share a common fixed class of frontier. This is, of course, unreasonable and ignores the real possibility that the observed performance of the economic unit may be affected by exogenous (i.e. random shock) as well as endogenous (i.e. inefficiency) factors. This argument is reinforced if one considers also the statistical noise that every empirical relationship contains. In addition to random shocks, statistical noise may be interpreted as having two sources: measurement error and misspecification of functional form. Both sources are as relevant for the production function as for any other model. To allocate all these influences, whether favourable and unfavourable or whether under or beyond the control of the economic unit, into a single disturbance term and to label the mixture as inefficiency is clearly a doubtful and inexact generalisation. In fact, to distinguish statistical noise from inefficiency, and to assume that the noise is one-sided, therefore, are both questionable assumptions to make. As a result, the parametric approach is highly sensitive to extreme outliers, thus causing an over- or under-estimation of the true extent of inefficiency. Rather than overcoming these problems through the extension and further development of deterministic frontiers, an alternative model based on the concept of a stochastic frontier model can be utilised.

The Stochastic Frontier Model

The stochastic frontier model (also often named the 'composed disturbance model') is motivated by the idea that deviations from the production frontier might not be entirely under the control of the economic unit being studied (Greene, 1993). Both Aigner *et al.* (1977) and Meeusen and van den Broeck (1977) independently constructed a more reasonable error structure than a purely one-sided one. They considered a linear model for the frontier production function as follows:

$$Y_{it} = f(X_{it}; \beta) \exp(\varepsilon_{it}), \qquad i = 1, 2, \ldots, N; \, t = 1, 2, \ldots, T \qquad (6.12)$$

....where i indexes firms and t time periods. Their disturbance term ε_{it} is defined as the following:

$$\varepsilon_{it} = v_{it} - u_{it} \tag{6.13}$$

The component v_{it} represents a *symmetric disturbance term* permitting random variation of the production function across economic units due not only to the effects of measurement and specification error, but also to those of exogenous shock beyond the control of the economic unit (e.g. luck, weather conditions, geography or machine performance). The other component u_{it} (≥ 0) is a *one-sided disturbance term* and represents 'productive inefficiency' relative to the stochastic production function. The non-negative disturbance u_{it} reflects the fact that output lies on or below its frontier. The deviation of an observation from the deterministic kernel of the above stochastic production function arises from two sources: (i) symmetric random variation of the deterministic kernel $f(X_{it}; \beta)$ across observations captured by the component v_{it} and (ii) asymmetric variation or productive inefficiency captured by the component u_{it}. The term u_{it} measures productive inefficiency in the sense that it measures the shortfall of output Y_{it} from that implied by its maximum frontier given by $f(X_{it}; \beta)$ $\exp(v_{it})$.

The measure of an economic unit's efficiency should be defined, therefore, by:

$$\frac{Y_{it}}{f(X_{it}; \beta)\exp(v_{it})} \tag{6.14}$$

....relative to the stochastic frontier $f(X; \beta) \exp(v)$, rather than by the ratio

$$\frac{Y_{it}}{f(X_{it}; \beta)} \tag{6.15}$$

....relative to the deterministic kernel of the stochastic frontier $f(X; \beta)$. Thus, the frontier $f(X; \beta) \exp(v)$ is stochastic since v consists of random factors which are beyond the control of the production unit.

Nevertheless, any estimate of a firm's efficiency level is not consistent, as it contains statistical noise as well as productive inefficiency.

In addition, stochastic frontier models suffer from two other difficulties. One is the requirement of specific assumptions about the distributions underlying productive inefficiency (e.g. half-normal and exponential) and statistical noise (e.g. normal). The other is the required assumption that the regressors (the input variables X) and productive inefficiency are independent. This may well be an unrealistic assumption since, if a firm knows its level of inefficiency, this should affect its input choices.

Choice of Approach

By virtue of its practical convenience, analytical tractability and theoretical superiority, the econometric (parametric) approach has been adopted as the appropriate analytical tool to apply in this research. Another justification for this choice is that econometric approaches have a strong policy orientation, especially in the assessment of alternative industrial organisations and in the evaluation of efficiency in government and other public agencies. Mathematical programming approaches, on the other hand, have a managerial decision-making orientation (Aigner and Schmidt, 1980; Fare *et al.*, 1994; Lovell, 1995). This property of the econometric approaches more closely supports the purpose of the research, especially since they have a grounding in economic theory (Forsund *et al.*, 1980; Pitt and Lee, 1981; Bauer, 1990).

In addition, several studies (e.g. Gong and Sickles, 1992; Oum and Waters, 1996) have compared the performance of alternative methods for measuring efficiency: the econometric method (in particular, the stochastic frontier model) and the mathematical programming method. The results show that the econometric approach generally produces better estimates than the latter approach, especially for measuring firm-specific efficiency when panel data are available. Greene (1993) notes that the main advantage of the econometric method lies in its ability to shift the harmful effect of measurement error away from estimates of efficiency.

The Use of Panel Data in Frontier Modelling

A further development in the modelling of frontiers lies with the use of estimation techniques which involve panel data. Initially, the stochastic frontier model (6.12) was developed for cross-sectional data. According to

Intriligator *et al.* (1996), panel data are a special type of pooled cross-section and/or time-series data in which the same individual units of observation are sampled over time and are generally microdata pertaining to individual economic agents, such as families and firms. Baltagi (1995, pp. 3-6) lists several benefits from using panel data, some of which are as follows:

- controlling for individual heterogeneity since panel data suggest that individuals, firms, states or countries are heterogeneous;
- giving more informative data, more variability, less collinearity among the variables, more degree of freedom and more efficiency;
- being better able to identify and measure effects that are simply not detectable in pure cross-sectional or pure time-series data;
- allowing the construction and testing of more complicated behavioural models than purely cross-sectional or time-series data, and also fewer restrictions being imposed in panels on a distributed lag model than in a purely time-series study; and
- gathering usually micro units, like individuals, firms and households, and biases resulting from aggregation over firms or individuals being eliminated.

In addition, a number of attractive features of panel data are suggested by Hausman and Taylor (1981) and Blundell (1996). Among them are (i) that panel data are able to control individual effects which may be correlated with other variables included in the specification of an economic relationship, thus making analysis on single cross-sections difficult, and (ii) that panel data allow an analyst to exploit the large variation in the circumstances of different individuals in any cross-section while still capturing temporal effects in behaviour.

With respect to the frontier production function, consistent estimates of the productive efficiency of an economic unit can be obtained as the number of time periods tends to infinity. This is true because adding more observations on the same unit yields information not attainable by adding more units. Secondly, unlike the techniques for cross-sectional analysis which draw evidence of inefficiency from skewness (e.g. Waldman, 1982), the technique of panel data analysis draws evidence of inefficiency in constancy over time. As a consequence, strong distributional assumptions are not necessary when panel data are available. Finally, the parameters and the economic unit's level of efficiency can be estimated without assuming that the input variables are uncorrelated with productive inefficiency. Therefore, as Schmidt and Sickles (1984) note, a variety of different estimates will be considered, depending on what one is willing to assume about the distribution of productive inefficiency and its potential correlation with the regressors.

The models noted earlier involved the estimation of the parameters of the stochastic frontier production function and the mean productive inefficiency for firms in the industry. Initially, it was claimed that productive efficiencies for individual firms could not be estimated and predicted. In an effort to explore this unsolved problem with the previous models along with the benefits from the aforementioned advantages of panel data, Pitt and Lee (1981) were the first to develop techniques using panel data to estimate the frontier production function. Their approach failed, however, to utilise the qualitative advantages of panel data and required strong assumptions, exactly as was the case for models using the cross-sectional data.

Jondrow *et al.* (1982) presented two estimators (i.e. for half-normal and exponential cases) for the firm-specific effect for an individual firm under the assumption that the parameters of the frontier production function were known and cross-sectional data were available for given sample firms. Schmidt and Sickles (1984) suggested three different estimators for individual firm effects and productive efficiencies for panel data. A major breakthrough in the area of panel data models was achieved by Battese and Coelli (1988), who presented a generalisation of the results of Jondrow *et al.* (1982) on the assumption of a more general distribution for firm effects to be applied to the stochastic frontier model. Ferrantino and Ferrier (1995) adopted the methods developed by Pitt and Lee (1981) and Battese and Coelli (1988) to derive firm-specific efficiency estimates based on available panel data for Indian vacuum-pan sugar producers.

Suppose that the frontier production function is of the following form:

$$Y_{it} = f(X_{it}; \beta) \exp(v_{it} - u_i), \qquad i = 1, 2, \ldots, N; \, t = 1, 2, \ldots, T \qquad (6.16)$$

.....where Y_{it} denotes the appropriate form of output for the *i*th firm at time *t*, X_{it} is a vector of inputs associated with the *i*th firm at time *t* and β is a vector of input coefficients for the associated independent variable in the production function. The main difference between models (6.12) and (6.16) is the absence of the subscript t associated with u in the latter, thus u captures firm-specific time invariant variables omitted from the previous production function.

The symmetric terms v_{it} are assumed to be identically and independently normally distributed with mean zero and variance σ_v^2, i.e., $v_{it} \sim N(0, \sigma_v^2)$. The one-sided terms u_i (≥ 0) are assumed to be identically and independently distributed non-negative random variables, which captures a *firm* effect but no *time* effect (Schmidt and Sickles, 1984). In addition, the error terms v_{it} and u_i are assumed to be independently distributed of the input variables as well as of one another.

The most frequently defined distribution for the u_i is the half-normal (often termed the absolute normal distribution), i.e., $u_i \sim |N(0, \sigma_u^2)|$. Other distributional assumptions for the terms u_i have been proposed by several researchers. For example, the exponential (Aigner *et al.*, 1977), the truncated normal (Stevenson, 1980) and the gamma (Greene, 1980).

As far as the productive efficiency of a firm is concerned, Battese and Coelli (1988) define it as the ratio of the firm's mean production (given its realised firm-specific effect) to the corresponding mean production with the firm effect being equivalent to zero. The productive efficiency of the ith firm (PE_i) is defined, therefore, as:

$$PE_i = \frac{E(Y_{it}^* \mid u_i, X_{it})}{E(Y_{it}^* \mid u_i = 0, X_{it})} \tag{6.17}$$

....where Y_{it}^* represents the output of production for the ith firm at time t, and the value of the PE_i lies between zero and one ($0 \leq PE_i \leq 1$). If a firm's productive efficiency is calculated as 0.65, for example, then this implies that, on average, the firm realises 65% of the production possible for a fully efficient firm having comparable input values. From the perspective of efficiency measurement, the definition contained in equation (6.17) has a thread of connection with that of equation (6.14).

If the model (6.16) is transformed to a logarithm of the production function, such as:

$$\ln Y_{it} = \ln f(X_{it}; \beta) + v_{it} - u_i \tag{6.18}$$

....then the measure of productive efficiency for the *i*th firm is defined by:

$$PE_i = \exp(-u_i) \tag{6.19}$$

The measure shown in equation (6.19) does not depend on the level of the input variables for the firm, while the definition provided by equation (6.17) for calculating the productive efficiency of a firm clearly shows that its estimation depends significantly on inferences concerning the distribution function of the unobservable firm effect u_i, given the sample observations.

In the early stages of its use, one problem with the stochastic frontier model was that the model provides estimates of productive efficiency only in terms of a sample mean, rather than of each observation. This is because v and u are unobservable. In order to solve this drawback, Jondrow *et al.* (1982) described a method for extracting estimates of productive efficiency for each observation in the sample, by decomposing the frontier residual $(v_{it} - u_i)$ into its components: statistical noise (v_{it}) and productive inefficiency (u_i). This decomposition can be conducted by finding the expected value of u_i under the conditional distribution of u_i given $(v_{it} - u_i)$.

This method provides unbiased, but inconsistent, estimation of u_i (Greene, 1993). Battese and Coelli (1988) refined the method of Jondrow *et al.* (1982) for the case of panel data. The elaborated technique by Battese and Coelli (1988) and Battese *et al.* (1989) was, however, for the case where productive efficiency is time-invariant. With regard to this time-invariant model for firm-level efficiency, Schmidt (1985, p. 313) states the following:

"Unchanging inefficiency over time is not a particularly attractive assumption....An important line of future research, in my opinion, is to allow inefficiency to change over time."

Battese and Coelli (1988, p. 393) admitted the shortcoming of their method by noting:

"Given the model (6.16), in which firm effects (and productive efficiencies) are time-invariant, the consistency of estimators for individual productive efficiencies requires that the number of time periods increases indefinitely. However, such a situation is unlikely to be realistic, because it is obvious that firm effects and productive efficiencies change, given a sufficiently long period of time."

With the assumption that productive efficiency does vary over time, an alternative approach has been adopted by econometricians such as Cornwell *et al.* (1990) and Kumbhakar (1990). None of these studies succeed, however, in completely separating inefficiency from individual firm effects (Kumbhakar and Hjalmarsson, 1993) and, in any case, the proposed method is too complicated for empirical application (Ferrantino and Ferrier, 1995).

In summary, in spite of the fact that the panel data model enables a researcher to relax certain assumptions, since the techniques of panel data analysis are focused on cross-sectional variation, this approach requires the additional assumption that individual firm inefficiency is invariant with time. At the same time, the problem remains that a restrictive functional form for technology is imposed on the model. Finally, the following remarks of Bauer (1990, p. 41) are worthy of note:

"Stronger assumptions generate stronger results, but they strain one's conscience more....The appropriate structure to impose can only be determined by a careful consideration of the data and the characteristics of the industry under study."

ESTIMATION ISSUES

In general, econometric analysis involves certain generic steps which include model specification, data development, estimation of the model and the use of the estimated model for research purposes such as forecasting and policy evaluation (Intriligator *et al.*, 1996). In contrast to the programming approach to efficiency measurement, the econometric approach uses statistical techniques for the estimation of a parametric representation of technology and of efficiency relative to that technology. The estimation stage can be implemented using certain techniques associated with each of the deterministic, stochastic, and panel data models. The estimation techniques may be differently or individually applied, depending on functional forms specified and assumptions made on the model components.

The commencement of estimation is based on the use of ordinary least squares (OLS), which treats the frontier residual (i.e. u for the deterministic case and $(v - u)$ for the stochastic case) as the inefficiency term. As previously discussed, however, this treatment is theoretically incorrect and in order to cope with this weakness, alternatives have been suggested as follows:

'Corrected' ordinary least squares (COLS) was initially proposed by Winsten (1957). This method does not make any assumption about the functional form of the efficiency component u. It estimates the parameters of the frontier model by OLS, and then corrects for the downward bias in the estimated OLS intercept by shifting it up until all corrected residuals are nonpositive and at least one is zero. The corrected residuals are then used to calculate the productive efficiency (PE) which, by construction, satisfy the requirement that $0 \leq PE \leq 1$. In other words, COLS provides exactly the same model as OLS, except for the constant term.

Maximum likelihood estimation (MLE) was initially proposed by Afriat (1972) and further developed by Greene (1980) and Stevenson (1980). Since their pioneering work, it has been in widespread use. MLE is conducted by assuming a functional form for the efficiency component u, and involves the estimation of all the technology parameters and the parameter(s) of the distribution of u at the same time. Unlike the case of a deterministic frontier, in that of a stochastic frontier, the resulting residuals obtained from MLE contain both statistical noise and inefficiency, which should be decomposed using the method suggested by Jondrow *et al.* (1982) and Battese and Coelli (1988). Since the inclusion of statistical noise allows the stochastic frontier to cover all observations, the estimates of u are inserted in the relevant equation for efficiency measurement, such as equations (6.14) and (6.19), to obtain estimates of productive efficiency (PE) which satisfy the condition that $0 < PE \leq 1$.

Figure 6.3 illustrates the OLS, COLS and MLE estimations of the deterministic frontier model. All these estimators are questionable since they make no accommodation for statistical noise and thus attribute all deviation from the frontier production function to productive inefficiency. In particular, COLS has one further disadvantage in that it adjusts only the OLS estimate of the intercept, leaving the remaining elements of the input coefficients β unchanged from its OLS estimates. As a consequence, the structure of an efficient frontier technology is the same as that of a less efficient frontier, thus assigning the same efficiency ranking as OLS does. MLE allows for a structural dissimilarity between OLS and the efficient frontier technology. Many studies (e.g. Greene, 1980), however, reveal that both OLS and MLE show significant differences in the structure of two technologies.

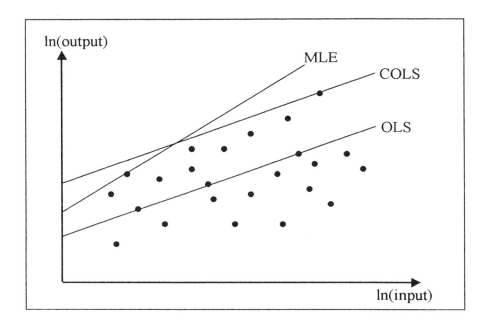

Figure 6.3 COLS and MLE for Deterministic Frontiers
Source: Lovell (1993, p. 22).

For the firm-effect efficiency of a panel sample, Schmidt and Sickles (1984) propose three estimators: the *'Within' estimator*, the *generalised least squares (GLS)*, and the *MLE*, the choice of which depends on whether or not one is willing to assume that the individual firm-specific efficiency is uncorrelated with the input variables and on whether or not one is willing to make certain distributional assumptions for the disturbance terms. For instance, the normal distribution is assumed for the symmetric disturbance term v_{it}, and the half-normal for the one-sided disturbance term u_i (capturing inefficiency).

The 'Within' estimator makes no distributional assumption on the one-sided disturbance terms u_i, and makes no assumption of independence between u_i and the input variables. The GLS makes no distributional assumption on u_i, but assumes that the error terms u_i are uncorrelated with the input variables in order to allow for the inclusion of time-invariant regressors in the frontier model. The MLE makes both distributional and independence assumptions. In the case of the 'Within' and GLS estimators, the estimated firm-effect efficiencies u_i are normalised so that the most efficient observation has $PE_i = 1$. The strongest case for the GLS is when the number of sample observations (N) is large and the time period (T) is small, while the GLS is useless when T is large and N is small. In the case where N and T are both large, the 'Within' estimator is more efficient than the GLS (Lovell, 1993).

In respect of efficiency, Schmidt and Sickles (1984) conclude that the MLE is generally more efficient (asymptotically) than the other estimators as it exploits distributional information which the others do not and distributional assumptions may be useful in estimating the parameters of frontiers. The MLE also has one major advantage: it is applicable to a wide variety of situations (Kleinbaum *et al.*, 1988).

In summary, many of the estimators are concerned with either how to make use of the consistent least squares estimates or how to modify the estimation techniques to account for the special nature of the disturbances. COLS can be employed for the deterministic frontier, MLE for all three models, and the 'Within' estimation and GLS are limited to panel data models.

PORT PRODUCTION FUNCTIONS

Measures of port efficiency (*or* port performance indicators) use a certain form of output relative to input which quantifies various aspects of port operation. UNCTAD (1975) lists several benefits associated with a properly used set of port performance indicators. These include improving the utilisation of port resources, highlighting the cause of congestion as well as providing information for port planning and a justification for capital development. To measure, however, port performance and to compare it between ports is a very delicate matter (Suykens, 1983), as there are great differences in their geographical location and this sometimes influences their technical structures. The various sizes of ports, the variability of the ships calling at them and goods passing through them impose more difficulties in defining and measuring such performance. De Monie (1987, p. 1) points out the difficulties as follows:

• the sheer number of parameters involved;

- the lack of up-to-date, factual and reliable data, collected in an accepted manner and available for publication;
- the absence of generally agreed and acceptable definitions;
- the profound influence of local factors on the data obtained; and
- the divergent interpretations given by various interests to identical results.

In addition to the awkwardness caused by factors such as these, another thing which greatly complicates measurement is the fact that the operational performance of a port or terminal is normally judged by measurements that are heavily dependent on factors over which the port or terminal has limited or no control (Dowd and Leschine, 1990). The limiting factors are either physical (e.g. geographical location of the port and the type of vessels visiting the port) or institutional factors (e.g. union work rules, customs regulations, and requirements imposed on the port operator by carriers) or a combination of both.

Traditionally, the performance of ports has been evaluated *either* by calculating cargo-handling productivity (e.g. Bendall and Stent, 1987) *or* by measuring a single factor productivity (e.g. labour as in the case of De Monie, 1987), *or* by comparing its actual throughput (i.e. tonnage or number of containers handled) with its optimum throughput for a specific period of time (e.g. Talley, 1988). The crucial aspect in the latter approach is how to determine the optimum throughput of a port, since port performance is a relative measure which depends on this measured optimum throughput. For its determination, a number of measurements have been undertaken using either an engineering approach or an economic approach. A definition of the two optimum throughputs is provided by Talley (1988, pp. 328-329):

- a port's *engineering* optimum throughput is the maximum throughput that can physically be handled by the port under certain conditions for a specified time period; and
- a port's *economic* optimum throughput is the throughput that satisfies an economic objective of the port for a specified time period.

Another argument put forward by Talley (1994) is that, in a competitive environment, ports should consider their economic optimum throughput when comparing actual to optimum throughput in evaluating their performance. The overall economic objective of a port may be to maximise profits *or* to maximise throughput subject to several constraints. In a case where reliable estimates of economic optimum throughput are not available, Talley (1988; 1994) suggests that performance indicators related to the port's economic objective may be used to evaluate its overall performance. In a private port, its economic objective may be to maximise profits while, in a public port, its objective may be to maximise throughput subject to a zero profit (or zero deficit) constraint. Such an approach, however, suffers from another problem, how should these indicators be selected?

In an effort to properly evaluate the efficiency or performance of a port, several methods have been suggested, such as estimation of a port cost function (De Neufville and Tsunokawa, 1981) or the estimation of the total factor productivity of a port (Kim and Sachish, 1986). Tongzon (1995) attempts to establish a model of port performance and efficiency and to quantify the relative contribution of each variable to overall performance and efficiency using multiple regression. In so doing, it is assumed that ports are throughput maximisers and that the definition of port performance is measured in terms of the number of containers moved through a port.

As noted by Braeutigam *et al.* (1984), various types of ports are of different sizes and face a variety of traffic mix. As such, the use of cross-sectional, time-series or even panel data may fail to show basic differences amongst ports, thus leading to a misjudgement of each port's performance. It is, therefore, crucial to estimate econometrically the structure of production in ports at the single port or terminal level using appropriate data such as the panel data for a terminal (Kim and Sachish, 1986).

In respect to attempts to derive a port production function, Chang (1978) focused on general cargo-handling as a measurement of port performance and assumed that port operations follow the conventional Cobb-Douglas case as expressed by:

$$Y = AK^{\alpha}L^{\beta}e^{\gamma(T/L)} \qquad (6.20)$$

....where Y is annual gross earnings (in real term), K is the real value of net assets in the port, L is the number of labourers per year and the average number of employees per month each year, and $e_{\gamma}^{(T/L)}$ a proxy for technological improvement, in which (T/L) shows the tonnage per unit of labour. Chang (1978) argued that, for the estimation of a production function such as (6.20), the output of a port should be measured in terms of *either* total tonnage handled at the port *or* its gross earnings. This was to be preferred to port services, since the production function of an organisation involves its internal operation. Bendall and Stent (1987) improved the model (6.20) to aid policy makers in assessing the merits of different ship types.

A more elaborate method of estimating the production function of a port was conducted by Liu (1995) who, under certain assumptions, econometrically estimated the production function of UK ports by employing frontier models such as those specified in equations (6.12) and (6.16). In the model adopted by Liu (1995), the output was measured by turnover, which consists of the amount receivable (except for sales of property) in respect of the port services provided to third parties. The labour input was measured by the value of total wage payments and the capital input by the net-book value of fixed capital assets including land, buildings, dredging, dock structures, roads, plants and equipment. Finally, all variables included in the model are deflated using appropriate price indices.

Regarding port production, Liu (1995, p. 268) mentions the following:

> "The process of port production is complex, consisting of pilotage, towage, berthing, cargo handling and warehousing. Also, modern ports tend to diversify beyond traditional port activities into distribution, related transport and property trading. Ideally it would be best to concentrate on one particular production process, for example, cargo handling. But this is impossible with the [reliable] data available."

As for a container terminal, its productivity is primarily concerned with the efficient use of labour, equipment and land (Dowd and Leschine, 1990). Terminal productivity measurement, therefore, is a means of quantifying the efficiency in utilising these three resources. Bernard (1991) questions whether total tonnage handled at a port, as a measure of the output of port production, should be applied to container terminals; since the basic unit of measurement is a container and since the facility inputs required for the movement of a container is more or less the same irrespective of size and weight, the use of total tonnage handled seems illogical. Some adjustments, therefore, are required to account for size change. Modern technology has, however, reduced the impact of the alteration. One possible solution of representing the output of a container terminal may be provided by measuring the throughput in terms of container movements across the quayside (i.e. TEUs).

REFERENCES

Afriat, S. (1972), Efficiency Estimation of Production Function, *International Economic Review*, Vol. 13, No. 3, pp. 568-598.

Aigner, D. and Chu, S. (1968), On Estimating the Industry Production Function, *American Economic Review*, Vol. 58, No. 4, pp. 826-839.

Aigner, D., Lovell, C. and Schmidt, P. (1977), Formulation and Estimation of Stochastic Frontier Production Function Models, *Journal of Econometrics*, Vol. 6, No. 1, pp. 21-37.

Aigner, D. and Schmidt, P. (1980), Editors' Introduction, *Journal of Econometrics*, Vol. 13, Supplement to the Journal of Econometrics: Specification and Estimation of Frontier Production, Profit and Cost Functions, pp. 1-3.

Baltagi, B. (1995), *Econometric Analysis of Panel Data*, John Wiley & Sons Ltd., Chichester.

Barrow, M. and Wagstaff, A. (1989), Efficiency Measurement in the Public Sector: An Appraisal, *Fiscal Studies*, Vol. 10, No. 1, pp. 72-97.

Battese, G. and Coelli, T. (1988), Prediction of Firm-Level Technical Efficiencies with a Generalised Frontier Production Function and Panel Data, *Journal of Econometrics*, Vol. 38, pp. 387-399.

Battese, G., Coelli, T. and Colby, T. (1989), Estimation of Frontier Production Functions and the Efficiencies of Indian Farms using Panel Data from Icrisat's Village Level Studies, *Journal of Quantitative Economics*, Vol. 5, No. 2, pp. 327-348.

Bauer, P. (1990), Recent Developments in the Econometric Estimation of Frontiers, *Journal of Econometrics*, Vol. 46, pp. 39-56.

Bendall, H. and Stent, A. (1987), On Measuring Cargo Handling Productivity, *Maritime Policy and Management*, Vol. 14, No. 4, pp. 337-343.

Bernard, J. (1991), *European Deep-Sea Container Terminals: Locational and Operational Perspectives*, PhD Thesis, University of Liverpool.

Blundell, R. (1996), Microeconometrics, in Greenaway, D., Bleaney, M. and Stewart, I. (eds.), *A Guide to Modern Economics*, Routledge, London, pp. 508-536.

Braeutigam, R., Daughety, A. and Turnquist, M. (1984), A Firm Specific Analysis of Economies of Density in the US Railroad Industry, *Journal of Industrial Economics*, Vol. 33, pp. 3-20.

Chang, S. (1978), Production Function, Productivities, and Capacity Utilisation of the Port of Mobile, *Maritime Policy and Management*, Vol. 5, pp. 297-305.

Charnes, A., Cooper, W. and Rhodes, E. (1978), Measuring the Efficiency of Decision-Making Units, *European Journal of Operational Research*, Vol. 2, No. 6, pp. 429-444.

Christensen, L., Jorgenson, D. and Lau, L. (1973), Transcendental Logarithmic Production Frontiers, *Review of Economics and Statistics*, Vol. 55, pp. 28-45.

Cobb, C. and Douglas, P. (1928), A Theory of Production, *American Economic Review*, Vol. 23, pp. 139-165.

Cornwell, C., Schmidt, P. and Sickles, R. (1990), Production Frontiers with Cross-Sectional and Time-Series Variation in Efficiency Levels, *Journal of Econometrics*, Vol. 46, pp. 185-200.

Debreu, G. (1951), The Coefficient of Resource Utilisation, *Review of Economic Studies*, Vol. 9, pp. 300-312.

De Monie, G. (1987), *Measuring and Evaluating Port Performance and Productivity*, UNCTAD Monograph No. 6 on Port Management, Geneva.

De Neufville, R. and Tsunokawa, K. (1981), Productivity and Returns to Scale of Container Ports, *Maritime Policy and Management*, Vol. 8, No. 2, pp. 121-129.

Devine, P., Lee, N. and Jones, R. (1985), *An Introduction to Industrial Economics* (4th ed.), George Allen and Unwin, London.

Dowd, T. and Leschine, T. (1990), Container Terminal Productivity: A Perspective, *Maritime Policy and Management*, Vol. 17, No. 2, pp. 107-112.

Fare, R., Grosskopf, S. and Lovell, C. (1994), *Production Frontiers*, Cambridge University Press, Cambridge.

Farrell, M. (1957), The Measurement of Productive Efficiency, *Journal of the Royal Statistical Society*, Vol. 120, No. 3, pp. 253-290.

Ferrantino, M. and Ferrier, G. (1995), The Technical Efficiency of Vacuum-Pan Sugar Industry of India: An Application of a Stochastic Frontier Production Function Using Panel Data, *European Journal of Operational Research*, Vol. 80, pp. 639-653.

Forsund, F., Lovell, C. and Schmidt, P. (1980), A Survey of Frontier Production Functions and of their Relationship to Efficiency Measurement, *Journal of Econometrics*, Vol. 13, pp. 5-25.

Gong, B. H. and Sickles, R. (1992), Finite Sample Evidence on the Performance of Stochastic Frontiers and Data Envelopment Analysis using Panel Data, *Journal of Econometrics*, Vol. 51, pp. 259-284.

Greene. W. (1980), Maximum Likelihood Estimation of Econometric Frontier Functions, *Journal of Econometrics*, Vol. 13, pp. 27-56.

Greene, W. (1993), The Econometric Approach to Efficiency Analysis, in Fried, H., Lovell, C. and Schmidt, S. (eds.), *The Measurement of Productive Efficiency: Techniques and Applications*, Oxford University Press, New York, pp. 68-119.

Hausman, J. and Taylor, W. (1981), Panel Data and Unobserved Individual Effects, *Econometrica*, Vol. 49, pp. 1377-1398.

Heathfield, D. and Wibe, S. (1987), *An Introduction to Cost and Production Functions*, Macmillan, London.

Intriligator, M., Bodkin, R. and Hsiao, C. (1996), *Econometric Models, Techniques and Applications* (2nd ed.), Prentice-Hall International, Inc., New Jersey.

Jondrow, J., Lovell, C., Materov, I. and Schmidt, P. (1982), On the Estimation of Technical Inefficiency in the Stochastic Frontier Production Model, *Journal of Econometrics*, Vol. 19, pp. 233-238.

Kalirajan, K. (1990), On Measuring Economic Efficiency, *Journal of Applied Econometrics*, Vol. 5, pp. 75-85.

Kim, M. and Sachish, A. (1986), The Structure of Production, Technical Change and Productivity in a Port, *Journal of Industrial Economics*, Vol. 35, No. 2, pp. 209-223.

Kleinbaum, D., Kupper, L. and Muller, K. (1988), *Applied Regression Analysis and Other Multivariable Methods* (2nd ed.), PWS-Kent Publishing Co., Boston.

Kumbhakar, S. (1990), Production Frontiers, Panel Data, and Time-Varying Technical Inefficiency, *Journal of Econometrics*, Vol. 46, pp. 201-211.

Kumbhakar, S. and Hjalmarsson, L. (1993), Technical Efficiency and Technical Progress in Swedish Dairy Farms, in Fried, H., Lovell, C. and Schmidt, S. (eds.), *The Measurement of Productive Efficiency: Techniques and Applications*, Oxford University Press, New York, pp. 256-270.

Leibenstein, H. (1966), Allocative Efficiency vs. X-inefficiency, *American Economic Review*, Vol. 56, pp. 392-415.

Liu, Z. (1995), The Comparative Performance of Public and Private Enterprises: the Case of British Ports, *Journal of Transport Economics and Policy*, Vol. 29, No. 3, pp. 263-274.

Lovell, C. (1993), Production Frontiers and Productive Efficiency, in Fried, H., Lovell, C. and Schmidt, S. (eds.), *The Measurement of Productive Efficiency: Techniques and Applications*, Oxford University Press, New York, pp. 1-67.

Lovell, C. (1995), Econometric Efficiency Analysis: A Policy-Oriented Review, *European Journal of Operational Research*, Vol. 80, No. 3, Special Issue of Productivity Analysis: Parametric and Non-Parametric Applications, pp. 452-462.

Mansson, J. (1996), Technical Efficiency and Ownership: the Case of Booking Centres in the Swedish Tax Market, *Journal of Transport Economics and Policy*, Vol. 30, No. 1, pp. 83-93.

Meeusen, W. and van den Broeck, J. (1977), Efficiency Estimation from Cobb-Douglas Production Functions with Composed Error, *International Economic Review*, Vol. 18, No. 2, pp. 435-444.

Newman, E. (1975), *A Civil Tongue*, Warner Books, New York.

Nicholson, W. (1995), *Microeconomic Theory: Basic Principles and Extensions* (6th ed.), Dryden Press, New York.

Oum, T. H. and Waters, W. (1996), A Survey of Recent Development in Transportation Cost Function Research, *Logistics and Transportation Review*, Vol. 32, No. 4, pp. 423-463.

Pitt, M. and Lee, L. (1981), The Measurement and Sources of Technical Efficiency in the Indonesian Weaving Industry, *Journal of Development Economics*, Vol. 9, pp. 43-64.

Schmidt, P. (1985), Frontier Production Functions, *Econometric Reviews*, Vol. 4, pp. 289-328.

Schmidt, P. and Sickles, R. (1984), Production Frontiers and Panel Data, *Journal of Business and Economic Statistics*, Vol. 2, No. 4, pp. 367-374.

Schotter, A. (1997), *Microeconomics: A Modern Approach* (2nd ed.), Addison-Wesley, Massachusetts.

Stevenson, R. (1980), Likelihood Functions for Generalised Stochastic Frontier Estimation, *Journal of Econometrics*, Vol. 13, pp. 57-66.

Suykens, F. (1983), A Few Observations on Productivity in Seaports, *Maritime Policy and Management*, Vol. 10, No. 1, pp. 17-40.

Talley, W. (1988), Optimum Throughput and Performance Evaluation of Marine Terminals, *Maritime Policy and Management*, Vol. 15, No. 4, pp. 327-331.

Talley, W. (1994), Performance Indicators and Port Performance Evaluation, *Logistics and Transportation Review*, Vol. 30, No. 4, pp. 339-352.

Thomas, R. (1993), *Introductory Econometrics* (2nd ed.), Longman, London.

Tongzon, J. (1995), Determinants of Port Performance and Efficiency, *Transportation Research* (Part A: Policy and Practice), Vol. 29A, No. 3, pp. 245-252.

UNCTAD (1975), *Port Performance Indicators*, TD/B/C.4/131, Geneva.

Vickers, J. and Yarrow, G. (1988), *Privatisation: An Economic Analysis*, MIT Press, Massachusetts.

Waldman, D. (1982), A Stationary Point for the Stochastic Frontier Likelihood, *Journal of Econometrics*, Vol. 18, pp. 275-279.

Winsten, C. (1957), Discussion on Mr Farrell's Paper, *Journal of the Royal Statistical Society*, Series A, Vol. 120, No. 3, pp. 282-284.

7 Productive Efficiency of Container Terminals: An Empirical Investigation

INTRODUCTION

Following the theoretical models discussed and developed in the previous chapter, this chapter aims to empirically estimate the productive efficiency of a sample set of container terminals in Korea and the UK. Based on the econometric frontier model developed in the previous chapter, the efficiency of the terminal operating companies based on both cross-sectional data and panel data is estimated. For the purpose of the research, prior to conducting the empirical investigation, the theoretical model is appropriately operationalised so that it can be converted into a working model. Finally, the empirical results derived are interpreted and assessed.

OPERATIONALISING THE MODEL

A conceptual or theoretical model is required to be transformed into a more realistic model for the purpose of empirical analysis. This procedure is defined by Simon and Burstein (1985) as the *operationalisation* of the theoretical concepts or models, a task which induces finding appropriate empirical proxies for the theoretical variables. The procedure of *operationalisation*, therefore, involves the final step of preparing and processing the data needed to undertake the empirical analysis together with the final specification of the model and the assumptions upon which it is based.

Data Sources

The data used in this research has been extracted from the annual reports and financial accounts published by each container terminal. For an international comparison with a country where port privatisation policies have had more time to work, the main container terminals in the UK have been included in the analysis. The UK terminals selected for inclusion account for a significant proportion of total UK container traffic and have different ownership attributes not only amongst themselves but, most importantly, as compared to their Korean counterparts.

The cross-sectional and panel observations on outputs and inputs for each terminal are established in terms of various terminal attributes. BCTOC (the operating company of the Jasungdae terminal) represents a purely public organisation, while PECT (the operator of the Shinsundae terminal) is a private company. These two operating companies carry out their activities within a Korean business environment in which the government is heavily involved.[1] The UK side includes the Tilbury Container Services Company which was formerly part of a trust port but which is now a private company, the Southampton Container Terminals Company which forms part of Associated British Ports PLC, and the purely private Felixstowe Dock and Railway Company operating the Trinity and Landguard terminals.[2] A summary description of the overall data set appears in Table 7.1.

Description of the Variables

Dowd and Leschine (1990) argue that the productivity of a container terminal depends on the efficient use of labour, land and equipment. It seems logical, therefore, to take labour and capital (including land, buildings and equipment) as the input variables for a terminal production function. An analysis of the average expenditure pattern of a port or a terminal over time in accordance with this conventional categorisation of inputs is shown in Figure 7.1.

---

(1) Since UTC, the operating company of the Uam terminal had only partially commenced its operation in 1996, the available data was judged insufficient for its inclusion in the analysis.

(2) Felixstowe Dock and Railway Company consists of five divisions including Dooley Terminal, Rail, and Warehouse and Dock Basin Divisions. Only the data associated with the operations of the two container terminal divisions have been used for this analysis.

Table 7.1 Summary of Data Set

Container Terminal Operators	Years	Observations
Busan Container Terminal Operation Corporation	1978 – 1996	19
Pusan East Container Terminal Company	1991 – 1996	6
Tilbury Container Services Company	1979 – 1996	18
Southampton Container Terminals Company	1987 – 1996	10
Felixstowe Dock and Railway Company	1985 – 1996	12
TOTAL		65

Source: Authors.

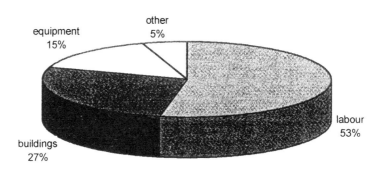

Figure 7.1 A Normal Port/Terminal Expenditure Pattern
Source: Derived from Sachish (1996, p. 347).

As a proxy for the capital input variable, the combined values of buildings and equipment (mainly cargo-handling equipment) accounts for an average of 42% of total expenditure. Thus, the labour and capital costs of a port or terminal together comprise 95% of the total cost structure of port or terminal operations. It seems reasonable enough to assume that this can be taken as sufficient, therefore, to describe the whole cost account.

Labour input can customarily be defined as an aggregate of the number of employees in a terminal operation. This will likely relate to two complementary, but fundamentally different groups of labourers: those hired directly by the terminal company and the stevedores employed by stevedoring companies who work on a sub-contract basis. With regard to the level of skill of labourers, the total wage bill (payments made for labour) which is quoted in value terms rather than in physical terms (the number of employees) may, to some extent, be a preferable input variable.

In practice, however, an accounting system adopted by one company may be different to that of others, a fact that puts a certain limitation on the collection of data necessary for the analysis. This problem is made worse by the fact that the required data is internationally dispersed. Under these circumstances, a possible solution is to collect only data which are consistently accounted for in financial statements in all areas of the world.

For this reason, the current research defines *labour input* as two different aggregates; one is the total remuneration of directors or executives for their managerial services (L_1) and the other, the total wages and salaries paid to employees (L_2). The input *capital variable* is also divided into two aggregates. One is the net book value of fixed equipment, buildings and land utilised for the purpose of terminal operations (K_1) and the other is the net book value of mobile and cargo handling equipment including container cranes, yard tractors and fork lifts (K_2).

As far as the output of a container terminal is concerned, there are two alternatives: a proxy either in value terms or in physical units. Financial output may be measured by annual 'turnover', while physical units such as 'TEU throughput' may also be used over a given time period.[3] This research defines, as *terminal output*, the turnover derived from container terminal services (Y), which excludes property sales. Finally, where relevant, the data for all variables collected are deflated by appropriate price indices to incorporate real values into the analysis and ensuing model estimation. A summary of the major properties of the variables is presented

---

(3) The unit of container TEU is regarded as a homogeneous product which is a very realistic assumption. The output of a terminal can, therefore, be measured in TEU throughput over a given time period. The present research, however, found the output 'turnover' more explicable of terminal production, in part due to the financial nature of the inputs into the model.

in Table 7.2.

Table 7.2 Statistical Properties of the Variables (Unit: £ 000s)

Variables	Mean	Median	Minimum	Maximum	Standard Deviation
Output (Y)	21929.75	14035.25	594.72	70771.91	20171.98
Labour (L$_1$)	208.00	146.40	0.00	1163.20	244.85
Labour (L$_2$)	9585.35	3049.91	15.14	40056.41	12400.42
Capital (K$_1$)	17287.38	536.13	14.90	110484.29	32046.35
Capital (K$_2$)	5107.37	220.88	32.56	34342.07	10309.40

Model Specification and Assumptions

The estimation of relative terminal operator efficiency is conducted by assuming the appropriateness of the log-linear Cobb-Douglas case.[4] Therefore, the logarithmic stochastic frontier model specified for the container terminal operating sector in the cross-sectional case is defined by:

$$\ln Y_{it} = \ln f(L_{1it}, L_{2it}, K_{1it}, K_{2it}; \beta) + v_{it} - u_{it}, \qquad (7.1)$$

$$i = 1, 2, ..., 5;$$
$$t = 1, 2, ..., T$$

....where Y_{it} represents the output of the ith container terminal operator at time t, L_{1it}, L_{2it}, K_{1it} and K_{2it} denote labour and capital input variables, associated with the ith terminal operator at time t, and β is a vector of input coefficients for the associated independent variables in the model and is the object of estimation. The disturbance term v_{it} represents the symmetric (statistical noise) component and u_{it} (≥ 0) the one-sided (inefficiency) component.

Concerning the sample data for the cross-sectional frontier model, the pooled data set is used and treated as if it were generated from the cross-sectional terminal operators in a single period.

---

(4) A number of other linear functions (e.g. the translog) are available, but the focus of this research is efficiency measurement, rather than the intricacies of selecting the function itself.

For the application of the panel data, the model (7.1) is transformed into:

$$\ln Y_{it} = \ln f(L_{1it}, L_{2it}, K_{1it}, K_{2it}; \beta) + v_{it} - u_i, \qquad (7.2)$$

$i = 1, 2, \ldots, 5;$
$t = 1, 2, \ldots T$

In the model (7.2), the one-sided disturbance term u_i (≥ 0) represents the 'terminal operator-specific time invariant inefficiency'.

For the purpose of the empirical analysis, some assumptions also have to be made. The overall objective of terminal operators is assumed to be the maximisation of their profits stemming from operational activities. In other words, a terminal operating company is regarded as a profit-maximiser. The terminal operators are also assumed to be price takers in their input markets. Hence, input prices may be treated as exogenous. Another assumption necessary for operationalising the models given in (7.1) and (7.2) is that they represent a single-output production function. This is justified on the basis that the main operational function of container terminals and the main issue of policy interest is *container handling*. Thus, earnings from sources such as the sales of terminal property are not classified as output and do not affect the production function frontier.

Finally, the concept of the *average* terminal frontier is applied as the definition of the frontier. Estimation of terminal efficiency is conducted using an econometric software package LIMDEP 7.0[5] (Greene, 1995).

Parameters and Likelihood Functions

The estimation commences with an ordinary least squares (OLS) estimation procedure which provides the starting values for ensuring the maximum likelihood estimation (MLE). The skewness of OLS residuals is

---

(5) LIMDEP 7.0 has several options concerning assumptions made on the disturbance distribution: the normal distribution is employed for v and the half-normal, exponential and truncated normal cases are available for u in the case of the cross-sectional model and the half-normal distribution for u in the panel data model. Moreover, the panel model can be estimated with balanced or unbalanced panels. The cross-sectional and panel models are estimated using OLS and MLE.

checked, however, prior to the implementation of the MLE. If the OLS residuals are positively skewed (skewed to the right), then the MLE for the frontier model is simply the OLS estimates for the coefficients, and σ_v^2 and $\sigma_u^2 = 0$. In theory, for the MLE estimation of the stochastic frontier model, the distribution of the OLS residuals must be skewed to the left (Waldman, 1982). The estimation procedure will therefore be ceased if the residuals are not negatively skewed, a situation that may arise due to an inappropriately specified model or to inconsistent data (Greene, 1993). In addition, Waldman (1982) suggests that the sign of the third moment of the OLS residuals be checked. The fact that the third moment is positive indicates the OLS residuals are inappropriately skewed for the continued application of the estimation procedure. Thus, the skewness of the sample residuals is informative about the extent of inefficiency (Greene, 1997).

MLE for the container terminal frontier is conducted by the David-Fletcher-Powell algorithm (Fletcher, 1980; Greene, 1997) which is an iterative and effective procedure. The MLE technique requires distributional assumptions on the symmetric component v and the one-sided component u. In models (7.1) and (7.2), the statistical noise v is identically and independently distributed as $N(0, \sigma_v^2)$ and two error components v and u are independent of one another and of the input variables. Based on these assumptions, three alternative formulations and specifications are taken into consideration for the inefficiency term u_{it} for the cross-sectional model (7.1).

- For the half-normal case (Aigner *et al.*, 1977):

$$f(u) = \sqrt{\frac{2}{\pi}} \exp\left[-\frac{1}{2}\left(\frac{u}{\sigma_u}\right)^2\right] \tag{7.3}$$

$$E(u) = \frac{\sigma\phi(0)}{\Phi(0)} = \sigma_u\sqrt{\frac{2}{\pi}} \tag{7.4}$$

....where $\sigma = \sqrt{(\sigma_v^2 + \sigma_u^2)}$ and, $\phi(\cdot)$ and $\Phi(\cdot)$ are, respectively, the probability density function (pdf) and the cumulative distribution function (cdf) of the standard normal distribution. A special note on the variance of u is necessary for the half-normal assumption; while the variance of v is σ_v^2, the variance of u is not σ_u^2, but rather:

$$Var(u) = \left(1 - \frac{2}{\pi}\right)\sigma_u^2 \tag{7.5}$$

Therefore, the estimation parameters may mislead as to the relative influence of u on the total variation in the disturbances (Greene, 1993).

- For the exponential case (Aigner *et al.*, 1977; Meeusen and van den Broeck, 1977):

$$f(u) = 6\exp(-6u) \tag{7.6}$$

$$E(u) = \frac{1}{\theta} \tag{7.7}$$

- For the truncated normal case (Stevenson, 1980):

$$f(u) = \frac{\left(\dfrac{1}{\sigma_u}\right)\phi\left[\dfrac{(u-\mu)}{\sigma_u}\right]}{\Phi\left(\dfrac{\mu}{\sigma_u}\right)} \tag{7.8}$$

$$E(u) = \mu + \frac{\sigma_u\phi\left(\dfrac{\mu}{\sigma_u}\right)}{\Phi\left(\dfrac{\mu}{\sigma_u}\right)} = \mu + \sigma_u\lambda \tag{7.9}$$

For accomplishing the MLE, the specification of a likelihood function is necessary (Kleinbaum *et al.*, 1988). The following log-likelihood functions for the cross-sectional model (7.1) are employed:

- For the half-normally distributed term u_{it}:

$$\sum_i \left[\ln \Phi \left(\frac{-\varepsilon_{it} \lambda}{\sigma} \right) - \frac{1}{2} \left(\frac{\varepsilon_{it}}{\sigma} \right)^2 \right] \tag{7.10}$$

....where N = the number of observations, $\varepsilon_{it} = (v_{it} - u_{it})$, and $\lambda = \sigma_u / \sigma_v$ (a useful indicator of the relative variability of the two disturbance terms, and hence is non-negative). One additional point to be noted is that the variance ratio (σ_u^2/σ^2) shows the influence of the inefficiency component in the overall variance.

- For the exponentially distributed term u_{it}:

$$n L (\alpha, \beta, \sigma_v, \theta) = N \left[\ln \theta + \frac{1}{2} (\theta \sigma_v)^2 \right] + \sum_i \left[\ln \Phi \left(\frac{-\varepsilon_{it}}{\sigma_v} - \theta \sigma_v \right) + \theta \varepsilon_{it} \right] \tag{7.11}$$

- For the truncated normally distributed term u_{it}:

$\ln L (\alpha, \beta, \sigma, \lambda, \mu) =$

$$- \sum_i \left[\ln \sigma + \frac{1}{2} \ln 2\pi + \frac{1}{2} \left(\frac{\varepsilon_{it}}{\sigma} \right)^2 \right.$$

$$\left. - \ln \left\{ 1 - \Phi \left[\frac{\varepsilon_{it} \lambda}{\sigma} + \frac{\mu}{(\sigma\lambda)} \right] \right\} + \ln \Phi \left(\frac{-\mu}{\sigma_u} \right) \right] \tag{7.12}$$

....where $\dfrac{\mu}{\sigma_u} = \dfrac{\sqrt{\mu(1+\lambda^2)}}{\lambda\sigma}$

For the log-likelihood function of the panel data model (7.2) where the composed error term $\varepsilon_{it} = (v_{it} - u_i)$, the half-normally distributed disturbance term u_i is utilised (Pitt and Lee, 1981; Battese and Coelli, 1988):

Ln L =

$$\sum_i \left\{ -\frac{1}{2}\left[T_i \ln 2\pi - \ln 2 + T_i \ln \sigma_v^2 + \ln(1 + \lambda T_i) - 2\ln \Phi\left(\frac{\mu}{\sigma_v} \right) \right] \right\}$$

$$\sum_i \left(-\frac{1}{2} \left\{ \frac{-\lambda}{(1+\lambda T_i)}\left[\sum_t \frac{(\varepsilon_{it} - \mu)}{\sigma_v} \right]^2 + \sum_t \left[\frac{(\varepsilon_{it} - \mu)}{\sigma_v} \right]^2 \right\} \right)$$

$$\sum_i \ln \Phi\left\{ \sqrt{\left(\frac{\lambda}{1+\lambda T_i} \right)} \frac{1}{\sigma_v}\left[\sum_t (\varepsilon_{it} - \mu) + T_i\mu\left(1 - \frac{1}{\lambda} \right) \right] \right\} \qquad (7.13)$$

....where T_i = the number of observations on the ith firm (terminal operator) and $\lambda = \sigma_u^2/\sigma_v^2$.

For statistical inference from MLE models, the likelihood ratio statistic is applied to test whether or not model coefficients are significantly different from zero. Since the maximum likelihood method is a large-sample estimation procedure (Maddala, 1992), it is required that an asymptotic test statistic be used; the likelihood ratio test is one of the general large-sample tests based on the MLE, which has a χ^2 distribution with degrees of freedom equal to the number of restrictions imposed. Under general conditions, the likelihood ratio test statistic (LR) can be expressed as follows (Engle, 1984):

$$LR = -2 \ln\left(\frac{L_R}{L_U} \right) \qquad (7.14)$$

....where L_R denotes 'restricted' likelihood function and L_U 'unrestricted' likelihood function.

Efficiency Estimation

The main theme of the frontier model as a technique of efficiency measurement is concerning the specification and estimation of u. The inefficiency term u, however, must be observed indirectly because the procedure estimates the residual ε, not u (Greene, 1993). In the case of a cross-sectional model such as (7.1), Jondrow *et al.* (1982) suggest the conditional expectation of u_{it}, conditioned on the realised value of the error term $\varepsilon_{it} = (v_{it} - u_{it})$, as an estimator of u_{it}. In other words, $E\left[u_{it}|\varepsilon_{it}\right]$ is the 'mean productive inefficiency' for the ith terminal operator in the industry at sample time t. This estimate enables us to measure the inefficiency for each observation in the cross-sectional framework.

- For the half-normal model:

$$E\left[u_{it}|\varepsilon_{it}\right] = \frac{\sigma\lambda}{\left(1+\lambda^2\right)}\left[\frac{\phi\left(\dfrac{\varepsilon_{it}\lambda}{\sigma}\right)}{\Phi\left(-\dfrac{\varepsilon_{it}\lambda}{\sigma}\right)} - \frac{\varepsilon_{it}\lambda}{\sigma}\right] \qquad (7.15)$$

- For the exponential model:

$$E\left[u_{it}|\varepsilon_{it}\right] = \left(\varepsilon_{it} - \theta\sigma_v^2\right) + \frac{\sigma_v\phi\left[\dfrac{\left(\varepsilon_{it} - \theta\sigma_v^2\right)}{\sigma_v}\right]}{\Phi\left[\dfrac{\left(\varepsilon_{it} - \theta\sigma_v^2\right)}{\sigma_v}\right]} \qquad (7.16)$$

- For the truncated normal model: the inefficiency term is obtained by replacing $(\varepsilon_{it}\lambda)/\sigma$ in equation (7.15) with

$$\left(\frac{\varepsilon_{it}\lambda}{\sigma} + \frac{\mu}{\sigma\lambda} \right) \tag{7.17}$$

These provide unbiased, but not consistent, estimates of the inefficiency component u. Greene (1993) argues that, regardless of the number of observations, the inconsistency stems from the fact that the variance of the estimate remains nonzero, not from the fact that the estimates converge to some other quantity. Again, Greene (1993) notes that, unfortunately, no improvement might be expected on this measure for the cross-sectional framework in the near future.

By generalising the cross-sectional results in Jondrow *et al.* (1982) to panel models, Battese and Coelli (1988) propose the estimation of the 'time-invariant terminal operator-specific inefficiency' u_i under the half-normal assumption:

$$E\left[u_i \middle| \varepsilon_{i1}, \ldots, \varepsilon_{iT}\right] = \mu_i^* + \sigma_{*i} \left[\frac{\phi\left(\frac{\mu_i^*}{\sigma_{*i}}\right)}{\Phi\left(-\frac{\mu_i^*}{\sigma_{*i}}\right)} \right] \tag{7.18}$$

where $\mu_i^* = \gamma_i \mu + \left(1 - \gamma_i\right)\left(-\bar{\varepsilon}_i\right)$, $\gamma_i = \dfrac{1}{\left(1 + \dfrac{\lambda}{T_i}\right)}$ and $\sigma_{*i} = \sqrt{\left(\dfrac{\sigma_u^2}{1 + \lambda T_i}\right)}$

Equations (7.15) to (7.18) as applied to the measurement of inefficiency require the calculation of the probability density and cumulative distribution functions of the standard normal distribution.[6]

---

(6) LIMDEP 7.0 provides these estimated inefficiencies for the cross-sectional and the panel cases as regression options along with a few matrix commands.

THE HYPOTHESIS FOR INVESTIGATION

The selected five terminal companies can be described by borrowing the concepts discussed in section 4.7.2 of Chapter 4 for testing the importance of container terminal ownership. Referring to the horizontal axis of Figure 4.3 in Chapter 4 and as illustrated in Figure 7.2, BCTOC may be located between B and C, PECT between D and E, Tilbury and Southampton between E and F, and Felixstowe at F. The panel observations on output and inputs for each terminal are established in terms of various terminal attributes according to Figure 7.2.

Based on the ownership characteristics of terminal operators illustrated in Figure 7.2, the research hypothesis is established for investigation as follows:

> "The productive efficiency of terminal operators improves as ownership moves along the continuum towards greater private sector participation (i.e. the movement away from A and towards F)."

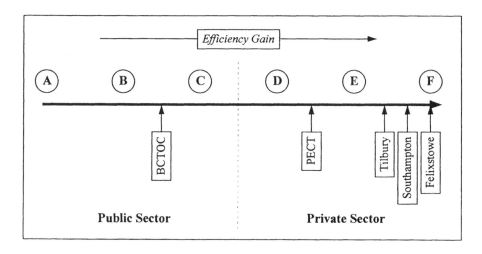

Figure 7.2 Terminal Ownership Attributes

THE PRODUCTIVE EFFICIENCY OF THE TERMINAL OPERATORS: THE CROSS-SECTIONAL MODEL

The first step in the estimation procedure is checking the sign of the third moment and the skewness of the OLS residuals associated with the sample data. The third moment for the terminal frontier model is -0.762, implying by its negative sign that the residuals are correctly (i.e. negatively) skewed. The histogram of the residuals shown in Figure 7.3 has a longer tail on the left side (or negative skewness), also implying that the residuals of the sample data is correctly shaped for the next step in the MLE procedure.

Based on the cross-sectional data, the OLS estimates and the MLEs for each of the three assumed distributions of the inefficiency terms in the terminal frontier model (7.1) are presented in Table 7.3. Although the OLS coefficients only have a limited usefulness, they do, however, provide a starting value for the MLE process. The goodness of fit of the estimated regression equation evaluated by R^2 using the OLS method, looks reasonably high at 0.785, revealing that the four inputs to the model do satisfactorily explain the model output. In addition, the *F*-statistic of 54.70 shows that a significant relationship is present between exogenous and endogenous variables at the 1% significance level and that all variables, except the first labour input (L_1), are statistically significant at the 5% level.

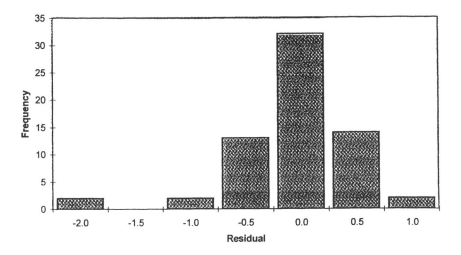

Figure 7.3 Skewness of the OLS Residuals

The MLEs under the three alternative cases yield parameters that are close to each other. An interesting point to be addressed here is that, except the second labour input (L_2), the MLEs differ only marginally from the OLS estimates. This is to be expected since both methods are consistent. Concerning statistical inference, the likelihood ratio test statistic (LR = $99.852)^7$ is significant at the 1% level, thus allowing the rejection of the null hypothesis that the coefficients in the model are equal to zero.

Table 7.3 Frontier Production Function of Container Terminals

Variables/ Parameters	OLS	MLE		
		half-normal	Exponential	Truncated normal
Constant	10.418	11.609	11.801	11.774
	(17.192)	(17.685)	(22.346)	(20.936)
ln L_1	0.043**	0.055*	0.048	0.048*
	(1.306)	(2.193)	(2.634)	(2.269)
ln L_2	0.123*	0.056**	0.049**	0.053**
	(2.267)	(1.348)	(1.278)	(1.318)
ln K_1	0.149	0.171	0.159	0.162
	(3.917)	(3.786)	(4.465)	(4.225)
ln K_2	0.129	0.120	0.120	0.119
	(2.981)	(2.576)	(3.086)	(2.721)
λ	-	4.078	2.026	5.811
σ_v^2	-	0.027	0.038	0.039
σ_u^2	-	0.449	0.156	1.317
θ	-	-	2.529	-
μ	-	-	-	1.798
Log-likelihood	-	-33.799	-31.019	-31.734

Notes: (1) * Not significant at the 1% level; ** Not significant at the 5% level.
(2) Figures in parentheses indicate t-ratios.

Mean Inefficiency and Disturbance Variation

The mean of the inefficiency component u by the specification (7.4) is $E(u)$ = 0.535 under the half-normal assumption. This means that the average

(7) According to (7.14), LR = -2 (-90.2997 + 40.3409) = 99.8516. The critical value at 5 degrees of freedom is 15.0863.

shortfall of output is 53.5% below its maximum possible frontier, equivalent to 58.6% efficiency.[8] For the exponential case, the inefficiency mean by equation (7.7) is $E(u) = 0.395$, implying an efficiency level of 67.4%. The mean of inefficiency component under the truncated normal assumption is $E(u) = 0.42$ by equation (7.9), yielding an average efficiency of 65.7%. These figures show us that the half-normal estimates of the mean of inefficiency u are slightly higher than under the other two assumptions. The overall productive inefficiency levels of terminal operators under the three assumptions over the sample period are illustrated in Figure 7.4, which shows graphically that the inefficiency trends are remarkably parallel over the period. In fact, the worst correlation over time between different inefficiency estimates for any operator is impressively high at 0.987.

The parameter λ $(=\sigma_u/\sigma_v)$ gives an insight into the relative variance of the two composite errors in the total variation in the overall structural disturbance. The two variances of the error components, along with λ, indicate that the inefficiency component u varies more widely than the uncontrolled exogenous component v. This means that the productive inefficiency u plays a more important part in total error variability in the cross-sectional frontier model. Under the half-normal assumption, as mentioned earlier, the variance of u is 0.714 by formulation (7.5), not $\sigma_u^2 = 0.449$. The ratio of σ_u^2 to σ^2 (again, $Var(u)$ in the case of the half-normal distribution) provides the information of how much the efficiency component u influences the overall variation of disturbances. The ratios are 96.4% in the half-normal case, 80.4% in the exponential case, and 97.1% under the truncated normal assumption. These figures indicate that the component u has a great effect on total error variation. In contrast, uncontrollable shocks, represented by the estimated variance of v (σ_v^2), were a less important source of variability. This may be due to the fact that uncontrolled shocks such as weather conditions do not seem to affect the business (outputs) of container terminals.

---

(8) The average efficiency is estimated by exp($-u$) as the counterpart of average inefficiency.

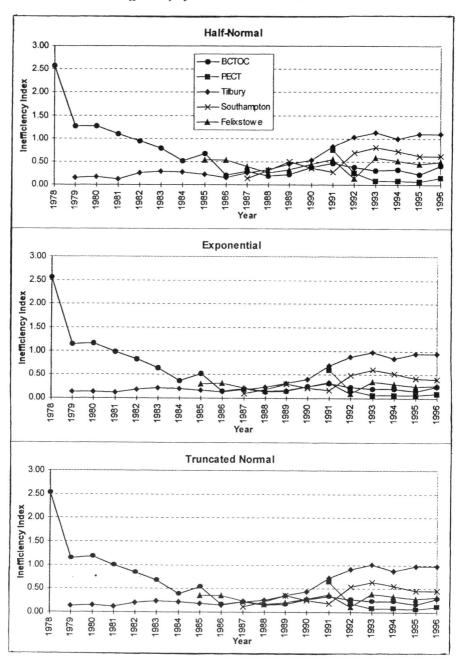

Figure 7.4 Overall Productive Inefficiency Levels under the Three Assumptions

Table 7.4 Average Productive Efficiency of Terminal Operators (%)

Container Terminal Operators	Half-Normal	Exponential	Truncated Normal
Busan Container Terminal Operation Corporation	52.0	57.7	56.7
Pusan East Container Terminal Company	78.9	83.4	82.3
Tilbury Container Services Company	59.3	65.1	63.6
Southampton Container Terminals Company	60.5	71.0	68.6
Felixstowe Dock and Rail Company	64.8	77.8	75.2

Note: Figures are computed by converting the inefficiency estimates using $\exp(-u)$.

Efficiency Level of Terminal Operators

With respect to the productive efficiency of each terminal operator for each time period, equations (7.15) to (7.17) are employed. Prior to analysing the efficiency level of each sampled terminal operator, it is useful to see the average efficiency level as shown in Table 7.4.

Throughout all three assumptions, the efficiency level of PECT is consistently highest followed by Felixstowe, Southampton, Tilbury and finally BCTOC. An intriguing result is that PECT (a quasi-private terminal operator in the context of Korean business circumstances) performs more efficiently than its UK counterparts which actually enjoy more freedom over the management of their terminal operations. The efficiency of the other four terminal operators ranks as expected according to the underlying privatisation theory. The estimated productive inefficiency of the five container terminal operators for the duration of the sample period is comprehensively shown in Appendix 4.

If the efficiency levels of BCTOC are examined before and after 1990, the year when PECT was established, we can discover whether or not the newly introduced competition has encouraged BCTOC to operate more efficiently. As can be seen in Figure 7.5, the average efficiency level of

BCTOC from 1979 to 1990[9] is 52.5%, while the average efficiency from 1991 to 1996 is 70.9%.

On average, therefore, the efficiency level improves significantly between the two periods. A significant improvement in the productive efficiency of BCTOC occurred, however, a few years before competition was introduced in the Korean port industry. This phenomenon probably verifies the assertion of contestable markets theory (Baumol *et al.*, 1982; Baumol, 1982), that merely the threat or anticipation of competition, rather than competition itself, is sufficient to stimulate a market response in the form of efforts to achieve greater efficiency. On the other hand, the efficiency improvement at BCTOC may merely be a coincidental and natural corollary of the increased availability and/or lower cost of advanced technology or simply the result of the ongoing more general liberalisation of the business environment in Korea.

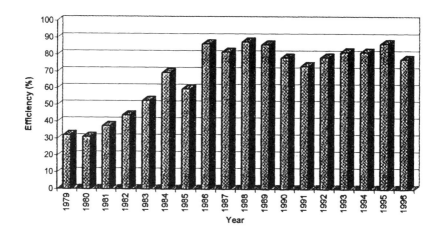

Figure 7.5 Productive Efficiency of BCTOC (1979-1996)
Note: Graph indicates the level of efficiency under the exponential case.

---

(9) The starting year 1978 has been treated as an outlier and has been excluded from the calculation due to the extraordinarily high level of inefficiency found to exist.

Moving to the UK side, the efficiency of the three terminals is ranked as expected. In general, as illustrated in Figure 7.6, except for 1990 and 1991 when the highest efficiency level was achieved by Southampton, the purely private operator Felixstowe was the most efficient operator over the research period, followed by Southampton and Tilbury.

TERMINAL OPERATOR-SPECIFIC EFFICIENCY: THE PANEL MODEL

The log-likelihood function in (7.13) for the panel model was again estimated by the David-Fletcher-Powell method under the assumptions that the two disturbances are independent of each other and $v_{it} \sim N(0, \sigma_v^2)$ and $u_i \sim N(0, \sigma_u^2)$. Based on the panel data, some of whose benefits for analysis are explained in section 6.4.4, the MLEs of the terminal frontier model (7.2) are presented in Table 7.5. As in the cross-sectional model, with a ratio of σ_u^2/σ^2 calculated at 93.7%, the inefficiency disturbance u is more important to the total variation of the error components, indicating that uncontrolled shocks (denoted by σ_v^2) do not significantly influence the overall variation.

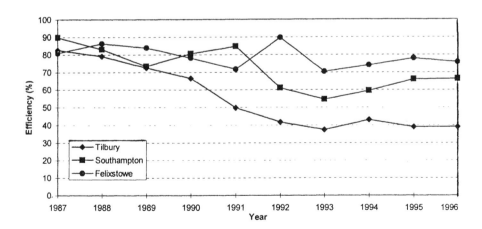

Figure 7.6 The Productive Efficiency of the Three UK Terminal Operators

Note: Graph indicates the level of efficiency under the exponential case.

Table 7.5 Maximum Likelihood Estimates of the Panel Frontier Model

	Coefficients	Asymptotic Standard Error
Constant	0.2114*	0.1179
ln L$_1$	0.2783**	0.0212
ln L$_2$	0.1137	0.0257
ln K$_1$	0.2838	0.0255
ln K$_2$	0.1536**	0.0497
λ	1.2251***	
$\sigma_v^{\,2}$	0.0702	
$\sigma_u^{\,2}$	0.0860	
Log-likelihood	-17.11002	

Note: *   Not significant at the 5% level.

               **   Not significant at the 10% level.

               *** $\lambda = \sigma_u^{\,2} / \sigma_v^{\,2}$

Given the parameters in Table 7.5, we are now able to measure the 'time invariant terminal operator-level efficiency' of each operator according to the formula in (7.18). Figure 7.7 shows the specific efficiency for the five sample container terminal operators.

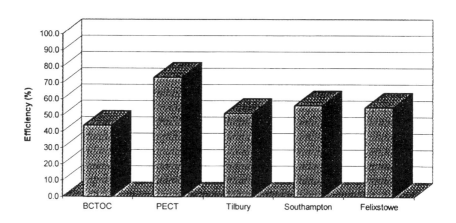

Figure 7.7 Terminal Operator-Specific Time Invariant Efficiency

As was the case in the cross-sectional model, PECT is ranked highest in terms of firm-specific efficiency at 75.7%, followed by 55.5% for

Southampton, 55.1% for Felixstowe, 51.9% for Tilbury and finally 41.1% for BCTOC. The difference between this result and that of the cross-sectional model is that the ranking among the UK terminal operators has changed with the efficiency level of Southampton now higher under the panel model than that of Felixstowe.

REFERENCES

Aigner, D., Lovell, C. and Schmidt, P. (1977), Formulation and Estimation of Stochastic Frontier Production Function Models, *Journal of Econometrics*, Vol. 6, No. 1, pp. 21-37.

Battese, G. and Coelli, T. (1988), Prediction of Firm-Level Technical Efficiencies with a Generalised Frontier Production Function and Panel Data, *Journal of Econometrics*, Vol. 38, pp. 387-399.

Baumol, W. (1982), Contestable Markets: An Uprising in the Theory of Industry Structure, *American Economic Review*, Vol. 72, No. 1, pp. 1-15.

Baumol, W., Panzar, J. and Willig, R. (1982), *Contestable Markets and the Theory of Industrial Structure*, Harcourt Brace Jovanovich, San Diego.

Dowd, T. and Leschine, T. (1990), Container Terminal Productivity: A Perspective, *Maritime Policy and Management*, Vol. 17, No. 2, pp. 107-112.

Engle, R. (1984), Wald, Likelihood Ratio and Lagrange Multiplier Tests in Econometrics, in Griliches, Z. and Intriligator, M. (eds.), *Handbook of Econometrics*, Volume II, Elsevier Science Publishers, Amsterdam, pp. 775-826.

Fletcher, R. (1980), *Practical Methods of Optimisation*, John Wiley and Sons, New York.

Greene, W. (1993), The Econometric Approach to Efficiency Analysis, in Fried, H., Lovell, C. and Schmidt, S. (eds.), *The Measurement of Productive Efficiency: Techniques and Applications*, Oxford University Press, New York, pp. 68-119.

Greene, W. (1995), *LIMDEP (Version 7.0) User's Manual*, Econometric Software, Inc., Castle Hill, Australia.

Greene, W. (1997), *Econometric Analysis* (3rd ed.), Prentice-Hall International, Inc., New Jersey.

Jondrow, J., Lovell, C., Materov, I. and Schmidt, P. (1982), On the Estimation of Technical Inefficiency in the Stochastic Frontier Production Model, *Journal of Econometrics*, Vol. 19, pp. 233-238.

Kleinbaum, D., Kupper, L. and Muller, K. (1988), *Applied Regression Analysis and Other Multivariable Methods* (2nd ed.), PWS-KENT Publishing, Boston.

Maddala, G. (1992), *Introduction to Econometrics* (2nd ed.), Macmillan Publishing Company, New York.

Meeusen, W. and van den Broeck, J. (1977), Efficiency Estimation from Cobb-Douglas Production Functions with Composed Error, *International Economic Review*, Vol. 18, No. 2, pp. 435-444.

Pitt, M. and Lee, L. (1981), The Measurement and Sources of Technical Efficiency in the Indonesian Weaving Industry, *Journal of Development Economics*, Vol. 9, pp. 43-64.

Sachish, A. (1996), Productivity Functions as a Managerial Tool in Israeli Ports, *Maritime Policy and Management*, Vol. 23, No. 4, pp. 341-369.

Simon, J. and Burstein, P. (1985), *Basic Research Methods in Social Science*, McGraw-Hill, Inc., New York.

Stevenson, R. (1980), Likelihood Functions for Generalised Stochastic Frontier Estimation, *Journal of Econometrics*, Vol. 13, pp. 57-66.

Waldman, D. (1982), A Stationary Point for the Stochastic Frontier Likelihood, *Journal of Econometrics*, Vol. 18, pp. 275-279.

8 Discussion, Policy Implications and Conclusions

INTERPRETATION OF EMPIRICAL RESULTS AND DISCUSSION

As the basis of the empirical investigation conducted within this study, it is hypothesised that the alteration of port ownership from public to private sector results in efficiency improvement. In other words, that a private terminal operator performs more efficiently than a public one. The findings drawn from an empirical analysis based on the use of the stochastic frontier model reveal, however, that ownership does not seem to be categorically related to efficiency in port operations. The overall results of the terminal frontier analysis have not provided clear-cut and indisputable evidence that the terminal operators who enjoy more freedom in carrying out their business perform more efficiently than the operators who implement their activities in an environment placing greater regulation upon them.

Under the more regulated business environment imposed by the Korean government, the private terminal operator PECT was found to have the highest level of efficiency during the sample period in both the cross-sectional and panel models. In contrast, the efficiency of all the private sector UK operators that carry on their activities in what is basically a deregulated environment showed lower levels of efficiency than PECT their counterpart in Korea. The efficiency of this group was, however, higher than that of the public sector operator BCTOC, which yielded the lowest estimate of productive efficiency in both models for the sample period covered by the research. With respect to the relative efficiency of PECT as compared to UK operators, the results contradict the research hypothesis. The results achieved from the analysis of both the cross-sectional and panel models reveal that PECT outperforms its UK counterparts.

The most convincing and consistent result stemming from the empirical analysis is that PECT, the Korean private sector organisation, operates a great deal more efficiently than its public rival BCTOC. PECT has the highest degree of productive efficiency whilst BCTOC operates with the lowest degree of productive efficiency in both cross-sectional and panel models. As far as the UK container terminal operators are concerned, the ranking of productive efficiency in the cross-sectional model concurs with the underlying theory of privatisation, whereas that in the panel model produces results which contradict the theory.

Unlike the claim made by privatisation theory (i.e. the theory of property rights and public choice), movement towards greater private sector participation does not seem to be a crucial factor in influencing efficiency levels, at least within Korean and UK container ports. Hence, it can be concluded that, according to the results derived from the terminal frontier analysis, merely changing the ownership of port assets is not sufficient to improve productive efficiency. Those interested and involved in port reforms and reorganisation, therefore, should recognise that port privatisation cannot provide the panacea that yields efficiency enhancement in port operations.

Vickers and Yarrow (1991) and Bishop and Thompson (1992), for example, suggest that to be a successful policy, privatisation must be planned and implemented, giving due consideration to the level of market regulation so that effective competition in the market is promoted. In addition, this view is supported by the contention that, in order to achieve what is expected from the conversion of property rights; that is, efficiency improvement, port privatisation should be considered and implemented against the whole background of the country concerned, its political and economic conditions and social culture (Goss, 1990; Thomas, 1994). This argument is highlighted in what follows.

IMPLICATIONS FOR THE FORMULATION OF PORT PRIVATISATION POLICY

Guislain (1997) notes that the main objectives driving an overall economic programme should be defined as the first step towards privatisation policy. This is because most industrial privatisation programmes within industrial sectors are an integral part of more comprehensive economic reform. In some sense, the development of a privatisation strategy involves (i) identifying government's overall objectives, (ii) analysing existing and/or possible constraints in implementing the programme, and (iii) deciding on an approach to accomplish the defined targets whilst taking the impediments into consideration. As part of establishing the port privatisation strategy, therefore, the characteristics of the country concerned and its port industry should be recognised. Figure 8.1 shows two sets of characteristics, relating to country and industry, which significantly impact upon port privatisation policy.

First, privatisation strategies need to be realistically geared to the specific circumstances and characteristics of the country; the political, institutional, economic and social setting must be carefully analysed. Second, privatisation programmes are also influenced by the existing structure of the industry such as the current nature of ownership, the financial situation and any applicable environmental obligations and restrictions.

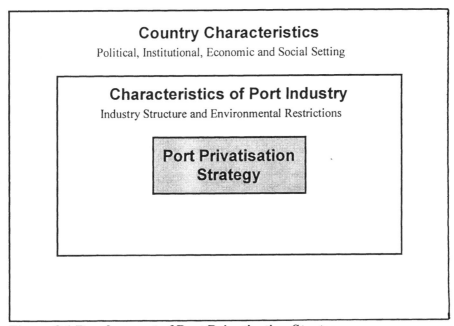

Figure 8.1 Development of Port Privatisation Strategy

According to this framework, the next sections examine the country characteristics of Korea; a nation that has launched ambitious general economic privatisation and deregulation programmes under which some form of port restructuring, such as privatisation, has been considered and implemented.

Country Characteristics

Since privatisation is, above all, a political process which is likely to radically disrupt the conditions of various stakeholders (Antal-Mokos, 1998), political decision-makers should attempt to predict possible obstacles to the programme. A variety of reluctance or resistance within, as well as outside, the government and the industry and/or company concerned can hinder the privatisation process or limit its success and/or scope. Guislain (1997) lists several reasons for such opposition including, among others, (i) the desire to retain national control over certain activities or interests perceived to be strategic, (ii) the sense that state ownership is needed to safeguard the public interest, (iii) a distrust of the private sector that is willing to become involved in the programme, and (iv) the protection of bureaucratic or other vested interests.

Turning to the Korean situation, all of the above reasons are likely obstacles to the implementation of any privatisation programme. In order to catch up with the industrialised countries within a short period of time, the Korean government maintained responsibility for overall industrial policies. As the nation's president in the 1960s and 1970s, Park (1970) asserted that, wherever necessary, the state has controlled production under the name of stimulating national development and that this authoritarian system, he believed, has protected the interests of the people. This command economy ideology does still exert considerable influence over the country's industries and has caused the present notorious bureaucracy which is characterised by a lack of enthusiasm, corruption and an inefficient and inflexible administrative system (Financial Times, 1998). The excessive domination of industry by government is regarded as a necessary evil and, in the past, has been accepted as a natural pre-condition to the nation's economic development. On the other hand, it now poses a serious barrier to further development at a time when more open and market-driven ideas predominate in international business.

As the 21st century approaches, by removing redundant traditions, the role of government and public authorities should be enhanced in terms of its quality of administration. Lodge (1987) suggested, for example, that tension mounts as business freedom to innovate and grow becomes increasingly essential to Korea's ability to develop still further. This suggestion sits alongside his assertion that the Korean society has been, and continues to be, dominated by authoritarian statists. These views are supported by Jun (1996) who suggests that the government should not directly control business activities and impose more regulations on the private sector, and that political and administrative institutions be transformed in order to remove constraints on individual growth as well as to further develop business activity, especially of privately managed companies. Again, Jun (1996) warns policy-makers and government bureaucrats that, to initiate an active and responsible society in the newly-emerged global environment, they should critically perceive the ever changing world and take actions to create challenging opportunities.

Another crucial factor influencing the structural reform of a country is its economic condition. Currently, Korea is in economic plight, the first important sign of which was the sharp depreciation of the nation's currency against the US dollar in late 1997. In attempting to deal with the sort of crisis that Korea has never experienced before, the winds of economic reform and restructuring are sweeping through all sectors of the domestic economy. Not surprisingly, public or state enterprises are emerging as the final bastion of vested interests; public corporations often called 'chaebols' (huge business conglomerates) without owners (Sohn, 1998a) have increasingly become the target of criticism for their loose and inefficient management. Present efforts toward economic reform will amount to nothing if the government or public authorities fail to restructure these public enterprises which contribute a large proportion of the nation's wealth (Economist, 1998).

Sohn (1998a) points out that the current crisis facing public sector companies can be attributed to two fundamental factors: inefficient management style and weakening competitiveness. Both factors derive from governmental intervention into their business activities and their monopolistic position. As far as fundamental reforms are concerned, the privatisation option is being actively and positively considered as a means of solving these problems (Chon, 1998).

Industry Characteristics

Characteristics specific to an industry can also dictate the measures that need to be taken to prepare for and implement a privatisation policy. In terms of the three types of port privatisation categorised by De Monie (1996), the Korean port industry can be described as a mixture of the first and third options: that is, a mixture of port management according to the landlord concept and a division of port activities based on the creation of mixed public and private enterprises where there is joint investment, management and operation of a port or a terminal. The overall approach to port privatisation pursued by the Korean government through its public port authority (i.e. the MMAF) can, therefore, be characterised as 'public ownership and private operation'; the MMAF retains all national ports and terminals under its ownership, while private companies operate them either under a concession or in a joint venture. This approach coincides closely with the classification of the PUBLIC/private port in which the operation function is the responsibility of the private sector while the regulatory and landowner functions are held by the public authority (Baird, 1995; 1997). This conceptualisation is further supported by the recent proclamation that the government will continue to strive to ease regulations which may adversely affect the free market system, combined with making every effort to strengthen environmental and safety regulations to ensure cleaner and safer seas (Sohn, 1998b).

As for the administrative structures of the container terminal sector in Korea is concerned, there exists an important feature worth focusing upon. On behalf of the MMAF as the public port authority, the KCTA has direct responsibility for the control and supervision of all container terminals in Korea. This hierarchical system can be seen as atypical since, in contrast to the vast majority of the world's other PUBLIC/private port ownership structures, the existence of KCTA adds another layer to the overall port administrative system. The initial objective for establishing the KCTA in 1990 was to diversify financial sources, thus enabling efficient and effective development and maintenance of the container terminal facilities. Almost a decade after its establishment, there is now increasing participation from private and foreign sectors, which already have a significant involvement in terminal development and operations. The main remaining function the KCTA may be required to undertake is the co-ordination of such involvement, a task that can easily be fulfilled by a mere department of the MMAF. The Port Construction Bureau under the supervision of the Assistant Minister for shipping and ports (see Appendix 1) is one possible department within the MMAF which may be capable of assuming this role.

Since a port can be considered as a facilitator of trade and, therefore, of great importance to the trade-oriented Korean economy, it is recommended that the overall principle of public ownership and private operation in the form of a modified landlord port (PUBLIC/private port) be maintained and reinforced.

Defining Approaches

Once the objectives and characteristics have been identified, the next step is to ascertain what approaches need to be undertaken to attain the defined objectives. Measures crucial to the success of the privatisation process should be established.

The empirical research carried out in the previous chapter consistently suggests that even within the context of the Korean business environment and compared to the UK container terminals, the private terminal company PECT performs most efficiently over the sample period. Logically, therefore, the most efficient policy for the most inefficient container terminal in the sample (i.e. the BCTOC, a Korean public entity) is for its administration and management structure to be transformed into one which is similar to that of PECT.

As pointed out by UNCTAD (1995) and Guislain (1997), a simultaneous and sustained effort on the part of the public authority to develop a consensus on the objectives of the privatisation process and attempts to explain the reasons for selecting specific approaches can be extremely beneficial in terms of establishing good public relations, especially with prospective port users (e.g. cargo and shipowning interests).

PROMOTING AND PROTECTING COMPETITION

A widespread view in economics is that competition forces economic entities to work harder. After analysing the effects of privatisation, a variety of literature (analysed in Chapters 4 and 5) reaches the same conclusion that a successful privatisation policy is relevant to the introduction, encouragement and protection of competition. Both the public and the private sectors must pursue the target of efficiency maximisation (i.e. cost minimisation and profit maximisation) so that they can maintain comparable prices and provide quality services. This objective can be best achieved through competition.[1] Goss (1995, pp. 16-

---

(1)   This is a rather controversial issue. Competition may be enhanced by privatisation, but it may also lead to a monopoly, in particular, a natural monopoly in the port industry due to geographical location and increasing returns to scale. If, however, characteristics of contestable markets theory (i.e. free entry and costless exit) are in place, then even natural monopolies are

17) warns that:

> "If they [governments] are to rely increasingly on the private sector then they will need to remember that it is competition which may make the private sector efficient; most of us have seen too many examples of private sector inefficiency caused by a lack of competition, as well as by obsolete rules and excessive bureaucracy."

The inexorability of the link between competition and efficiency was found in several works. For example, Hart (1983), Nalebuff and Stiglitz (1983), Horn *et al.* (1994), Graziano and Parigi (1998), all found that more competition increases economic efficiency. The definition of 'more competition', however, has to be clarified. Stigler (1987) defines competition as a rivalry between individuals (or groups or nations) which arises whenever two or more parties strive for something which all cannot obtain. Vickers (1995) adopts a general working definition with the identification of two components concerning 'more competition': more firms and markets closer to perfect competition. In other words, these components can be distinguished as follows: (i) an increase in the number of rivals, (ii) the greater freedom of rivals, such as the freedom to enter an industry following the removal of legal monopoly rights or barriers to business, and (iii) a move away from collusion towards more independent behaviour between rivals. All three perceptions are closely interlinked. For example, freedom of entry may result in a greater number of firms that may lead to a breakdown of collusion. Finally, Mookherjee (1984) asserts that competition may improve incentives for efficiency by allowing performance comparisons, which is referred to as 'competition-by-comparison'.

With this context in mind, the port authority MMAF has to establish and maintain some sort of intra-port competition, thus motivating all parties in port administration and operations to carry on their work more efficiently. Ultimately, this will contribute to the nation's further development.

---

forced to behave competitively by the threat of entry (Baumol, 1982; Shepherd, 1984). This view has recently been criticised on the grounds that even if there are very slight entry costs, incumbent firms may be able to exercise considerable monopoly power (Stiglitz, 1988; Martin, 1993).

RECOMMENDATIONS FOR KOREAN PORTS POLICY

The analysis and discussion up to this point leads to the following overall recommendation on the approaches and measures the Korean port authority should adopt:

- to sustain the principle of 'public ownership and private operation';
- to strengthen the monitoring function, especially a regular-based monitoring over all parties involved in port activities through 'competition-by-comparison';
- to continue to reduce regulation that inevitably unfavourably affects market-driven activities;
- to transform the administrative and management structure of BCTOC into one which is similar to that of PECT, UTC and other similar organisations;
- to abolish the KCTA and shift its responsibilities to a division of MMAF (e.g. the Bureau of Port Construction); and
- to engender good public relations, especially with port users.

CONTRIBUTION OF THE RESEARCH

The main motivation for the current research was the Korean government's comprehensive privatisation, liberalisation and deregulation programme as applied to the whole economy, but especially as applicable to the port industry. Subsequently, this initial motivation has been stimulated by the current increasing and urgent demand for the rationalisation of the nation's industry as it has entered a new era of financial crisis. The objectives for this research were to evaluate the critical features of port privatisation together with the economic theory relating to privatisation, to establish an analytical framework for efficiency measurement which is applicable to the port industry, and to deduce policy implications for the Korean government and public authority with reference to a privatisation strategy and its implementation to the nation's ports and terminals. This research makes an original contribution to knowledge in three respects:

- Korean port privatisation has, for the first time, been scientifically investigated on the basis of the economic theory of privatisation;

- The industry was analysed through the application of recently developed econometric and efficiency techniques based on the estimation of two stochastic frontier models (i.e. the cross-sectional and panel models); and
- The research undoubtedly provides the Korean government, its port authority and other interested parties with information and guidelines for implementing the policy of port privatisation.

RESEARCH LIMITATIONS AND FURTHER RESEARCH AREAS

It should be recognised that any research project has limitations of various kinds. The following limitations are recognised within the research contained herein.

First, a limitation associated with the nature of port privatisation may be considered. In the context of port privatisation, it is difficult to dichotomously define a specific port or terminal as either private or public sector. As mentioned in Chapter 5, 'port privatisation' can be defined as the actual transfer of property ownership from the public to the private sector, or the actual application of private capital to finance investment in port development and maintenance as well as port activities; 'port ownership' can be explained in terms of who provides the port facilities and services. These definitions may lead to confusion. Ultimately, however, a port or a terminal is likely to be either in public or in private sector ownership or in joint ownership by both (i.e. placed somewhere on a continuum of private sector participation between the two former extremes).

In addition, the main theme pursued by this research is 'privatisation' but the analysis and discussion has, to some extent, incorporated the rather different issues of deregulation and liberalisation. Controlling for the individual effects of these three interacting characteristics may allow greater fine tuning in policy assessment and/or formulation. These three concepts, however, have a feature in common; all are concerned with the introduction of more market-oriented forces; a policy that the Korean government and public authorities should contemplate as a solution for dealing with the nation's current difficulties.

Second, it should be acknowledged that the small sample size for data collection within this research does inevitably undermine the comprehensiveness of the results achieved. Since the process of port privatisation in Korea is in its very early stages, the available data from the private sector, such as PECT and UCT, was extremely limited. With more data, the greater cross-sectional variation in the combinations of the variables extracted from both the Korean and UK sides, with their great diversity in geography and political economy, may permit the isolation of differences in their static effects. On the other hand, time-series variation in the sample may facilitate the assessment of the dynamic impacts of changes in policy. In addition, as the data collected are related only to container port operations, a generalisation of the research implications may also be confined. This restriction could be alleviated on the grounds that the container trade accounts for a major proportion (in value terms) of current international trade.

Third, in the case of the panel model, the efficiency level of each terminal operator is estimated as 'time-invariant' over the sample period. As mentioned in Chapter 6, time-invariant efficiency is not an attractive assumption. Given the lack of available techniques fully capable of overcoming the implausibility of this assumption for empirical application, however, the results based on the time-invariant terminal operator level efficiency still provide a useful insight for those interested in port administration and management.

Fourth, another limitation of the methodology with respect to two sources of inefficiency may be identified. This research was concerned with productive (in)efficiency only. The production process of a container terminal operator (e.g. the cargo handling process) may exhibit productive inefficiency, allocative inefficiency or both simultaneously. As discussed in Chapter 6, allocative inefficiency exists when the marginal rate of technical substitution between any two of its inputs is not equal to the ratio of corresponding input prices. Reasons for allocative inefficiency may include regulatory constraints and incremental adjustment to price changes, which have lots of policy implications, none of which are addressed within the boundaries set for this study.

Finally, a number of research areas for further investigation can be identified in light of these research limitations. First, in order to validate and generalise the research results, more and wider data should be collected from ports and terminals in terms of types of cargo handled. This would also strengthen the justification for the use of the asymptotic MLE. Second, a more sophisticated but empirically applicable model should be investigated so that it can embrace the 'time-varying' efficiency. Third, for more precise policy and strategy development a model which is able to assess allocative efficiency should be developed. Finally, the application of alternative efficiency models to the existing data set will reveal the robustness of the various alternative methodologies. Certainly, within this study, it has been shown that within the family of stochastic frontier models, estimates of relative container terminal efficiency have proved remarkably consistent. It would be interesting to determine if this were also so for other families of models such as deterministic frontier models or those based on quadratic programming such as Data Envelopment Analysis (DEA).

REFERENCES

Antal-Mokos, Z. (1998), *Privatisation, Politics and Economic Performance in Hungary*, Cambridge University Press, Cambridge.

Baird, A. (1995), UK Port Privatisation: In Context, *Proceedings of UK Port Privatisation Conference*, Scottish Transport Studies Group, 21 September, Edinburgh.

Baird, A. (1997), Port Privatisation: An Analytical Framework, *Proceedings of International Association of Maritime Economist Conference*, 22-24 September, City University, London.

Baumol, W. (1982), Contestable Markets: An Uprising in the Theory of Industry Structure, *American Economic Review*, Vol. 72, No. 1, pp. 1-15.

Bishop, M. and Thompson, D. (1992), Regulatory Reform and Productivity Growth in the UK's Public Utilities, *Applied Economics*, Vol. 24, No. 11, pp. 1181-1190.

Chon, S.Y. (1998), Government Meeting Unveils Economic Reform Programmes, *Korea Herald*, 11 March.

De Monie, G. (1996), Privatisation of Port Structures, in Bekemans, L. and Beckwith, S. (eds.), *Ports for Europe: Europe's Maritime Future in a Changing Environment*, European Interuniversity Press, Brussels, pp. 267-298.

Economist (1998), A Survey of East Asian Economies: Frozen Miracle, 7 March.

Financial Times (1998), Special Report on Asia in Crisis: The Country that Invested Its Way into Trouble, 15 January.

Goss, R. (1990), Economic Policies and Seaports: 2. The Diversity of Port Policies, *Maritime Policy and Management*, Vol. 17, No. 3, pp. 221-234.

Goss, R. (1995), The New Role of Port Authorities, *Proceedings of UK Port Privatisation Conference*, Scottish Transport Studies Group, 21 September, Edinburgh.

Graziano, C. and Parigi, B. (1998), Do Managers Work Harder in Competitive Industries?, *Journal of Economic Behaviour and Organisation*, Vol. 34, pp. 489-498.

Guislain, P. (1997), *The Privatisation Challenge: A Strategic, Legal and Institutional Analysis of International Experience*, World Bank, Washington, D.C.

Hart, O. (1983), The Market Mechanism as An Incentive Scheme, *Bell Journal of Economics*, Vol. 14, pp. 366-383.

Horn, H., Lang, H. and Lundgren, S. (1994), Competition, Long Run Contracts and Internal Inefficiencies in Firms, *European Economic Review*, Vol. 38, pp. 213-233.

Jun, J.S. (1996), The Political and Administrative Challenges in Korea's Future: Thinking Globally, Acting Locally, Perceiving Critically, in Ro, C.-H. (ed.), *Korea in the Era of Post-Development and Globalisation: the Tasks of Public Administration*, Korea Institute of Public Administration, KIPA Publication Series II, Seoul, pp. 67-100.

Lodge, G. (1987), Introduction: Ideology and Country Analysis, in Lodge, G. and Vogel, E. (eds.), *Ideology and National Competitiveness: An Analysis of Nine Countries*, Harvard Business School Press, Boston.

Martin, S. (1993), *Advanced Industrial Economics*, Blackwell Publishers, Oxford.

Mookherjee, D. (1984), Optimal Incentive Schemes with Many Agents, *Review of Economic Studies*, Vol. 51, pp. 433-446.

Nalebuff, B. and Stiglitz, J. (1983), Information, Competition and Markets, *American Economic Review*, Vol. 73, pp. 278-283.

Park, C.H. (1970), *Our Nation's Path*, Hollym Corporation, Seoul.

Shepherd, W. (1984), "Contestability" vs. Competition, *American Economic Review*, Vol. 74, No. 4, pp. 572-587.

Sohn, T.S. (1998a), Restructuring Wave Reaching State Enterprises to Enhance Efficiency, *Korea Herald*, 14 March.

Sohn, T.S. (1998b), Korea to Emerge as Marine Superpower in the 21st Century: the Ministry of Maritime Affairs and Fishers Celebrates the 3rd Ocean's Day, 1998 International Year of Ocean, *Korea Herald*, 1 June.

Stigler, G. (1987), Competition, in Eatwell, J., Milgate, M. and Newman, P. (eds.), *The New Palgrave*, Macmillan, London.

Stiglitz, J. (1988), *Economics of the Public Sector* (2nd ed.), W.W.Norton & Company, New York.

Thomas, B. (1994), The Need for Organisational Change in Seaports, *Marine Policy*, Vol. 18, No. 1, pp. 69-78.

UNCTAD (1995), *Comparative Experience with Privatisation: Policy Insights and Lessons Learned*, UNCTAD/DTCI/23, New York.

Vickers, J. and Yarrow, G. (1988), *Privatisation: An Economic Analysis*, MIT Press, Cambridge, Massachusetts.

Vickers, J. and Yarrow, G. (1991), Economic Perspectives on Privatisation, *Journal of Economic Perspective*, Vol. 5, No. 2, pp. 111-132.

Vickers, J. (1995), Concepts of Competition, *Oxford Economic Papers*, Vol. 47, No. 1, pp. 1-23.

Bibliography

Abbott, P. (1995), Privatisation: Enhancing Efficiency of Ports of Latin America, *World Wide Shipping*, Vol. 58, No. 4, pp. 14-16.

Adams, G. (1973), *Organisation of the British Port Transport Industry*, National Ports Council, London.

Afriat, S. (1972), Efficiency Estimation of Production Function, *International Economic Review*, Vol. 13, No. 3, pp. 568-598.

Agerschou, H., Lundgren, H. and Sorensen, T. (1983), *Planning and Design of Ports and Marine Terminals*, John Wiley and Sons, Chichester.

Aigner, D. and Chu, S. (1968), On Estimating the Industry Production Function, *American Economic Review*, Vol. 58, No. 4, pp. 826-839.

Aigner, D., Lovell, C. and Schmidt, P. (1977), Formulation and Estimation of Stochastic Frontier Production Function Models, *Journal of Econometrics*, Vol. 6, No. 1, pp. 21-37.

Aigner, D. and Schmidt, P. (1980), Editors' Introduction, *Journal of Econometrics*, Vol. 13, Supplement to the Journal of Econometrics: Specification and Estimation of Frontier Production, Profit and Cost Functions, pp. 1-3.

Alchian, A. (1965), Some Economics of Property Rights, *Il Politico*, Vol. 30, No. 4, pp. 816-829.

Alchian, A. and Demsetz, H. (1972), Production, Information Costs and Economic Organisation, *American Economic Review*, Vol. 62, pp. 777-795.

Amsden, A. (1989), *Asia's Next Giant: South Korea and Late Industrialisation*, Oxford University Press, New York.

Antal-Mokos, Z. (1998), *Privatisation, Politics and Economic Performance in Hungary*, Cambridge University Press, Cambridge.

Aoki, M., Murdock, K. and Okuno-Fujiwara, M. (1996), Beyond the East Asian Market: Introducing the Market-Enhancing View. In Aoki, M., Kim, H.K. and Okuno-Fujiwara, M. (eds.), *The Role of Government in East Asian Economic Development: Comparative Institutional Analysis*, Clarendon Press, Oxford, pp. 1-37.

Aquarone, M.C. (1988), French Marine Policy in the 1970s and 1980s, *Ocean Development and International Law*, Vol. 19, pp. 267-285.

Arrow, K. (1971), Political and Economic Evaluation of Social Effects and Externalities. In Intriligator, M. (ed.), *Frontier of Quantitative Economics*, North-Holland, Amsterdam.

Baird, A. (1995), Privatisation of Trust Ports in the United Kingdom: Review and Analysis of the First Sales, *Transport Policy*, Vol. 2, No. 2, pp. 135-143.

Baird, A. (1995), UK Port Privatisation: In Context, *Proceedings of UK Port Privatisation Conference*, Scottish Transport Studies Group, 21 September, Edinburgh.

Baird, A. (1996), Containerisation and the Decline of the Upstream Urban Port in Europe, *Maritime Policy and Management*, Vol. 23, No. 2, pp. 145-156.

Baird, A. (1997), Port Privatisation: An Analytical Framework, *Proceedings of International Association of Maritime Economist Conference*, 22-24 September, City University, London.

Baker, G. (1998), US Looks to G7 Backing on Asian Crisis, *Financial Times*, 20 February.

Baltagi, B. (1995), *Econometric Analysis of Panel Data*, John Wiley & Sons Ltd., Chichester.

Bang, H.S. (1984), *Factors Affecting Container Terminal Development: A Critique of the Approach Applied in Korean Port*, PhD Thesis, UWIST.

Bank of Korea (several years), *Economic Statistics Yearbook*, Seoul.

Barrow, M. and Wagstaff, A. (1989), Efficiency Measurement in the Public Sector: An Appraisal, *Fiscal Studies*, Vol. 10, No. 1, pp. 72-97.

Barzel, Y. (1989), *Economics Analysis of Property Rights*, Cambridge University Press, New York.

Bassett, K. (1993), British Port Privatisation and Its Impact on the Port of Bristol, *Journal of Transport Geography*, Vol. 1, No. 4, pp. 255-267.

Battese, G. and Coelli, T. (1988), Prediction of Firm-Level Technical Efficiencies with a Generalised Frontier Production Function and Panel Data, *Journal of Econometrics*, Vol. 38, pp. 387-399.

Battese, G., Coelli, T. and Colby, T. (1989), Estimation of Frontier Production Functions and the Efficiencies of Indian Farms using Panel Data from Icrisat's Village Level Studies, *Journal of Quantitative Economics*, Vol. 5, No. 2, pp. 327-348.

Baudelaire, J. (1997), Some Thoughts about Port Privatisation. In *Essays in Honour and in Memory of Late Professor Emeritus of Maritime Economics Dr Basil Metaxas*, Piraeus, Greece, pp. 255-260.

Bauer, P. (1990), Recent Developments in the Econometric Estimation of Frontiers, *Journal of Econometrics*, Vol. 46, pp. 39-56.

Baumol, W. (1982), Contestable Markets: An Uprising in the Theory of Industry Structure, *American Economic Review*, Vol. 72, No. 1, pp. 1-15.

Baumol, W., Panzar, J. and Willig, R. (1982), *Contestable Markets and the Theory of Industrial Structure*, Harcourt Brace Jovanovich, San Diego.

Beesley, M. and Littlechild, S. (1988), Privatisation: Principles, Problems and Priorities. In Johnson, C. (ed.), *Lloyds Bank Annual Review: Privatisation and Ownership*, Printer Publisher Ltd., London, pp. 1-29.

Begg, D., Fisher, S. and Dornbusch, R. (1991), *Economics* (3rd ed.), McGraw-Hill International UK Ltd., London.

Bendall, H. and Stent, A. (1987), On Measuring Cargo Handling Productivity, *Maritime Policy and Management*, Vol. 14, No. 4, pp. 337-343.

Bernard, J. (1991), *European Deep-Sea Container Terminals: Locational and Operational Perspectives*, PhD Thesis, University of Liverpool.

Beth, H. (1985), Economic Effects of Port Congestion. In Beth, H. (ed.), *Port Management Textbook: Containerisation*, Institute of Shipping Economic and Logistics, Bremen.

Bishop, M. and Kay, J. (1988), *Does Privatisation Work?: Lessons from the UK*, London Business School, London.

Bishop, M. and Kay, J. (1989), Privatisation in the United Kingdom: Lessons for Experience, *World Development*, Vol. 17, No. 5, pp. 643-657.

Bishop, M. and Thompson, D. (1992), Regulatory Reform and Productivity Growth in the UK's Public Utilities, *Applied Economics*, Vol. 24, No. 11, pp. 1181-1190.

Blackstone, L. and Franks, D. (1986), *Guide to Management Buy-outs*, Economist Publications Ltd., London.

Blundell, R. (1996), Microeconometrics. In Greenaway, D., Bleaney, M. and Stewart, I. (eds.), *A Guide to Modern Economics*, Routledge, London, pp. 508-536.

Boardman, A. and Vining, A. (1989), Ownership and Performance in Competitive Environments: A Comparison of the Performance of Private, Mixed and State-Owned Enterprises, *Journal of Law and Economics*, Vol. 32, pp. 1-33.

Borooah, V. (1996), Widening Public Choice. In Pardo, J. and Schneider, F. (eds.), *Current Issues in Public Choice*, Edward Elgar, Cheltenham, pp. 43-50.

Braeutigam, R., Daughety, A. and Turnquist, M. (1984), A Firm Specific Analysis of Economies of Density in the US Railroad Industry, *Journal of Industrial Economics*, Vol. 33, pp. 3-20.

Brittan, S. (1984), The Politics and Economics of Privatisation, *Political Quarterly*, Vol. 55, pp. 109-128.

Brown, C. and Jackson, P. (1990), *Public Sector Economics* (4th ed.), Basil Blackwell Ltd., Oxford.

Buchanan, J. (1980), Rent Seeking and Profit Seeking. In Buchanan, J. and Tollison, D. and Tullock, G. (eds.), *Toward a Theory of the Rent-Seeking Society*, A&M Press, Texas, pp. 3-15.

Burton, J. (1997), Asian Financial Markets: South Korea - A Puddle to Fight a Big Fire, *Financial Times*, 9 May, p. 8.

Canna, E. (1995), Japanese Cargo Shifts to Korea, *American Shipper*, Vol. 37, No. 10, p. 34.

Cargo Systems (1996), *Top 100 Container Ports*, March, Supplement.

Cass, S. (1996), *Port Privatisation: Process, Players and Progress*, Cargo Systems Report, London.

Chang, S. (1978), Production Function, Productivities, and Capacity Utilisation of the Port of Mobile, *Maritime Policy and Management*, Vol. 5, pp. 297-305.

Charnes, A., Cooper, W. and Rhodes, E. (1978), Measuring the Efficiency of Decision-Making Units, *European Journal of Operational Research*, Vol. 2, No. 6, pp. 429-444.

Chen, M. (1995), *Asian Management Systems: Chinese, Japanese and Korean Styles of Business*, Routlege, London.

Chenery, H. and Syrquin, M. (1986), The Semi-Industrial Countries. In Chenery, H., Robinson, S. and Syrquin, M. (eds.), *Industrialisation and Growth: A Comparative Study*, Oxford University Press, London, pp. 84-118.

Chon, S.Y. (1998), Government Meeting Unveils Economic Reform Programmes, *Korea Herald*, 11 March.

Christensen, L., Jorgenson, D. and Lau, L. (1973), Transcendental Logarithmic Production Frontiers, *Review of Economics and Statistics*, Vol. 55, pp. 28-45.

Chung, B.M. (1995), Estimation of Congestion Costs in Container Traffic in Pusan Port, *Korea Maritime Review*, Vol. 129, pp. 7-17.

Chung, J.S. (1996), Korean Economy. In *The Far East and Australasia 1996*, Europa Publications Ltd., London.

Clementi, D. (1985), The Experience of the United Kingdom. In Asian Development Bank, *Privatisation*, pp. 167-182.

Cobb, C. and Douglas, P. (1928), A Theory of Production, *American Economic Review*, Vol. 23, pp. 139-165.

Collins, S. (1990), Lessons for Development from the Experience in Asia: Lessons from Korean Economic Growth, *American Economic Review*, Vol. 80, No. 2, pp. 104-107.

Comptroller and Auditor General (1993), *Department of Transport: The First Sales of Trust Ports*, National Audit Office, HMSO, London.

Containerisation International (1996), Congestion: the Carrier's Three-Pronged Defence, April, pp. 56-59.

Containerisation International (1997), Post-Panamax Passion, February, pp. 44-46.

Containerisation International Yearbook (several years), Emap Business Communications, Ltd., London.

Cornwell, C., Schmidt, P. and Sickles, R. (1990), Production Frontiers with Cross-Sectional and Time-Series Variation in Efficiency Levels, *Journal of Econometrics*, Vol. 46, pp. 185-200.

Cullinane, K. and Khanna, M. (1997), Large Containerships and the Concentration of Load Centres, *Proceedings of Port Strategy and Development II*, 23-25 February, Port Training Institute, Egypt.

Cullis, J. and Jones, P. (1989), *Microeconomics and the Public Economy: A Defence of Leviathan*, Basil Blackwell, Oxford.

De Alessi, L. (1980), The Economics of Property Rights: A Review of the Evidence, *Research in Law and Economics*, Vol. 2, pp. 1-47.

Debreu, G. (1951), The Coefficient of Resource Utilisation, *Review of Economic Studies*, Vol. 9, pp. 300-312.

De Monie, G. (1987), *Measuring and Evaluating Port Performance and Productivity*, UNCTAD Monograph No. 6 on Port Management, Geneva.

De Monie, G. (1994), The Combined Effects of Competition and Privatisation on Ports, *Proceedings of the Future Role of Ports in the G.C.C.*, 3-5 December, Kuwait Ports Authority.

De Monie, G. (1995), Restructuring the Indian Ports System, *Maritime Policy and Management*, Vol. 22, No. 3, pp. 255-260.

De Monie, G. (1996), Privatisation of Port Structures. In Bekemans, L. and Beckwith, S. (eds.), *Ports for Europe: Europe's Maritime Future in a Changing Environment*, European Interuniversity Press, Brussels, pp. 267-298.

De Neufville, R. and Tsunokawa, K. (1981), Productivity and Returns to Scale of Container Ports, *Maritime Policy and Management*, Vol. 8, No. 2, pp. 121-129.

De Salvo, J. (1994), Measuring the Direct Impacts of a Port, *Transportation Journal*, Vol. 30, No. 4, pp. 33-42.

Devine, P., Lee, N. and Jones, R. (1985), *An Introduction to Industrial Economics* (4th ed.), George Allen and Unwin, London.

Douglas, R. and Geen, G. (1993), *The Law of Harbours and Pilotage* (4th ed.), Lloyd's of London Press, London.

Dowd, T. and Leschine, T. (1990), Container Terminal Productivity: A Perspective, *Maritime Policy and Management*, Vol. 17, No. 2, pp. 107-112.

Drewry Shipping Consultants (1996), *Global Container Markets: Prospects and Profitability in a High Growth Era*, Drewry Shipping Consultants, London.

Dunkerley, J. and Hare, P. (1991), Nationalised Industries. In Crafts, N. and Woodward, N. (eds.), *The British Economy Since 1945*, Clarendon Press, Oxford.

Dunleavy, P. (1986), Explaining the Privatisation Boom: Public Choice versus Radical Approaches, *Public Administration*, Vol. 64, No. 1, pp. 13-34.

Dunsire, A., Hartley, K., Parker, D. and Dimitriou, B. (1988), Organisational Status and Performance: A Conceptual Framework for Testing Public Choice Theories, *Public Administration*, Vol. 66, No. 4, pp. 363-388.

Economic Planning Board (1988), *White Paper on Public Enterprises*, EPB, Seoul.

Economist (1998), A Survey of East Asian Economies: Frozen Miracle, 7 March.

Economist Intelligence Unit (1996), *Country Profile: South Korea and North Korea 1995-96*, EIU, London.

Engle, R. (1984), Wald, Likelihood Ratio and Lagrange Multiplier Tests in Econometrics. In Griliches, Z. and Intriligator, M. (eds.), *Handbook of Econometrics*, Volume II, Elsevier Science Publishers, Amsterdam, pp. 775-826.

Evans, A. (1969), *Technical and Social Changes in the World's Ports*, International Labour Office, Geneva.

Everett, S. and Robinson, R. (1998), Port Reform in Austria: Issues in the Ownership Debate, *Maritime Policy and Management*, Vol. 25, No. 1, pp. 41-62.

Eyre, J. (1990), Maritime Privatisation, *Maritime Policy and Management*, Vol. 17, No. 2, pp. 113-121.

Fairplay (1993), World Ports: Free to Grow, 25 March, p. 16.

Fairplay (1995), Pusan Takes Action to Relieve Pressure, 10 August, p. 25.

Fairplay (1996), A New Deal for Ports: Multi-national Operators Show Their Hand, 13 June, pp. 12-14.

Fairplay (1996), Port Policies Open Up, 8 August, p. 30.

Fare, R., Grosskopf, S. and Logan, J. (1985), The Relative Performance of Publicly Owned and Privately Owned Electric Utilities, *Journal of Public Economics*, Vol. 26, pp. 89-106.

Fare, R., Grosskopf, S. and Lovell, C. (1994), *Production Frontiers*, Cambridge University Press, Cambridge.

Farrell, M. (1957), The Measurement of Productive Efficiency, *Journal of the Royal Statistical Society*, Vol. 120, No. 3, pp. 253-290.

Faust, P. (1978), The Role of Ports in Economic Development. In Beth, H. L. (ed.), *Port Management Textbook*, Institute of Shipping Economics, Bremen, pp. 15-24.

Ferrantino, M. and Ferrier, G. (1995), The Technical Efficiency of Vacuum-Pan Sugar Industry of India: An Application of a Stochastic Frontier Production Function Using Panel Data, *European Journal of Operational Research*, Vol. 80, pp. 639-653.

Financial Times (1986), Best-seller with a Choice of Ending, 10th December.

Financial Times (1995), South Korea: Trade, Industry and Finance, 20 October.

Financial Times (1996), Kim calls for Accelerated State Sector Reform and Privatisation, 18 June.

Financial Times (1998), Special Report: Asia in Crisis, 13-16 January.

Financial Times (1998), Special Report on Asia in Crisis: The Country that Invested Its Way into Trouble, 15 January.

Fleming, D. (1997), World Container Port Rankings, *Maritime Policy and Management*, Vol. 24, No. 2, pp. 175-181.

Flere, W. (1967), *Port Economics* (2nd ed.), Foxlow Publications, London.

Fletcher, R. (1980), *Practical Methods of Optimisation*, John Wiley and Sons, New York.

Forsund, F., Lovell, C. and Schmidt, P. (1980), A Survey of Frontier Production Functions and of their Relationship to Efficiency Measurement, *Journal of Econometrics*, Vol. 13, pp. 5-25.

Fossey, J. (1997), Regional Focus - South Korea: Boxes Galore, *Containerisation International*, January, p. 71.

Frankel, E. (1987), *Port Planning and Development*, John Wiley and Sons, New York.

Frankel, E. (1992), Debt-Equity Conversion and Port Privatisation, *Maritime Policy and Management*, Vol. 19, No. 3, pp. 201-209.

Gilman, S. (1983), *The Competitive Dynamics of Container Shipping*, Gower Publishing Company, Aldershot.

Gong, B. H. and Sickles, R. (1992), Finite Sample Evidence on the Performance of Stochastic Frontiers and Data Envelopment Analysis using Panel Data, *Journal of Econometrics*, Vol. 51, pp. 259-284.

Goss, R. (1979), The Economic Efficiency of Seaports, *Proceedings of Ports: Policy and Practice*, 22-23 May, Nautical Institute, Cardiff.

Goss, R. (1981), Editorial: The Public and Private Sectors in Ports, *Maritime Policy and Management*, Vol. 8, No. 2, pp. 69-71.

Goss, R. (1986), Seaports Should Not Be Subsidised, *Maritime Policy and Management*, Vol. 13, No. 2, pp. 83-104.

Goss, R. (1990), Economic Policies and Seaports: 1. The Economic Functions of Seaports, *Maritime Policy and Management*, Vol. 17, No. 3, pp. 207-219.

Goss, R. (1990), Economic Policies and Seaports 2: The Diversity of Port Policies, *Maritime Policy and Management*, Vol. 17, No. 3, pp. 221-234.

Goss, R. (1990), Economic Policies and Seaports: 3. Are Port Authorities Necessary?, *Maritime Policy and Management*, Vol. 17, No. 4, pp. 257-271.

Goss, R. (1995), The New Role of Port Authorities, *Proceedings of UK Port Privatisation Conference*, Scottish Transport Studies Group, 21 September, Edinburgh.

Goss, R. (1998), British Ports Policies Since 1945, *Journal of Transport Economics and Policy*, Vol. 32, No. 1, pp. 51-71.

Graziano, C. and Parigi, B. (1998), Do Managers Work Harder in Competitive Industries?, *Journal of Economic Behaviour and Organisation*, Vol. 34, pp. 489-498.

Greene. W. (1980), Maximum Likelihood Estimation of Econometric Frontier Functions, *Journal of Econometrics*, Vol. 13, pp. 27-56.

Greene, W. (1993), The Econometric Approach to Efficiency Analysis. In Fried, H., Lovell, C. and Schmidt, S. (eds.), *The Measurement of Productive Efficiency: Techniques and Applications*, Oxford University Press, New York, pp. 68-119.

Greene, W. (1995), *LIMDEP (Version 7.0) User's Manual*, Econometric Software Inc., Castle Hill, Australia.

Greene, W. (1997), *Econometric Analysis* (3rd ed.), Prentice-Hall International Inc., New Jersey.

Guislain, P. (1997), *The Privatisation Challenge: A Strategic, Legal and Institutional Analysis of International Experience*, World Bank, Washington, D.C.

Haarymeyer, D. and Yorke, P. (1993), *Port Privatisation: An International Perspective*, Reason Foundation, Los Angeles.

Hanink, D. (1994), *The International Economy: A Geographical Perspective*, John Wiley and Sons, New York.

Haralambides, H. and Veenstra, A. (1996), Ports as Trade Facilitators in the Export-led Growth Strategies of Developing Countries. In Valleri, M. (ed.), *L'industria Portuale Per Uno Sviluppo Sostenibile Dei Porti*, Cacucci Editore, Bari.

Hart, O. (1983), The Market Mechanism as An Incentive Scheme, *Bell Journal of Economics*, Vol. 14, pp. 366-383.

Hartley, K. and Parker, D. (1991), Privatisation: A Conceptual Framework. In Ott, A. and Hartley, K. (eds.), *Privatisation and Economic Efficiency: A Comparative Analysis of Developed and Developing Countries*, Edward Elgar Publishing Ltd., Aldershot, pp. 11-25.

Hartley, K., Parker, D. and Martin, S. (1991), Organisational Status, Ownership and Productivity, *Fiscal Studies*, Vol. 12, No. 2, pp. 46-60.

Hausman, J. and Taylor, W. (1981), Panel Data and Unobserved Individual Effects, *Econometrica*, Vol. 49, pp. 1377-1398.

Haynes, K., Hsing, Y. and Stough, R. (1997), Regional Port Dynamics in the Global Economy: The Case of Kaohsiung, Taiwan, *Maritime Policy and Management*, Vol. 24, No. 1, pp. 93-113.

Heald, D. (1982), Privatising Public Enterprises: An Analysis of the Government's Case, *Political Quarterly*, Vol. 53, pp. 333-340.

Heald, D. (1984), Privatisation: Analysing its Appeal and Limitations, *Fiscal Studies*, Vol. 5, No. 1, pp. 36-46.

Heathfield, D. and Wibe, S. (1987), *An Introduction to Cost and Production Functions*, Macmillan, London.

Heaver, T. (1995), The Implications of Increased Competition among Ports for Port Policy and Management, *Maritime Policy and Management*, Vol. 22, No. 2, pp. 125-133.

Heggie, I. (1974), Charging for Port Facilities, *Journal of Transport Economics and Policy*, Vol. 8, No. 1, pp. 3-25.

Hershman, M. (1988), Harbour Management: A New Role of the Public Port. In Hershman, M. (ed.), *Urban Ports and Harbour Management: Responding to Change along US Waterfronts*, Taylor and Francis, New York, pp. 3-25.

HMSO (1974), *British Industry Today - Ports*, HMSO, London.

HMSO (1991), *Ports Act 1991*, HMSO, London.

Hong, S.Y. (1995), Marine Policy in the Republic of Korea, *Marine Policy*, Vol. 19, No. 2, pp. 97-113.

Horn, H., Lang, H. and Lundgren, S. (1994), Competition, Long Run Contracts and Internal Inefficiencies in Firms, *European Economic Review*, Vol. 38, pp. 213-233.

Hoyle, B. (1983), *Seaport and Development: The Experience of Kenya and Tanzania*, Gordon and Breach, London.

Hutchinson, G. (1991), Efficiency Gains through Privatisation of UK Industries. In Ott, A. and Hartley, K. (eds.), *Privatisation and Economic Efficiency: A Comparative Analysis of Developed and Developing Countries*, Edward Elgar Publishing Ltd., Aldershot, pp. 87-107.

Iheduru, O. (1993), Rethinking Maritime Privatisation in Africa, *Maritime Policy and Management*, Vol. 20, No. 1, pp. 31-49.

Imakita, J. (1978), *A Techno-Economic Analysis of the Port Transport System*, Saxon House Teakfield Limited, Westmead.

International Monetary Fund (1989), *International Financial Statistics Yearbook*, IMF, Washington, D.C.

International Monetary Fund (1996), *International Financial Statistics Yearbook*, IMF, Washington, D.C.

Intriligator, M., Bodkin, R. and Hsiao, C. (1996), *Econometric Models, Techniques and Applications* (2nd ed.), Prentice-Hall International Inc., New Jersey.

Jackson, P. and Price, C. (1994), Privatisation and Regulation: A Review of the Issues. In Jackson, P. and Price, C. (eds.), *Privatisation and Regulation: A Review of the Issues*, Longman Group Ltd., Essex, pp. 1-34.

Jansson, J. and Shneerson, D. (1982), *Port Economics*, MIT Press, Cambridge, Massachusetts.

Jasinski, P. and Yarrow, G. (1996), Privatisation: An Overview of the Issues. In Yarrow, G. and Jasinski, P. (eds.), *Privatisation: Critical Perspectives on the World Economy*, Routledge, London, pp. 1-46.

Jensen, M. and Meckling, W. (1976), Theory of the Firm: Managerial Behaviour, Agency Costs and Ownership Structure, *Journal of Financial Economics*, Vol. 3, pp. 305-360.

John, M. (1995), Port Productivity: A User's View, *Proceedings of UK Port Privatisation Conference*, Scottish Transport Studies Group, 21 September, Edinburgh.

Jondrow, J., Lovell, C., Materov, I. and Schmidt, P. (1982), On the Estimation of Technical Inefficiency in the Stochastic Frontier Production Model, *Journal of Econometrics*, Vol. 19, pp. 233-238.

Jones, L. (1975), *Public Enterprise and Economic Development: The Korean Case*, Korea Development Institute, Seoul.

Juhel, M. (1998), Global Challenges for Ports and Terminals in the New Era, *Proceeding of SingaPort '98*, 24-27 March, Singapore.

Jun, J.S. (1996), The Political and Administrative Challenges in Korea's Future: Thinking Globally, Acting Locally, Perceiving Critically. In Ro, C.H. (ed.), *Korea in the Era of Post-Development and Globalisation: the Tasks of Public Administration*, Korea Institute of Public Administration, KIPA Publication Series II, Seoul, pp. 67-100.

Kalirajan, K. (1990), On Measuring Economic Efficiency, *Journal of Applied Econometrics*, Vol. 5, pp. 75-85.

Kang, S.I. (1988), *A Study on Privatisation of Public Enterprises*, Korea Development Institute, Seoul.

Kay, J. and Tompson, D. (1986), Privatisation: A Policy in Search of a Rationale, *Economic Journal*, Vol. 96, pp. 18-32.

Kim, M. and Sachish, A. (1986), The Structure of Production, Technical Change and Productivity in a Port, *Journal of Industrial Economics*, Vol. 35, No. 2, pp. 209-223.

Kleinbaum, D., Kupper, L. and Muller, K. (1988), *Applied Regression Analysis and Other Multivariable Methods* (2nd ed.), PWS-Kent Publishing Co., Boston.

Koo, B.H. (1991), The Korean Economy: Structural Adjustment for Future Growth. In Lee, C.-S. (ed.), *Korea Briefing, 1990*, Westview Press, Oxford.

Korea Chamber of Commerce and Industry (1995), *Privatisation of Public Enterprises and Changing Role of Public and Private*, KCCI Working Paper No. 264, Seoul.

Korea Container Terminal Authority (1993), *Public Notice on the Scheme for Financing from Private Sector for the Development of Container Terminals*, KCTA, Pusan.

Korea Container Terminal Authority (1996), *Report on Operations*, KCTA Internal Document, KCTA, Pusan.

Korea Maritime and Port Administration (1979), *Introduction to Functions of Korea Maritime and Port Administration*, KMPA, Seoul.

Korea Maritime and Port Administration (1989), *Report on Basic Plan for Development of Pusan Port* (Vol. 3), KMPA, Seoul.

Korea Maritime and Port Administration (1992), *Report on the 3rd Phase Container Terminal Development in Pusan*, KMPA, Seoul.

Korea Maritime and Port Administration (1992), *The Calculation of Optimum Port Capacity and Basic Development Plan*, KMPA, Seoul.

Korea Maritime and Port Administration (1993), *Statistical Yearbook of Shipping and Ports*, KMPA, Seoul.

Korea Maritime and Port Administration (1996), *Statistical Yearbook of Shipping and Ports*, KMPA, Seoul.

Korea Maritime Institute (1996), *A Study on Privatisation Schemes of the BCTOC* (The Interim Report), KMI, Seoul.

Korea Maritime Institute (1996), *A Study on Privatisation Schemes of the BCTOC* (The Final Report), KMI, Seoul.

Korean National Statistical Office (1996), *Major Statistics of Korean Economy*, Seoul.

Korean Overseas Information Service (1993), *A Handbook of Korea* (9th ed.), Hollym Co., Seoul.

Krause, L. (1981), Summary of the Eleventh Pacific Trade and Development Conference on Trade and Growth of the Advanced Developing Countries. In Hong, W. and Krause, L. (eds.), *Trade and Growth of the Advanced Developing Countries in the Pacific Basin*, Korea Development Institute, Seoul.

Krieger, I. (1990), *Management Buy-Outs*, Butterworths, London.

Kumbhakar, S. (1990), Production Frontiers, Panel Data, and Time-Varying Technical Inefficiency, *Journal of Econometrics*, Vol. 46, pp. 201-211.

Kumbhakar, S. and Hjalmarsson, L. (1993), Technical Efficiency and Technical Progress in Swedish Dairy Farms. In Fried, H., Lovell, C. and Schmidt, S. (eds.), *The Measurement of Productive Efficiency: Techniques and Applications*, Oxford University Press, New York, pp. 256-270.

Kuznets, P. (1988), An East Asian Model of Economic Development: Japan, Taiwan, and South Korea, *Economic Development and Cultural Change*, Supplement Vol. 36, pp. s11-s44.

Lee, T.W. (1998), Keeping the Maritime Sector Afloat, *Lloyd's List*, 6 January.

Lee, T.W. (1998), Korea: Chaebol Dilemmas, *Lloyd's Shipping Economist*, April, pp. 10-12.

Leibenstein, H. (1966), Allocative Efficiency vs. X-inefficiency, *American Economic Review*, Vol. 56, pp. 392-415.

Lim, J.S. and Shin, S.J. (1993), *A Study on the Cargo Handling System of the Container Terminal*, KMI Working Paper No. 85, Seoul.

Liu, Z. (1992), *Ownership and Productive Efficiency: with Reference to British Ports*, PhD Thesis, Queen Mary and Westfield College, University of London.

Liu, Z. (1995), The Comparative Performance of Public and Private Enterprises: The Case of British Ports, *Journal of Transport Economics and Policy*, Vol. 29, No. 3, pp. 263-274.

Liu, Z. (1995), Ownership and Productive Efficiency: The Experience of British Ports. In McConville, J. and Sheldrake, J. (eds.), *Transport in Transition: Aspects of British and European Experience*, Avebury, Aldershot, pp. 163-182.

Lloyd's List (1995), South Korean Ports Development Plan Launched, 25 October.

Lloyd's List (1997), Korean Shipping Firms Slump, 14 March.

Lloyd's List (1998), New-look PSA Gets Down to Business, 30 January, p. 9.

Lloyd's List Maritime Asia (1995), Unlimited Capacity?, June.

Lloyd's Shipping Economist (1998), Korean Crisis: Korean Pride Comes Before a Fall, February, pp. 16-18.

Lodge, G. (1987), Introduction: Ideology and Country Analysis. In Lodge, G. and Vogel, E. (eds.), *Ideology and National Competitiveness: An Analysis of Nine Countries*, Harvard Business School Press, Boston.

Lovell, C. (1993), Production Frontiers and Productive Efficiency. In Fried, H., Lovell, C. and Schmidt, S. (eds.), *The Measurement of Productive Efficiency: Techniques and Applications*, Oxford University Press, New York, pp. 1-67.

Lovell, C. (1995), Econometric Efficiency Analysis: A Policy-Oriented Review, *European Journal of Operational Research*, Vol. 80, No. 3, Special Issue of Productivity Analysis: Parametric and Non-Parametric Applications, pp. 452-462.

Maddala, G. (1992), *Introduction to Econometrics* (2nd ed.), Macmillan Publishing Company, New York.

Maekyung Business (1997), The History of Privatising Public Enterprises, 15 October, p. 18.

Mansson, J. (1996), Technical Efficiency and Ownership: the Case of Booking Centres in the Swedish Tax Market, *Journal of Transport Economics and Policy*, Vol. 30, No. 1, pp. 83-93.

Martin, S. (1993), *Advanced Industrial Economics*, Blackwell Publishers, Oxford.

Meeusen, W. and van den Broeck, J. (1977), Efficiency Estimation from Cobb-Douglas Production Functions with Composed Error, *International Economic Review*, Vol. 18, No. 2, pp. 435-444.

Meyer, R. (1975), Publicly Owned versus Privately Owned Utilities: a Policy Choice, *Review of Economics and Statistics*, Vol. 57, pp. 391-399.

Millward, R. (1982), The Comparative Performance of Public and Private Ownership. In Roll, E. (ed.), *The Mixed Economy*, Macmillan Press, London, pp. 58-93.

Millward, R. and Parker, D. (1983), Public and Private Enterprise: Comparative Behaviour and Relative Efficiency. In Millward, R., Parker, D., Rosenthal, L., Sumnar, M. and Topham, N. (eds.), *Public Sector Economics*, Longman Group Ltd., New York, pp. 199-274.

Montagnon, P. (1997), This is an Unusual Situation, *Financial Times*, 9 December, p. 19.

Mookherjee, D. (1984), Optimal Incentive Schemes with Many Agents, *Review of Economic Studies*, Vol. 51, pp. 433-446.

Moon, S.H. (1992), *The Economic Impact of the Korean Port Industry on the National Economy: A Port Planning and Development Perspective*, PhD Thesis, University of Wales College of Cardiff.

Moon, S.H. (1995), Port Economic Impact Model (PIM) and Its Planning Applications, *Maritime Policy and Management*, Vol. 22, No. 4, pp. 363-387.

Moore, J. (1986), *Why Privatise?* In Kay, J., Mayer, C. and Thompson, D. (eds.), *Privatisation and Regulation: The UK Experience*, Clarendon Press, Oxford, pp. 78-93.

Morita, A. (1987), *Made in Japan*, Fontana and Collins, London.

Nah, H.J. (1994), KCTA Puts Its Case, *Containerisation International*, December, pp. 92-94.

Nagorski, B. (1972), *Port Problems in Developing Countries: Principles of Port Planning and Organisation*, International Association of Ports and Harbours, Tokyo.

Nalebuff, B. and Stiglitz, J. (1983), Information, Competition and Markets, *American Economic Review*, Vol. 73, pp. 278-283.

National Ports Council (1973), *Functions and Powers of the Council*, National Ports Council, London.

Newman, E. (1975), *A Civil Tongue*, Warner Books, New York.

Newman, N. (1980), Denationalisation: Private Problem for Public Ports, *Management Today*, December, pp. 66-74.

Nicholson, W. (1995), *Microeconomic Theory: Basic Principles and Extensions* (6th ed.), Dryden Press, New York.

Niskanen, W. (1971), *Bureaucracy and Representative Government*, Aldine-Altherton, New York.

Olson, D. (1988), Public Port Accountability: A Framework for Evaluation. In Hershman, M. (ed.), *Urban Ports and Harbour Management: Responding to Change along US Waterfronts*, Taylor and Francis, New York, pp. 307-333.

Oum, T. H. and Waters, W. (1996), A Survey of Recent Development in Transportation Cost Function Research, *Logistics and Transportation Review*, Vol. 32, No. 4, pp. 423-463.

Oxford English Dictionary (1993), Clarendon Press, Oxford.

Pack, H. and Westphal, W. (1986), Industrial Strategy and Technological Change: Theory versus Reality, *Journal of Economic Development*, Vol. 11, pp. 87-128.

Park, C.H. (1970), *Our Nation's Path*, Hollym Corporation, Seoul.

Park, M.D. (1995), *The Development of the New Kwangyang Container Terminal in Korea*, MSc thesis, University of Plymouth.

Park, Y.C. (1990), Development Lessons from Asia: The Role of Government in South Korea and Taiwan, *American Economic Review*, Vol. 80, No. 2, pp. 118-121.

Parker, D. (1991), Privatisation Ten Years on: A Critical Analysis of its Rationale and Results, *Economics*, Vol. 27, Part 4, No. 116, pp. 154-163.

Parker, D. (1993), Ownership, Organisational Changes and Performance. In Clarke, T. and Pitelis, C. (eds.), *The Political Economy of Privatisation*, Routledge, London, pp. 31-50.

Parker, D. (1994), Nationalisation, Privatisation, and Agency Status within Government: Testing for the Importance of Ownership. In Jackson, P. and Price, C. (eds.), *Privatisation and Regulation: A Review of the Issues*, Longman Group Ltd., Essex, pp. 149-169.

Pearson, R. (1988), *Container Ships and Shipping*, Fairplay Publications, London.

Pirie, M. (1988), *Privatisation*, Adam Smith Institute, London.

Pitt, M. and Lee, L. (1981), The Measurement and Sources of Technical Efficiency in the Indonesian Weaving Industry, *Journal of Development Economics*, Vol. 9, pp. 43-64.

Port Development International (1993), Port Privatisation: Privates on Parade, December / January, pp. 33-55.

Port Development International (1995), Bursting Pusan, September, pp. 59-61.

Port Development International (1997), Singapore: State of Independence, May, pp. 35-37.

Porter, M. (1990), *The Competitive Advantage of Nations*, Macmillan Press, London.

Posner, M. (1984), Privatisation: the Frontier between Public and Private, *Policy Studies*, Vol. 5, pp. 22-23.

Posner, R. (1975), The Social Costs of Monopoly and Regulation, *Journal of Political Economy*, Vol. 83, pp. 807-827.

Pryke, R. (1982), The Comparative Performance of Public and Private Enterprise, *Fiscal Studies*, Vol. 3, No. 2, pp. 68-81.

Ranis, G. (1989), *The Political Economy of Development Policy Change: A Comparative Study of Taiwan and Korea*, KDI Working Paper No. 8916, Korea Development Institute, Seoul.

Raven, J. (1982), *Ports and Politics*, Paper presented at the International Association of Ports and Harbours, Nagoya.

Rees, R. (1985), The Theory of Principal and Agent, *Bulletin of Economic Research*, Vol. 37, pp. 3-26.

Ro, C.H. (1996), Introduction: Korea in the Era of Post-Development and Globalisation - The Tasks of Public Administration. In Ro, C.H. (ed.), *Korea in the Era of Post-Development and Globalisation: The Tasks of Public Administration*, Korea Institute of Public Administration, KIPA Publication Series II, Seoul, pp. 25-35.

Robinson, R. (1998), Asian Hub/Feeder Nets: the Dynamics of Restructuring, *Maritime Policy and Management*, Vol. 25, No. 1, pp. 21-40.

Rowthorn, B. and Chang, H.-J. (1993), Public Ownership and the Theory of the State. In Clarke, T. and Pitelis, C. (eds.), *The Political Economy of Privatisation*, Routledge, London, pp. 51-69.

Ryoo, S.Y. (ed.) (1997), *Privatisation and Korean Economy*, Samsung Economic Research Institute, SERI Economic Research No. 3, Seoul.

Sachish, A. (1996), Productivity Functions as a Managerial Tool in Israeli Ports, *Maritime Policy and Management*, Vol. 23, No. 4, pp. 341-369.

Sappington, D. (1991), Incentives in Principal-Agent Relationships, *Journal of Economic Perspectives*, Vol. 5, No. 2, pp. 45-66.

Saundry, R. and Turnbull, P. (1997), Private Profit, Public Loss: the Financial and Economic Performance of UK Ports, *Maritime Policy and Management*, Vol. 24, No. 4, pp. 319-334.

Schmidt, P. (1985), Frontier Production Functions, *Econometric Reviews*, Vol. 4, pp. 289-328.

Schmidt, P. and Sickles, R. (1984), Production Frontiers and Panel Data, *Journal of Business and Economic Statistics*, Vol. 2, No. 4, pp. 367-374.

Schotter, A. (1997), *Microeconomics: A Modern Approach* (2nd ed.), Addison-Wesley, Massachusetts.

Shepherd, W. (1984), "Contestability" vs. Competition, *American Economic Review*, Vol. 74, No. 4, pp. 572-587.

Sherman, R. (1995), Privatisation of Seaports?, *Transportation Quarterly*, Vol. 49, No. 3, pp. 93-100.

Simon, J. and Burstein, P. (1985), *Basic Research Methods in Social Science*, McGraw-Hill Inc., New York.

SingaPort '98 (1998), First Step Towards Privatisation, p. 6.

Singh, A. (1975), Takeovers, Economic Natural Selection and the Theory of the Firm, *Economic Journal*, Vol. 85, pp. 497-515.

Slack, B. (1993), Pawn in the Game: Ports in a Global Transportation System, *Growth and Change*, Vol. 24, pp. 579-588.

Slack, B., Comtois, C. and Sletmo, G. (1996), Shipping Lines as Agents of Change in the Port Industry, *Maritime Policy and Management*, Vol. 23, No. 3, pp. 289-300.

Smith, A. (1776), *An Inquiry into the Nature and Causes of the Wealth of Nations*, edited by Sutherland, K. (1993), Oxford University Press, Oxford.

Sohn, T.S. (1998), Restructuring Wave Reaching State Enterprises to Enhance Efficiency, *Korea Herald*, 14 March.

Sohn, T.S. (1998), Korea to Emerge as Marine Superpower in the 21st Century: the Ministry of Maritime Affairs and Fishers Celebrates the 3rd Ocean's Day, 1998 International Year of Ocean, *Korea Herald*, 1 June.

Song, B.N. (1990), *The Rise of the Korean Economy*, Oxford University Press, Hong Kong.

Song, B.N. (1994), *The Rise of the Korean Economy* (Updated ed.), Oxford University Press, Hong Kong.

Song, D.H. (1986), The Role of the Public Enterprises in the Korean Economy. In Lee, K.U. (ed.), *Industrial Development Policies and Issues*, Korea Development Institute, Seoul.

Stehli, H. (1978), Typology of Ports. In Beth, H. (ed.), *Port Management Textbook*, Institute of Shipping Economics, Bremen, pp. 25-35.

Stevenson, R. (1980), Likelihood Functions for Generalised Stochastic Frontier Estimation, *Journal of Econometrics*, Vol. 13, pp. 57-66.

Stigler, G. (1987), Competition. In Eatwell, J., Milgate, M. and Newman, P. (eds.), *The New Palgrave*, Macmillan, London.

Stiglitz, J. (1988), *Economics of the Public Sector* (2nd ed.), W.W. Norton and Company, New York.

Suykens, F. (1983), A Few Observations on Productivity in Seaports, *Maritime Policy and Management*, Vol. 10, No. 1, pp. 17-40.

Suykens, F. (1985), Administration and Management at the Port of Antwerp, *Maritime Policy and Management*, Vol. 12, No. 3, pp. 181-194.

Suykens, F. (1989), The City and its Port: An Economic Appraisal, *Geoforum*, Vol. 20, No. 4, pp. 437-445.

Talley, W. (1988), Optimum Throughput and Performance Evaluation of Marine Terminals, *Maritime Policy and Management*, Vol. 15, No. 4, pp. 327-331.

Talley, W. (1994), Performance Indicators and Port Performance Evaluation, *Logistics and Transportation Review*, Vol. 30, No. 4, pp. 339-352.

Taylor, R. (1983), Thatcher's Public Putsch, *Management Today*, May, pp. 54-59.

The Times Atlas of the World (1995), Times Books and Bartholomew, Edinburgh.

Thomas, B. (1976), Port Administration (I): A Review of the Different Forms of Port Ownership and the Numerous Functions Undertaken within Ports. In *Manual on Port Management*, Part I, UNCTAD, pp. 95-102.

Thomas, B. (1994), The Privatisation of United Kingdom Seaports, *Maritime Policy and Management*, Vol. 21, No. 2, pp. 135-148.

Thomas, B. (1994), The Need for Organisational Change in Seaports, *Marine Policy*, Vol. 18, No. 1, pp. 69-78.

Thomas, R. (1993), *Introductory Econometrics* (2nd ed.), Longman, London.

Tongzon, J. (1995), Determinants of Port Performance and Efficiency, *Transportation Research*, Vol. 29A, No. 3, pp. 245-252.

Transport (1991), Ports Industry Review: Privatisation Problems, Vol. 12, No. 2, pp. 39-43.

Tullock, G. (1967), The Welfare Costs of Tariffs, Monopolies and Theft, *Western Economic Journal*, Vol. 5, pp. 224-232.

Turnbull, P. (1991), Labour Market De-regulation and Economic Performance: the Case of Britain's Docks, *Work, Employment and Society*, Vol. 5, No. 1, pp. 17-35.

UNCTAD (1975), *Port Performance Indicators*, TD/B/C.4/131, Geneva.

UNCTAD (1985), *Port Development: A Handbook for Planners in Developing Countries*, TD/B/C.4/175/Rev.1, New York.

UNCTAD (1992), *Port Marketing and the Challenge of the Third Generation Port*, TD/B/C.4/AC.7/14, Geneva.

UNCTAD (1995), *Comparative Experiences with Privatisation: Policy Insights and Lessons Learned*, UNCTAD/DTCI/23, New York.

UNCTAD (1995), *Comparative Analysis of Deregulation, Commercialisation and Privatisation of Ports*, UNCTAD / SDD / PORT / 3, Geneva.

Underdal, A. (1980), Integrated Marine Policy - What? Why? How?, *Marine Policy*, Vol. 4, No. 3, pp. 159-169.

Veljanovski, C. (1987), *Selling the State: Privatisation in Britain*, Butler and Tanner Ltd., London.

Vickers, J. and Yarrow, G. (1988), *Privatisation: An Economic Analysis*, MIT Press, Cambridge, Massachusetts.

Vickers, J. and Yarrow, G. (1991), Economic Perspectives on Privatisation, *Journal of Economic Perspectives*, Vol. 5, No. 2, pp. 111-132.

Vickers, J. (1995), Concepts of Competition, *Oxford Economic Papers*, Vol. 47, No. 1, pp. 1-23.

Vogel, R. (1994), The Future Role of Ports, *Proceedings of the Future Role of Ports in the G.C.C.*, 3-5 December, Kuwait Ports Authority.

Vuylsteke, C. (1988), *Techniques of Privatisation of State-Owned Enterprises: Methods and Implementation* (Volume I), World Bank, Washington, D.C.

Wade, R. (1990), *Governing the Market: Economic Theory and the Role of Government in East Asian Industrialisation*, Princeton University Press, Princeton.

Waldman, D. (1982), A Stationary Point for the Stochastic Frontier Likelihood, *Journal of Econometrics*, Vol. 18, pp. 275-279.

Wild, P., Fells, H. and Dearing, J. (1995), *International Ports*, Lloyd's Business Intelligence Centre, Lloyd's of London Press, London.

Wilder, R. and Pender, D. (1979), Economic Behaviour of Public Ports in the United Sates, *Journal of Transport Economics and Policy*, Vol. 13, No. 2, pp. 169-181.

Wiltshire, K. (1988), *Privatisation: The British Experience*, Longman Cheshire Pty Ltd., Melbourne.

Winsten, C. (1957), Discussion on Mr Farrell's Paper, *Journal of the Royal Statistical Society*, Series A, Vol. 120, No. 3, pp. 282-284.

Wolf, C. (1979), A Theory of Non-market Behaviour: Framework for Implementation Analysis, *Journal of Law and Economics*, Vol. 22, No. 2, pp. 107-140.

Wolf, C. (1993), *Markets or Governments: Choosing between Imperfect Alternatives* (2nd ed.), MIT Press, Cambridge, Massachusetts.

World Bank (1993), *The East Asian Miracle: Economic Growth and Public Policy*, Oxford University Press, Washington, D.C.

World Bank (1995), *Bureaucrats in Business: The Economics and Politics of Government Ownership*, Oxford University Press, Washington, D.C.

Wright, M. and Coyne, J. (1985), *Management Buy-Outs*, Croom Helm, London.

Yarrow, G. (1986), Privatisation in Theory and Practice, *Economic Policy*, April, pp. 323-377.

Yoo, C.M. (1997), Heavy Logistic Costs Eat into Exports, *Korea Herald*, 20 June.

Appendices

Appendix 1   Organisation Structure of the MMAF

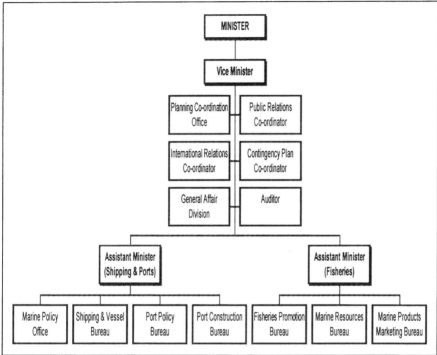

Note : The Maritime Police Administration is an independent government
organisation under the supervision of the MMAF.

Source: Drawn from the Administrative Structure of the Government as of 1997.

Appendix 2   Container Terminals in the Port of Pusan

Ownership Status of the World's Top 30 Container Ports

	Port	PUBLIC	PUBLIC/ private	PRIVATE/ Public	PRIVATE
1	Hong Kong			●	
2	Singapore	●			
3	Kaohsiung		●		
4	Rotterdam		●		
5	**Pusan**		●		
6	Hamburg		●		
7	Long Beach		●		
8	Yokohama		●		
9	Los Angeles		●		
10	Antwerp		●		
11	New York/NJ		●		
12	Keelung		●		
13	Dubai		●		
14	**Felixstowe**				●
15	Tokyo		●		
16	San Juan		●		
17	Bremen		●		
18	Oakland		●		
19	Shanghai	●			
20	Seattle		●		
21	Nagoya		●		
22	Bangkok		●		
23	Kobe		●		
24	Tanjung Priok		●		
25	Algeciras		●		
26	Klang				●
27	Hawaii		●		
28	Tacoma		●		
29	Osaka		●		
30	La Spezia		●		
44	Southampton				●
82	Tilbury			●	

Note: Classified as defined by the Port Function Matrix due to Baird (1995b, 1997).

Source: Extracted from Cass (1996, p. 167).

Appendix 3 Full Data Set

	Year	Variables (Unit: £)				
		Y	L₁	L₂	K₁	K₂
BCTOC	1978	594715.85	91102.10	143170.48	28776.03	84113.51
	1979	3907891.46	290024.49	568335.66	175050.71	124006.54
	1980	2656501.48	187684.93	475417.62	14901.55	219622.38
	1981	3442511.11	222501.82	530737.86	22021.61	209897.53
	1982	4225824.24	248584.57	674588.12	30603.90	174798.86
	1983	5836149.32	243498.49	896459.67	56534.54	220883.94
	1984	9206373.58	312034.83	1338214.81	125704.49	226390.86
	1985	7511103.26	259349.98	1100565.98	58293.82	547841.24
	1986	10760576.87	291100.72	1271422.23	80246.62	67542.09
	1987	11275862.08	240290.66	1321415.02	89875.54	291791.19
	1988	14059197.42	326452.34	2295618.35	74859.64	363979.30
	1989	18442737.41	434421.89	3122703.17	149672.11	1730162.60
	1990	14035252.22	358479.23	2548689.28	119952.02	1501233.33
	1991	12489386.29	327591.08	2395173.70	100366.54	1707948.88
	1992	11595999.42	426417.81	3049909.51	175969.34	152917.93
	1993	12394464.71	440830.55	3079998.69	215205.69	113523.41
	1994	14800350.62	438273.63	3213378.59	314846.81	299836.65
	1995	17039008.55	538766.88	3901768.08	412414.57	168586.38
	1996	14494531.66	457980.50	3772617.22	536128.43	237432.52
PECT	1991	7743920.13	146401.94	2061951.64	228349.89	233621.76
	1992	23629585.36	474377.70	5977118.68	1876735.79	458597.72
	1993	32898808.42	703362.79	6863020.33	1301105.91	322517.53
	1994	35872434.50	808116.75	7823161.18	1103179.41	606747.41
	1995	43335196.97	1163197.75	9877723.37	1527466.01	926403.47
	1996	36868168.19	1116078.05	9643067.12	1463880.05	2974341.53
Tilbury	1979	8737000.00	17902.00	20000.00	145000.00	61000.00
	1980	8514056.60	20332.08	16943.40	192307.55	40664.15
	1981	8946684.65	20443.51	15143.34	177177.07	32558.18
	1982	9039262.42	21613.35	2256155.28	130377.33	41135.09
	1983	7742918.40	22649.85	1816651.34	88600.89	33974.78
	1984	7170663.37	22227.72	1616908.06	51441.30	33659.12
	1985	7334864.00	20354.67	1523008.00	40110.67	34124.00
	1986	7712847.94	10414.95	1682592.78	30666.24	34716.49
	1987	6722774.75	23339.11	1630959.16	25561.88	40565.59
	1988	6847382.53	34987.01	1645449.82	32866.59	56191.26
	1989	6053385.54	36883.90	2226803.94	33933.19	47703.18
	1990	5555926.00	35471.00	2121974.00	31879.00	61064.00
	1991	3863774.32	21167.14	2538821.53	27559.02	49606.23
	1992	5590009.11	20037.34	2691955.37	1159712.20	33531.88
	1993	5352160.54	23356.05	2228892.38	1448075.34	44698.65
	1994	6434881.01	23962.38	2455947.51	1950773.40	40461.07
	1995	6433626.92	37480.41	2339465.93	3209164.40	41304.94
	1996	6316529.02	42815.09	1970611.11	2839571.31	41698.18

Appendix 3 (*continued*)

	Year	Variables (Unit: £)				
		Y	L_1	L_2	K_1	K_2
	1987	22183000.00	5449.00	10964000.00	2789000.00	147000.00
	1988	20166936.95	36249.17	12491653.15	4242106.27	134503.48
	1989	17903539.82	40707.96	13407079.65	7578761.06	119469.03
	1990	20222204.27	75145.44	9705882.35	6603102.78	105042.02
S	1991	22900198.38	39676.48	10027468.34	9314054.63	94613.15
	1992	21342262.12	44153.36	10415041.58	13359334.76	1504157.77
	1993	20386956.52	52173.91	9491304.35	16036956.52	2074637.68
	1994	22119327.02	55846.18	7916725.58	17105188.75	1889580.09
	1995	25333103.92	60564.35	8378527.19	20290433.59	1710254.65
	1996	26380142.03	63647.33	9161865.20	25735629.10	1565724.24
	1985	46389000.00	160000.00	29947000.00	61343000.00	8509000.00
	1986	52408182.99	197164.95	33634020.62	59182345.36	22513530.93
	1987	60692450.50	176361.39	33785272.28	58927908.42	21471534.65
	1988	70768299.88	107142.86	37804604.49	70154663.52	19302538.37
	1989	70771905.81	179901.42	40056407.45	73881982.48	27654709.75
F	1990	63671250.00	157500.00	37251000.00	102501000.00	25417500.00
	1991	56208215.30	97733.71	32922804.53	95221671.39	34342067.99
	1992	52405737.70	0.00	33183060.11	110484289.62	31389344.26
	1993	54698878.92	180269.06	33595964.13	87086098.65	28976905.83
	1994	58884514.44	253280.84	33107611.55	83898293.96	28595144.36
	1995	62959114.14	290034.07	33856686.54	81682921.64	25798977.85
	1996	63088308.46	241293.53	33199004.98	94363805.97	33929104.48

Notes: Y = Turnover derived from container terminal services (excluding property sales)

L_1 = Total remuneration of directors or executives for their managerial services

L_2 = Total wages and salaries paid to employees (including pension and social security costs)

K_1 = Net book value of fixed equipment (e.g. building and land)

K_2 = Net book value of mobile and cargo handling equipment (e.g. crane, forklifts, tractors)

S = Southampton

F = Felixstowe

Data Incompatibilities

As the accounting system adopted by both countries sampled is not identical, this research compiled only the data appearing commonly in financial statements of each container terminal company. More specifically, the financial accounts for the output and two labour variables are broken down in a similar way, thus allowing a relatively easy comparison of these items between the terminal companies. On the side of capital proxies, however, there is a noticeable discrepancy between the two countries. Under the account of tangible assets, which include the capital items associated with cargo handling and its supporting activities, the UK companies provide a rather simply separated record; that is, the capital assets are broadly divided into two different components – (i) fixed assets (e.g. civil works, dock structures, buildings, land and machinery for general operations), and (ii) mobile, especially cargo handling related, assets (e.g. cranes, fork lifts and tractors). In the Korean counterparts, these assets are cut up into the more detailed categories; that is, without division of fixed and mobile assets, they report the capital associated items individually, such as machinery, dock structures, land and buildings for the purpose of operations, cargo handling equipment (e.g. container cranes, yard tractors, yard chassis, fork lifts and transfer cranes) and electronic facilities (e.g. network connected computers).

To cope with these discrepancies existing in the capital variables, each account for the capital inputs in the Korean terminal companies was accordingly divided into two categories based on its nature of whether or not it is mobile, so as to permit a consistent comparison with the UK counterparts. This compilation may not have any serious effects on the findings, which is again supported by the fact that all the items in both countries are reported in terms of net book value.

Data Sources and Contacts

- The data of 'BCTOC' and 'PECT' were extracted from the Annual Financial Reports, which were kindly provided by the Korea Container Terminal Authority (KCTA).
- The data of 'Tilbury Container Services Company' and 'Southampton Container Terminal Company' were collected through the Company Houses, Cardiff, U.K.
- The data of 'Felixstowe Dock and Railway Company' were compiled by the Annual Report and Accounts, which were cordially provided by the Financial Division of the Port of Felixstowe.

Appendix 4   Productive Inefficiency of Container Terminal Operators

Terminal Operators	Year	Estimated Productive Inefficiency		
		Half-Normal	Exponential	Truncated Normal
BCTOC	1978	2.5694	2.5623	2.5261
	1979	1.2604	1.1402	1.1511
	1980	1.2610	1.1707	1.1758
	1981	1.0888	0.9823	0.9938
	1982	0.9459	0.8253	0.8428
	1983	0.7804	0.6422	0.6664
	1984	0.5160	0.3656	0.3955
	1985	0.6646	0.5194	0.5459
	1986	0.2007	0.1460	0.1620
	1987	0.2981	0.2036	0.2249
	1988	0.1802	0.1332	0.1474
	1989	0.2191	0.1512	0.1673
	1990	0.3708	0.2463	0.2708
	1991	0.4555	0.3123	0.3397
	1992	0.3716	0.2431	0.2705
	1993	0.3154	0.2052	0.2296
	1994	0.3208	0.2063	0.2304
	1995	0.2166	0.1453	0.1630
	1996	0.4034	0.2569	0.2864
PECT	1991	0.7618	0.6062	0.6366
	1992	0.2633	0.1634	0.1845
	1993	0.0872	0.0738	0.0813
	1994	0.0826	0.0711	0.0781
	1995	0.0742	0.0654	0.0716
	1996	0.1534	0.1072	0.1194
Tilbury	1979	0.1555	0.1301	0.1407
	1980	0.1660	0.1360	0.1473
	1981	0.1268	0.1113	0.1202
	1982	0.2566	0.1818	0.2047
	1983	0.2995	0.2114	0.2370
	1984	0.2802	0.2022	0.2261
	1985	0.2291	0.1714	0.1916
	1986	0.1594	0.1307	0.1458
	1987	0.2585	0.1915	0.2136
	1988	0.3264	0.2342	0.2600
	1989	0.4404	0.3199	0.3517
	1990	0.5336	0.4040	0.4372
	1991	0.8185	0.6985	0.7276
	1992	1.0206	0.8739	0.9046
	1993	1.1281	0.9856	1.0122
	1994	0.9973	0.8431	0.8748
	1995	1.1008	0.9448	0.9738
	1996	1.0974	0.9428	0.9709

	1987	0.1405	0.1063	0.1208
	1988	0.3008	0.1851	0.2130
	1989	0.4906	0.3086	0.3505
	1990	0.3588	0.2152	0.2471
Southampton	1991	0.2679	0.1642	0.1893
	1992	0.6942	0.4921	0.5342
	1993	0.8072	0.6065	0.6458
	1994	0.7240	0.5201	0.5608
	1995	0.6194	0.4136	0.4553
	1996	0.6167	0.4081	0.4504
	1985	0.5268	0.3105	0.3511
	1986	0.5334	0.3145	0.3543
	1987	0.3865	0.2125	0.2433
	1988	0.2571	0.1459	0.1674
	1989	0.3225	0.1758	0.2018
Felixstowe	1990	0.4466	0.2469	0.2822
	1991	0.5540	0.3312	0.3723
	1992	0.1404	0.1081	0.1250
	1993	0.5790	0.3501	0.3918
	1994	0.5191	0.2993	0.3381
	1995	0.4491	0.2481	0.2827
	1996	0.4902	0.2768	0.3139